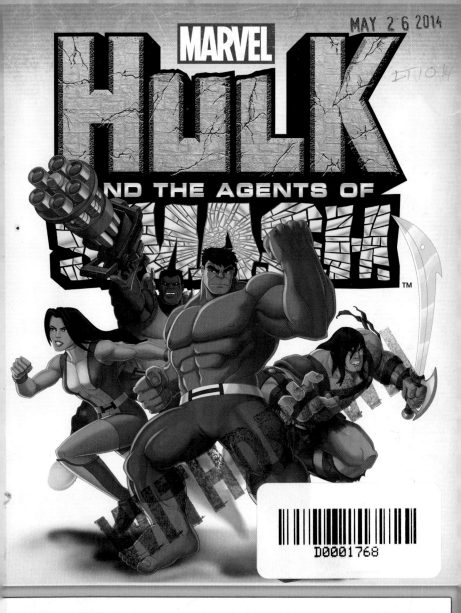

MAY 2 6 2014

D0001768

MARVEL UNIVERSE HULK: AGENTS OF S.M.A.S.H.. Contains material originally published in magazine form as MARVEL UNIVERSE HULK: AGENTS OF S.M.A.S.H. #1-4 and FREE COMIC BOOK DAY 2013. First printing 2014. ISBN# 978-0-7851-8925-1. Published by MARVEL WORLDWIDE, INC., a subsidiary of MARVEL ENTERTAINMENT, LLC. OFFICE OF PUBLICATION: 135 West 50th Street, New York, NY 10020. Copyright © 2013 and 2014 Marvel Characters, Inc. All rights reserved. All characters featured in this issue and the distinctive names and likenesses thereof, and all related indicia are trademarks of Marvel Characters, Inc. No similarity between any of the names, characters, persons, and/or institutions in this magazine with those of any living or dead person or institution is intended, and any such similarity which may exist is purely coincidental. **Printed in the U.S.A.** ALAN FINE, EVP - Office of the President, Marvel Worldwide, Inc. and EVP & CMO Marvel Characters B.V.; DAN BUCKLEY, Publisher & President - Print, Animation & Digital Divisions; JOE QUESADA, Chief Creative Officer; TOM BREVOORT, SVP of Publishing; DAVID BOGART, SVP of Operations & Procurement, Publishing; C.B. CEBULSKI, SVP of Creator & Content Development; DAVID GABRIEL, SVP Print, Sales & Marketing; JIM O'KEEFE, VP of Operations & Logistics; DAN CARR, Executive Director of Publishing Technology; SUSAN CRESPI, Editorial Operations Manager; ALEX MORALES, Publishing Operations Manager; STAN LEE, Chairman Emeritus. For information regarding advertising in Marvel Comics or on Marvel.com, please contact Niza Disla, Director of Marvel Partnerships, at ndisla@marvel.com. For Marvel subscription inquiries, please call 800-217-9158. **Manufactured between 2/14/2014 and 3/24/2014 by SHERIDAN BOOKS, INC., CHELSEA, MI, USA.**

10 9 8 7 6 5 4 3 2 1

Based on the TV series episodes by
**PAUL DINI,
HENRY GILROY, EUGENE SON
& STEVEN MELCHING**

Adapted by
JOE CARAMAGNA

Editor
SEBASTIAN GIRNER

Consulting Editor
JON MOISAN

Senior Editor
MARK PANICCIA

Special thanks to Jeph Loeb, Cort Lane, Todd Casey,
Eric Radomski & Jen Chapman

Collection Editor
ALEX STARBUCK

Editors, Special Projects
JENNIFER GRÜNWALD & **MARK D. BEAZLEY**

Senior Editor, Special Projects
JEFF YOUNGQUIST

SVP Print, Sales & Marketing
DAVID GABRIEL

Book Designer
NELSON RIBEIRO

Editor In Chief
AXEL ALONSO

Chief Creative Officer
JOE QUESADA

Publisher
DAN BUCKLEY

Executive Producer
ALAN FINE

MARVEL

HULK AND THE AGENTS OF S.M.A.S.H.

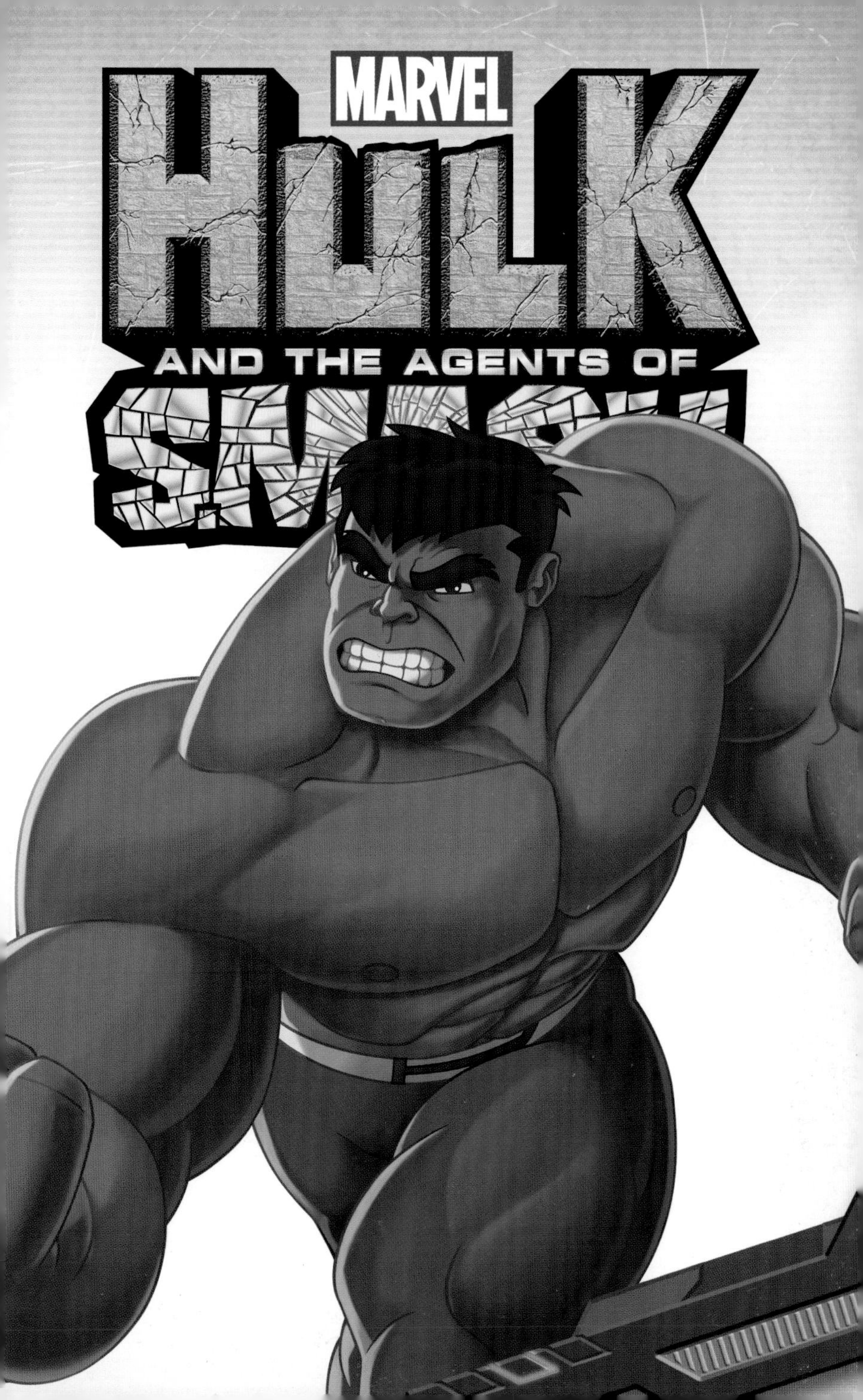

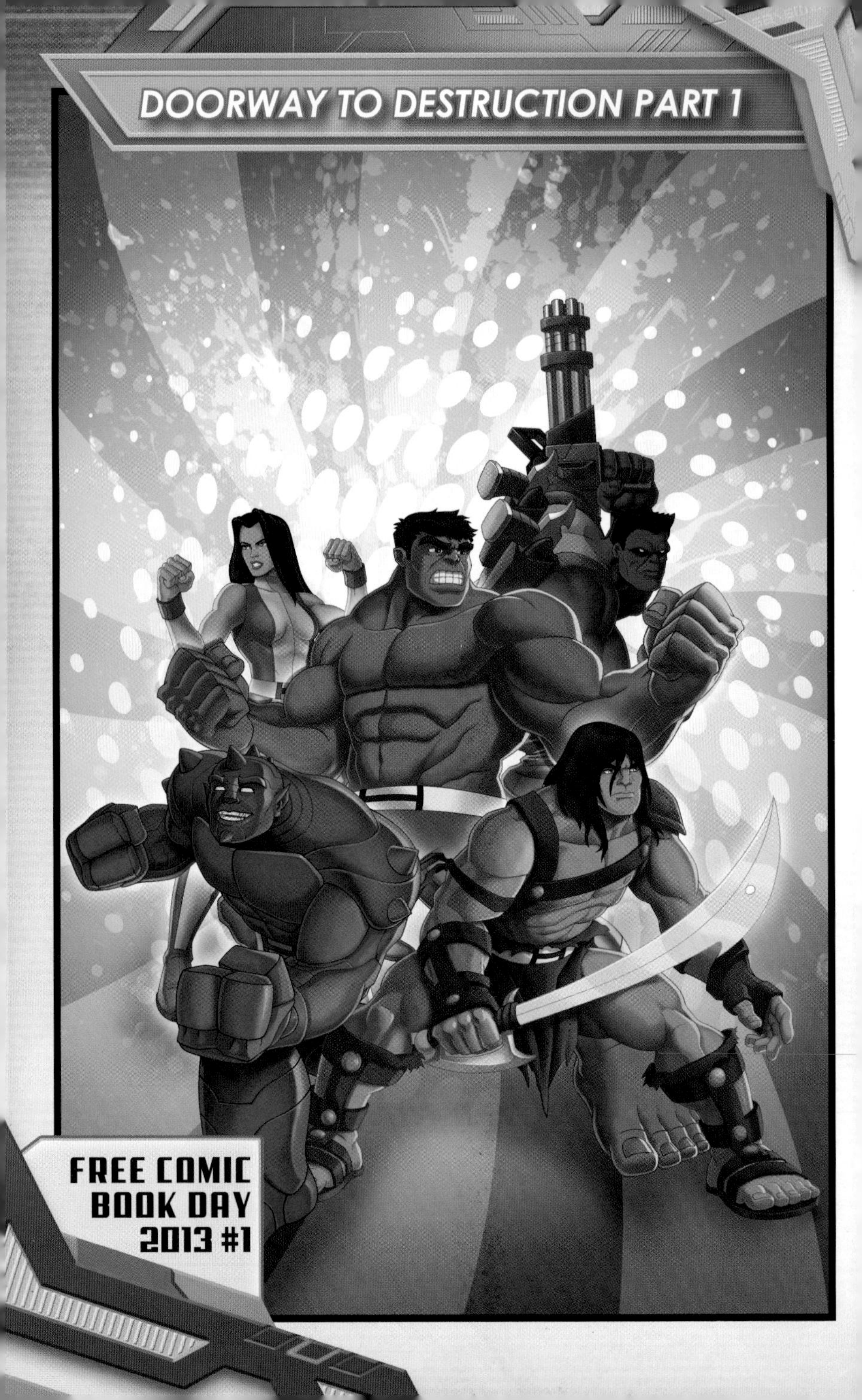
DOORWAY TO DESTRUCTION PART 1
FREE COMIC
BOOK DAY
2013 #1

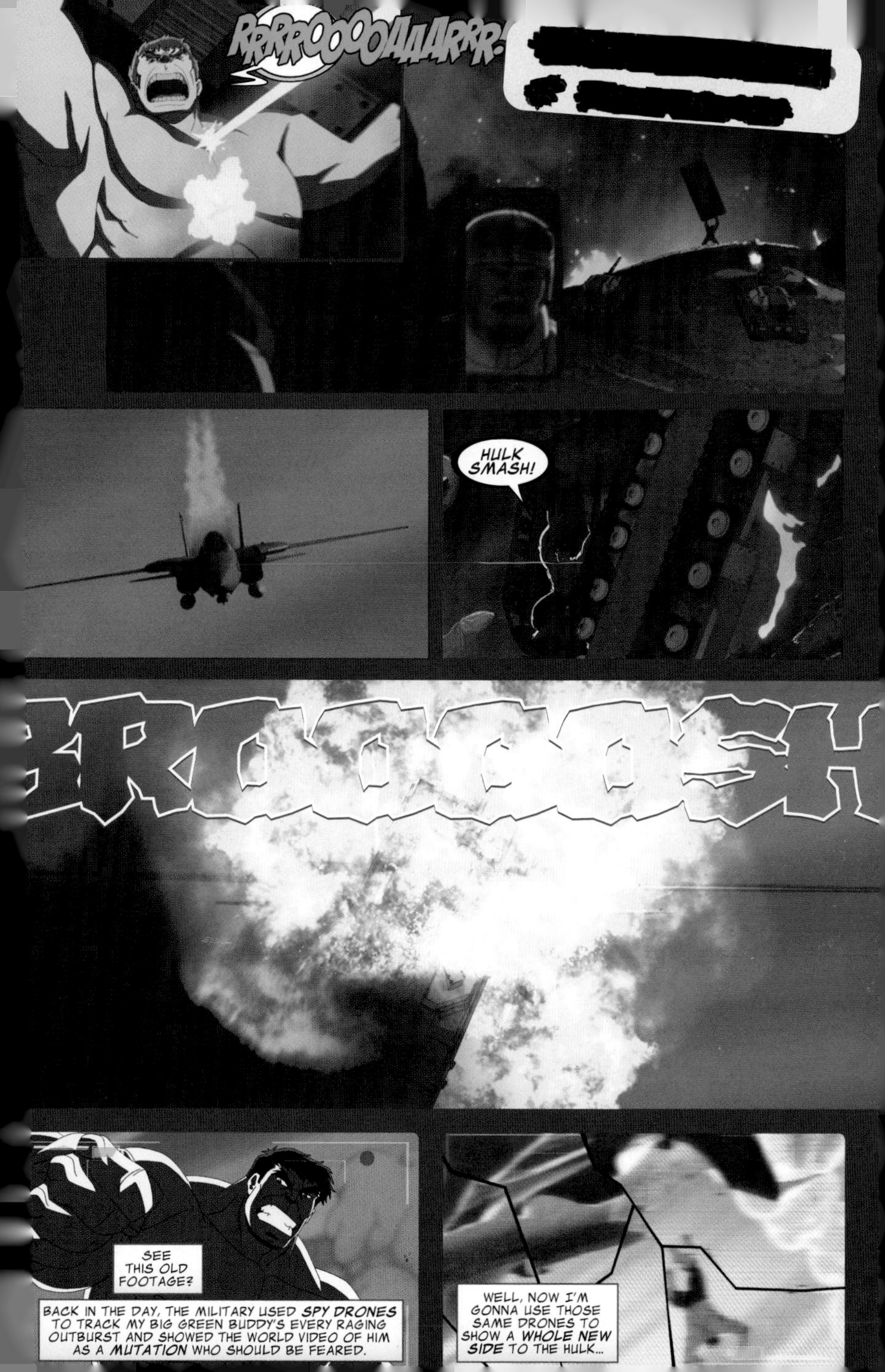

RRRROOOOAAARRR!
[redacted]
HULK SMASH!
SEE THIS OLD FOOTAGE?
BACK IN THE DAY, THE MILITARY USED *SPY DRONES* TO TRACK MY BIG GREEN BUDDY'S EVERY RAGING OUTBURST AND SHOWED THE WORLD VIDEO OF HIM AS A *MUTATION* WHO SHOULD BE FEARED.
WELL, NOW I'M GONNA USE THOSE SAME DRONES TO SHOW A *WHOLE NEW SIDE* TO THE HULK...

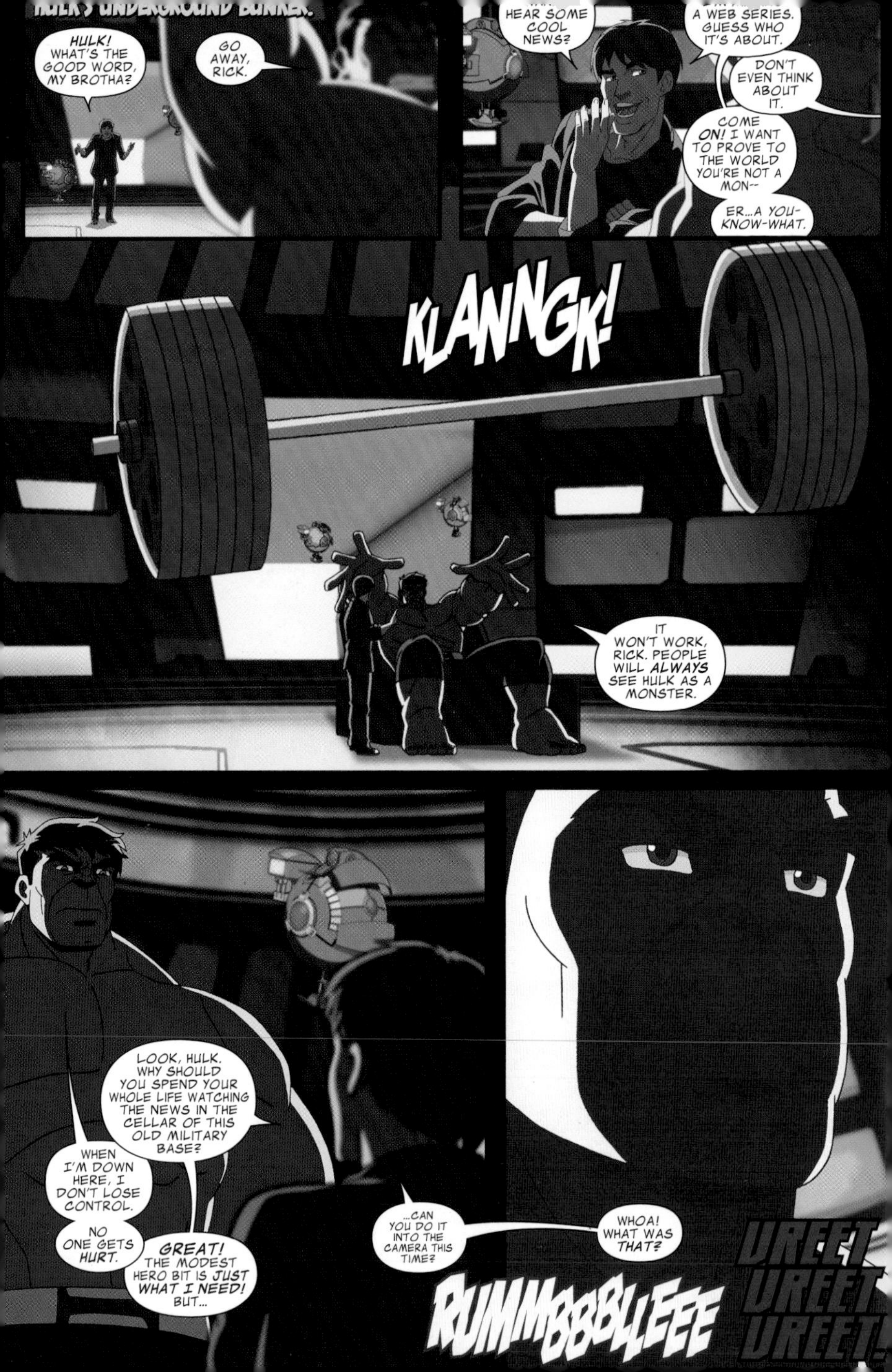
HULK'S UNDERGROUND BUNKER.
HULK! WHAT'S THE GOOD WORD, MY BROTHA?
GO AWAY, RICK.
HEAR SOME COOL NEWS?
A WEB SERIES. GUESS WHO IT'S ABOUT.
DON'T EVEN THINK ABOUT IT.
COME ON! I WANT TO PROVE TO THE WORLD YOU'RE NOT A MON--
ER...A YOU-KNOW-WHAT.
KLANNGK!
IT WON'T WORK, RICK. PEOPLE WILL ALWAYS SEE HULK AS A MONSTER.
LOOK, HULK. WHY SHOULD YOU SPEND YOUR WHOLE LIFE WATCHING THE NEWS IN THE CELLAR OF THIS OLD MILITARY BASE?
WHEN I'M DOWN HERE, I DON'T LOSE CONTROL.
NO ONE GETS HURT.
GREAT! THE MODEST HERO BIT IS JUST WHAT I NEED! BUT...
...CAN YOU DO IT INTO THE CAMERA THIS TIME?
WHOA! WHAT WAS THAT?
RUMMBBBLLEEE
UREET UREET UREET!

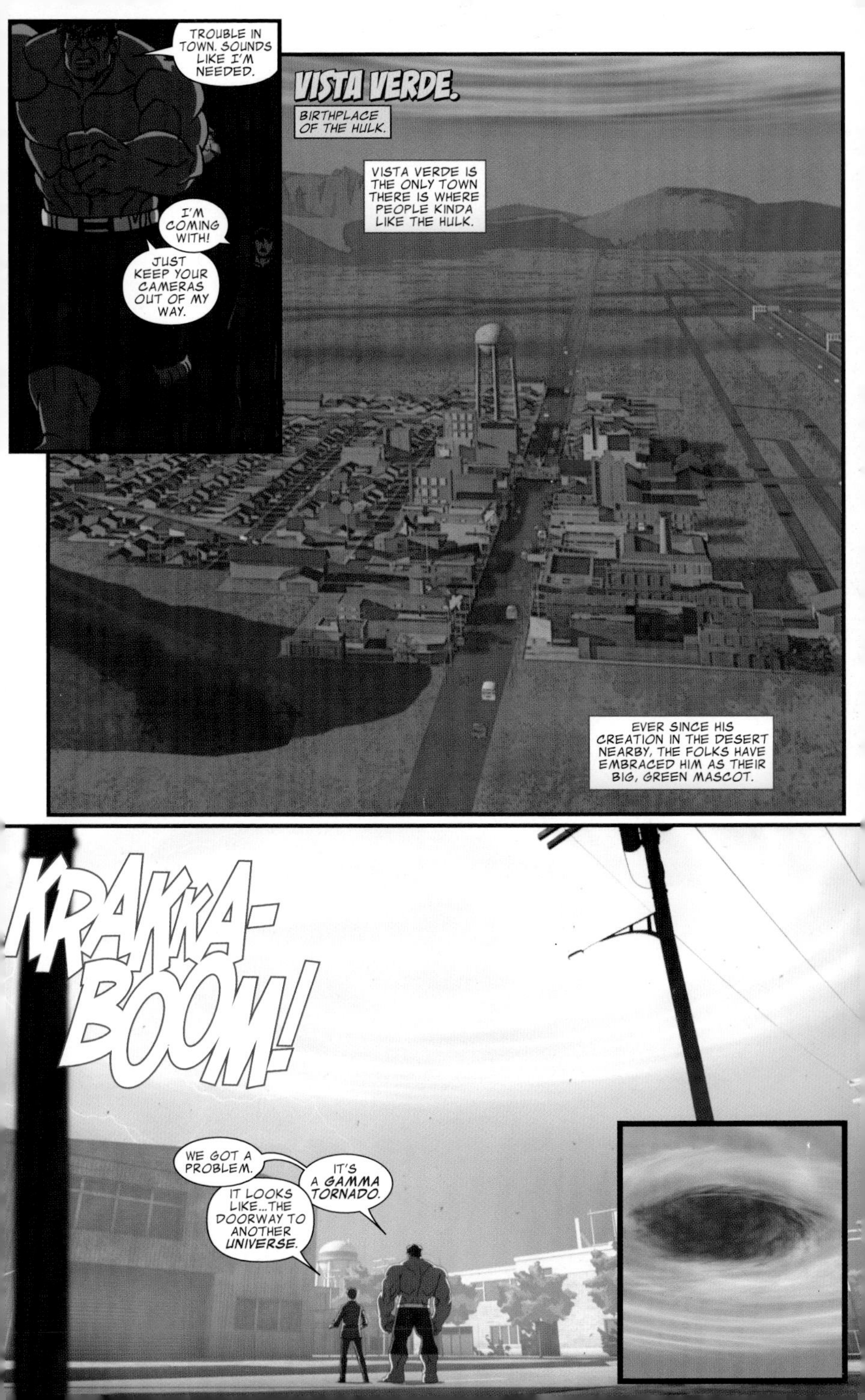
TROUBLE IN TOWN. SOUNDS LIKE I'M NEEDED.
I'M COMING WITH!
JUST KEEP YOUR CAMERAS OUT OF MY WAY.
VISTA VERDE.
BIRTHPLACE OF THE HULK.
VISTA VERDE IS THE ONLY TOWN THERE IS WHERE PEOPLE KINDA LIKE THE HULK.
EVER SINCE HIS CREATION IN THE DESERT NEARBY, THE FOLKS HAVE EMBRACED HIM AS THEIR BIG, GREEN MASCOT.
KRAKKA-BOOM!
WE GOT A PROBLEM.
IT'S A GAMMA TORNADO.
IT LOOKS LIKE... THE DOORWAY TO ANOTHER UNIVERSE.

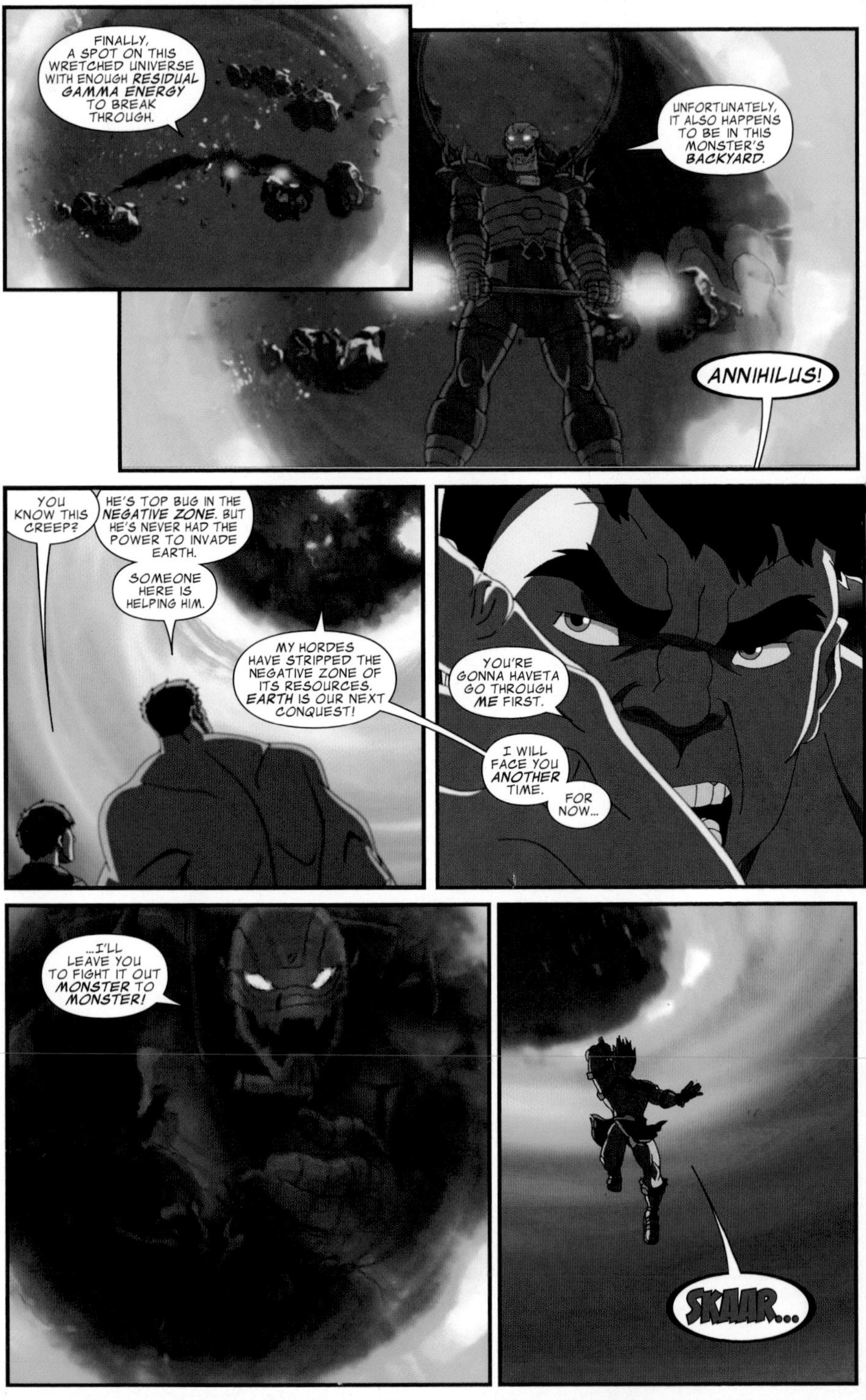
FINALLY, A SPOT ON THIS WRETCHED UNIVERSE WITH ENOUGH RESIDUAL GAMMA ENERGY TO BREAK THROUGH.
UNFORTUNATELY, IT ALSO HAPPENS TO BE IN THIS MONSTER'S BACKYARD.
ANNIHILUS!
YOU KNOW THIS CREEP?
HE'S TOP BUG IN THE NEGATIVE ZONE. BUT HE'S NEVER HAD THE POWER TO INVADE EARTH.
SOMEONE HERE IS HELPING HIM.
MY HORDES HAVE STRIPPED THE NEGATIVE ZONE OF ITS RESOURCES. EARTH IS OUR NEXT CONQUEST!
YOU'RE GONNA HAVETA GO THROUGH ME FIRST.
I WILL FACE YOU ANOTHER TIME.
FOR NOW...
...I'LL LEAVE YOU TO FIGHT IT OUT MONSTER TO MONSTER!
SKAAR...

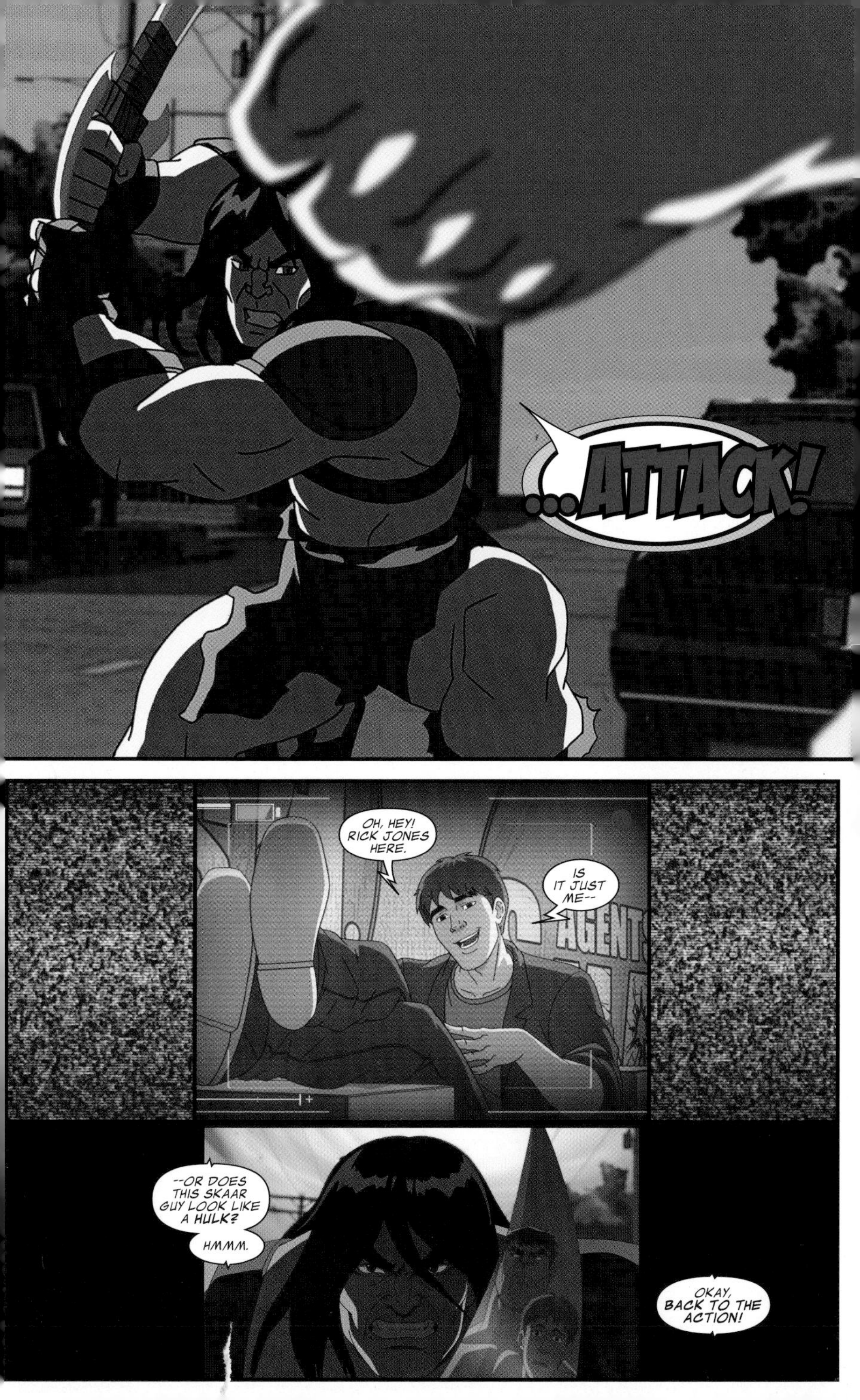
...ATTACK!
OH, HEY! RICK JONES HERE.
IS IT JUST ME--
AGENTS
--OR DOES THIS SKAAR GUY LOOK LIKE A HULK?
HMMM.
OKAY, BACK TO THE ACTION!

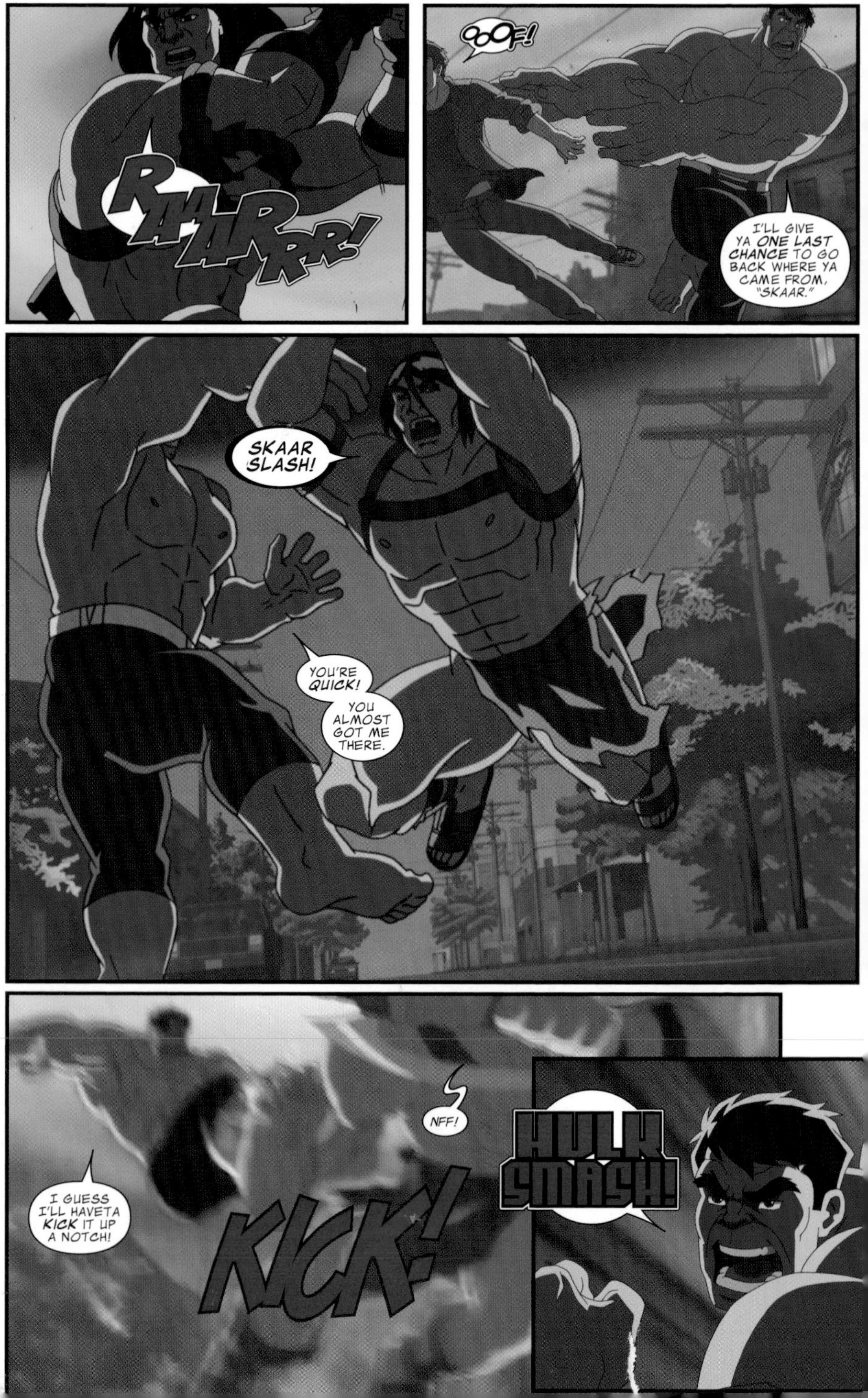
RAAARRRR!
OOOF!
I'LL GIVE YA ONE LAST CHANCE TO GO BACK WHERE YA CAME FROM, "SKAAR."
SKAAR SLASH!
YOU'RE QUICK!
YOU ALMOST GOT ME THERE.
I GUESS I'LL HAVETA KICK IT UP A NOTCH!
NFF!
KICK!
HULK SMASH!

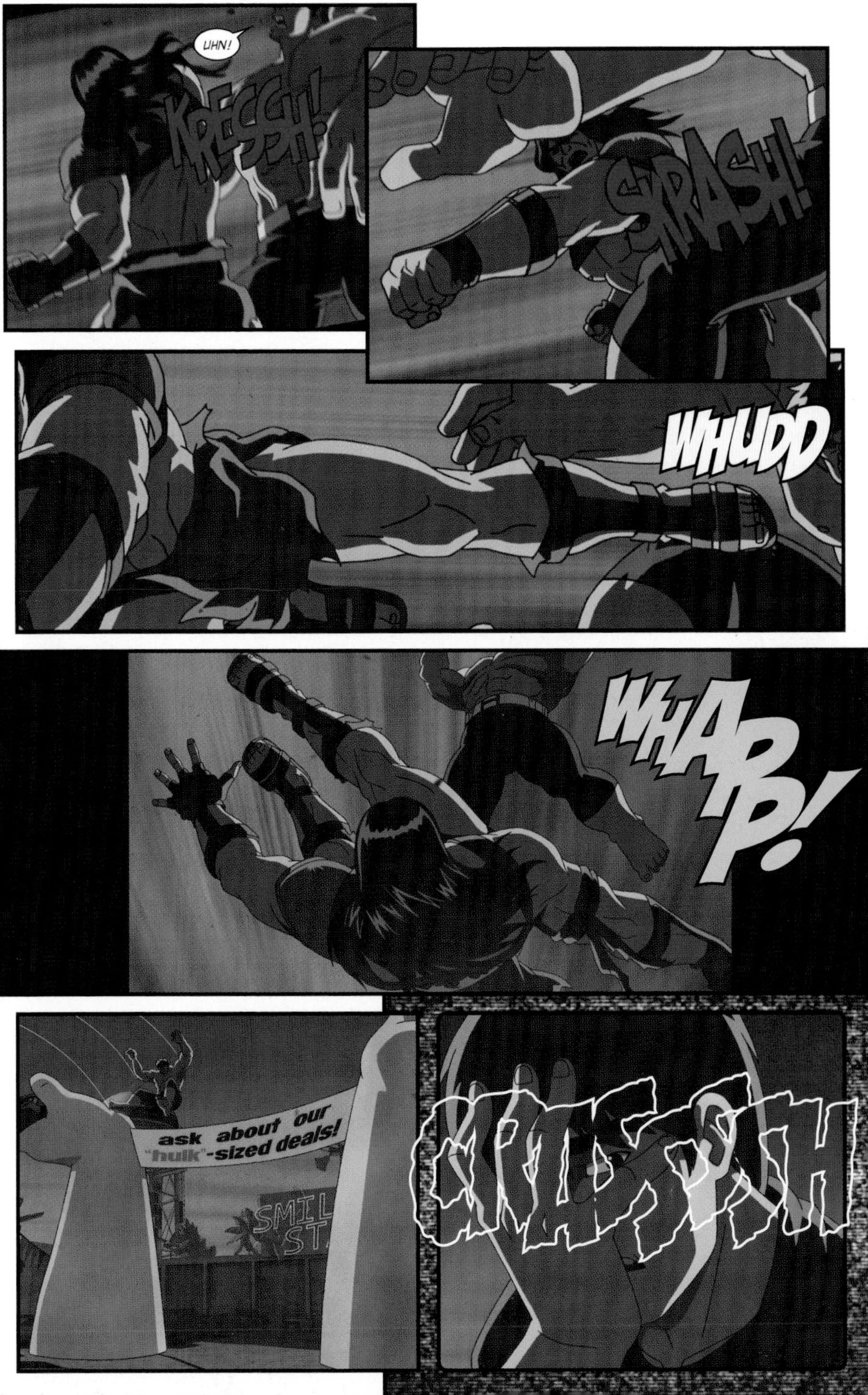
UHN!
KRESSH!
SRASH!
WHUDD
WHAP!
ask about our "hulk"-sized deals!
CRUSSH

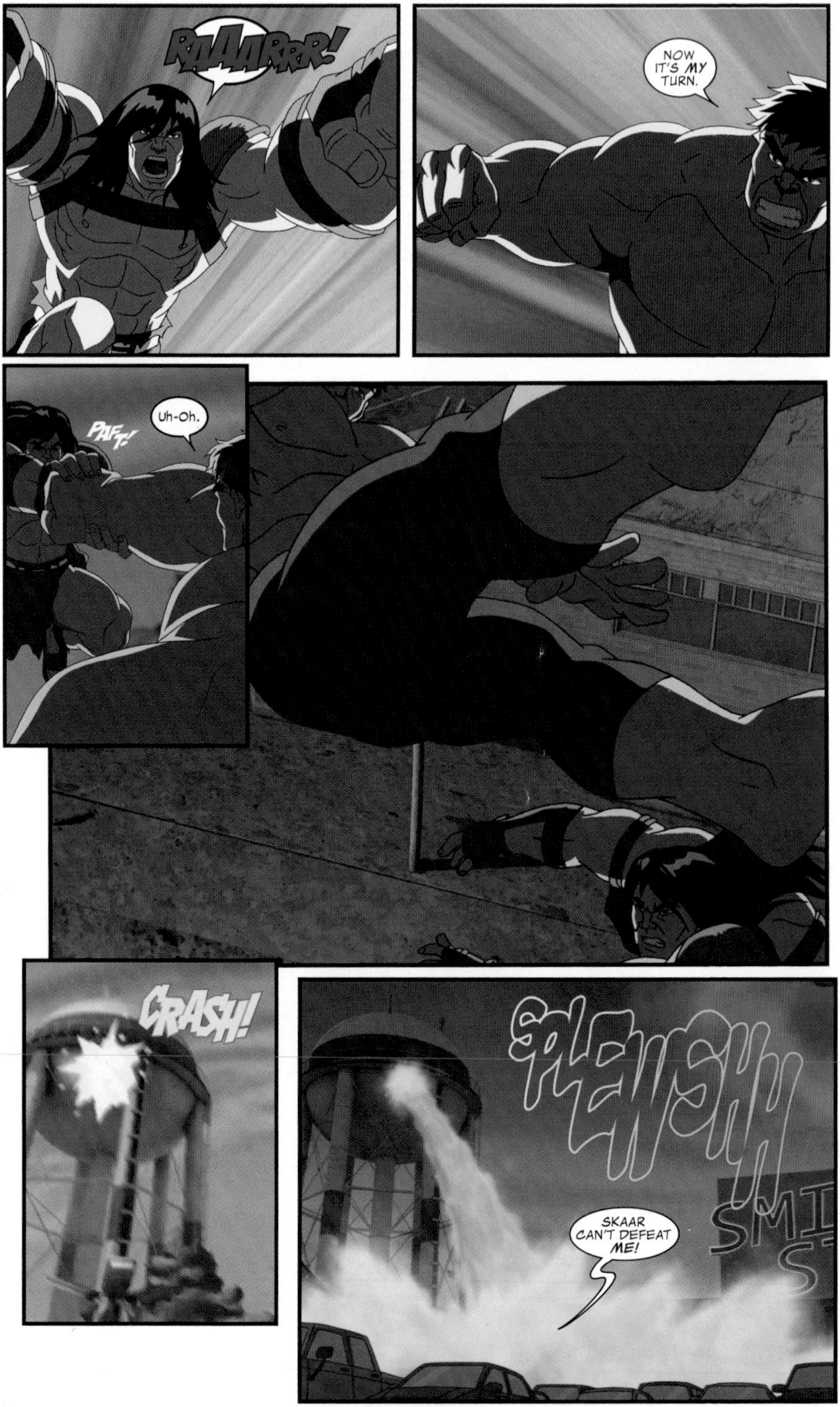
RAAAARRR!
NOW IT'S MY TURN.
PAFT!
Uh-Oh.
CRASH!
SPLEWSHH
SKAAR CAN'T DEFEAT ME!

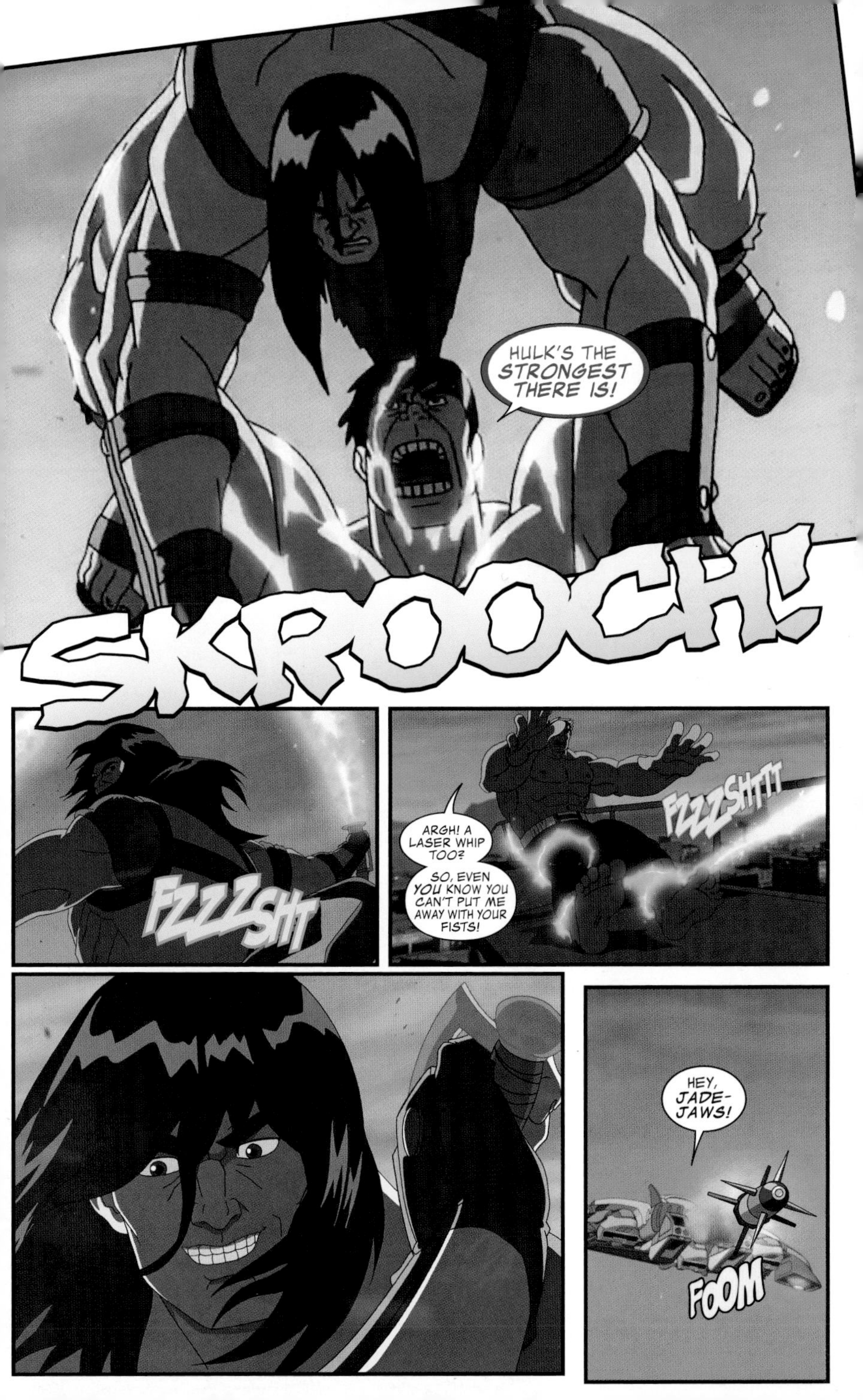
HULK'S THE STRONGEST THERE IS!
SKROOCH!
FZZZSHT
ARGH! A LASER WHIP TOO?
SO, EVEN *YOU* KNOW YOU CAN'T PUT ME AWAY WITH YOUR FISTS!
FZZZSHTTT
HEY, JADE-JAWS!
FOOM

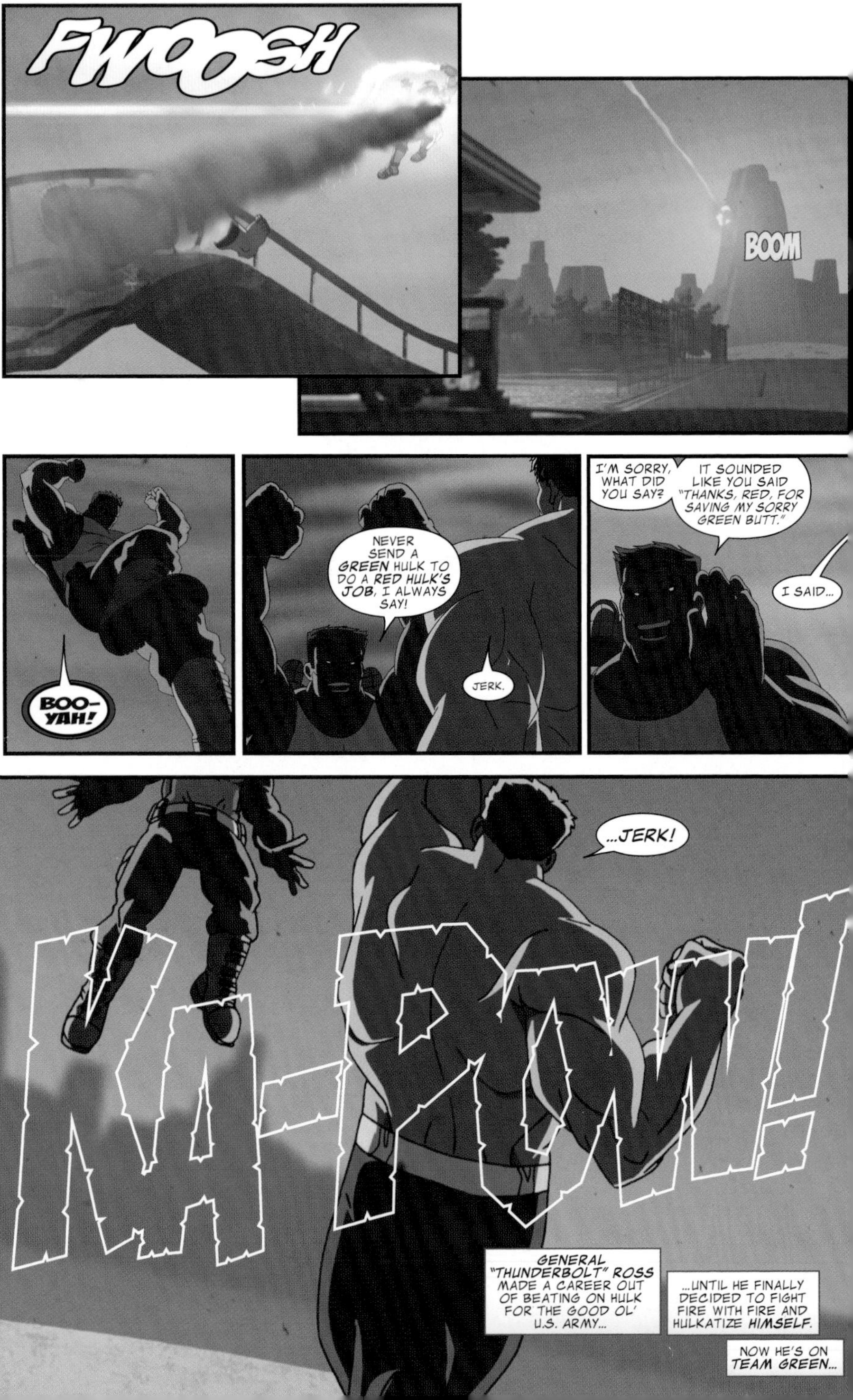
FWOOSH
BOOM
BOO-YAH!
NEVER SEND A GREEN HULK TO DO A RED HULK'S JOB, I ALWAYS SAY!
JERK.
I'M SORRY, WHAT DID YOU SAY?
IT SOUNDED LIKE YOU SAID "THANKS, RED, FOR SAVING MY SORRY GREEN BUTT."
I SAID...
...JERK!
KA-POW!!
GENERAL "THUNDERBOLT" ROSS MADE A CAREER OUT OF BEATING ON HULK FOR THE GOOD OL' U.S. ARMY...
...UNTIL HE FINALLY DECIDED TO FIGHT FIRE WITH FIRE AND HULKATIZE HIMSELF.
NOW HE'S ON TEAM GREEN...

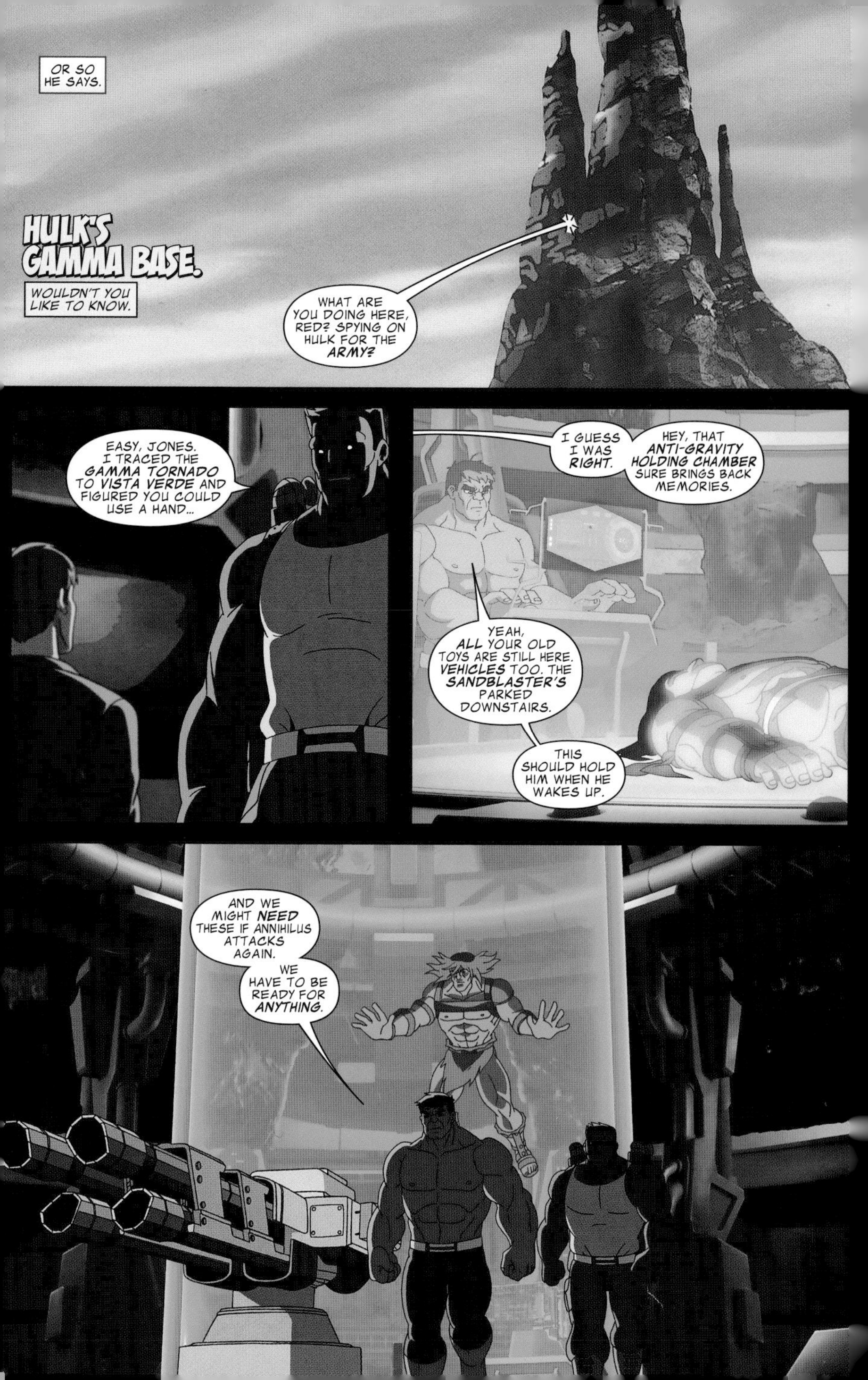
OR SO HE SAYS.
HULK'S GAMMA BASE.
WOULDN'T YOU LIKE TO KNOW.
WHAT ARE YOU DOING HERE, RED? SPYING ON HULK FOR THE ARMY?
EASY, JONES. I TRACED THE GAMMA TORNADO TO VISTA VERDE AND FIGURED YOU COULD USE A HAND...
I GUESS I WAS RIGHT.
HEY, THAT ANTI-GRAVITY HOLDING CHAMBER SURE BRINGS BACK MEMORIES.
YEAH, ALL YOUR OLD TOYS ARE STILL HERE. VEHICLES TOO. THE SANDBLASTER'S PARKED DOWNSTAIRS.
THIS SHOULD HOLD HIM WHEN HE WAKES UP.
AND WE MIGHT NEED THESE IF ANNIHILUS ATTACKS AGAIN.
WE HAVE TO BE READY FOR ANYTHING.

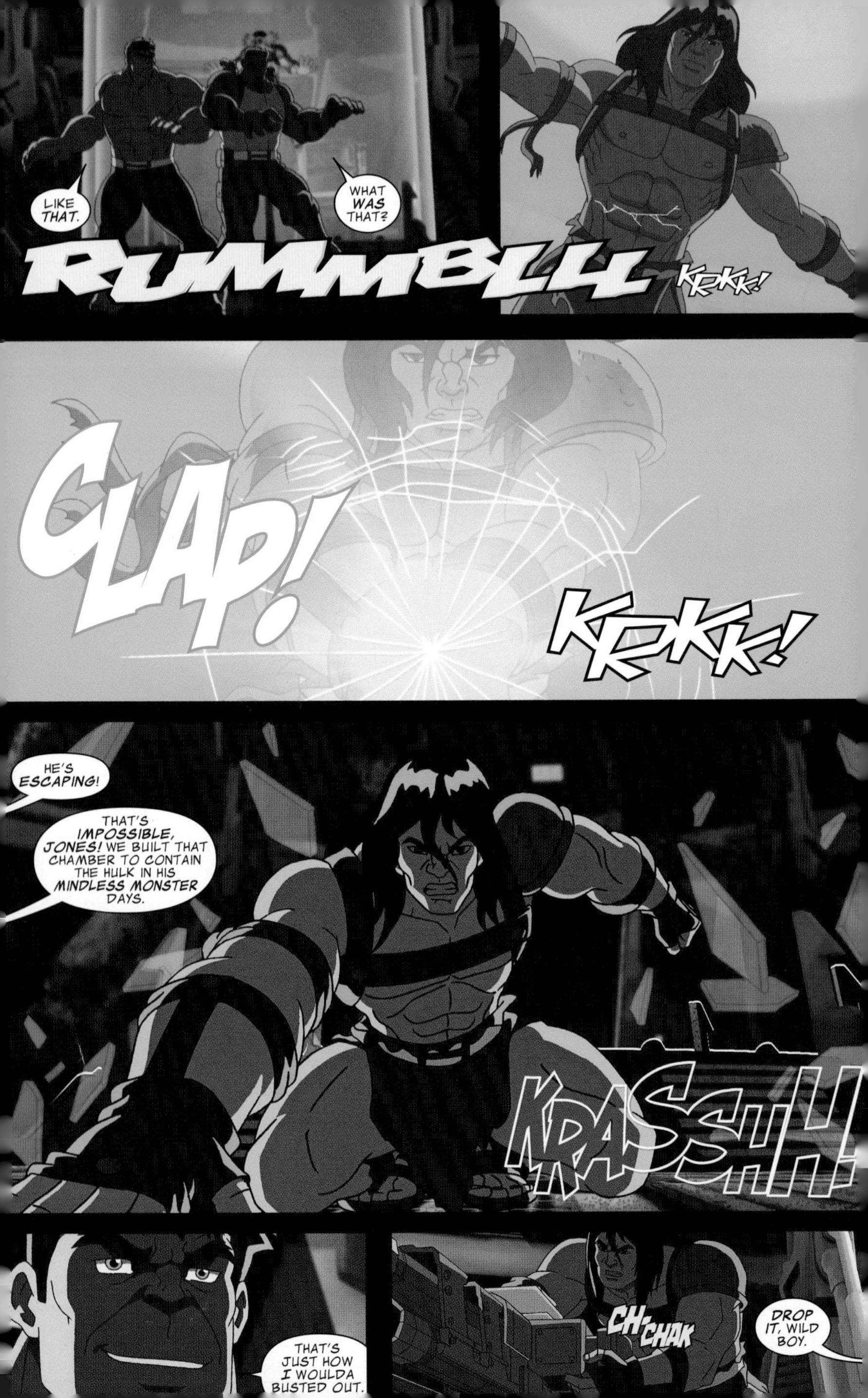

LIKE THAT.
WHAT WAS THAT?
RUMMBLLL
KRKKK!
CLAP!
KRKKK!
HE'S ESCAPING!
THAT'S IMPOSSIBLE, JONES! WE BUILT THAT CHAMBER TO CONTAIN THE HULK IN HIS MINDLESS MONSTER DAYS.
KRASSHH!
THAT'S JUST HOW I WOULDA BUSTED OUT.
CH-CHAK
DROP IT, WILD BOY.

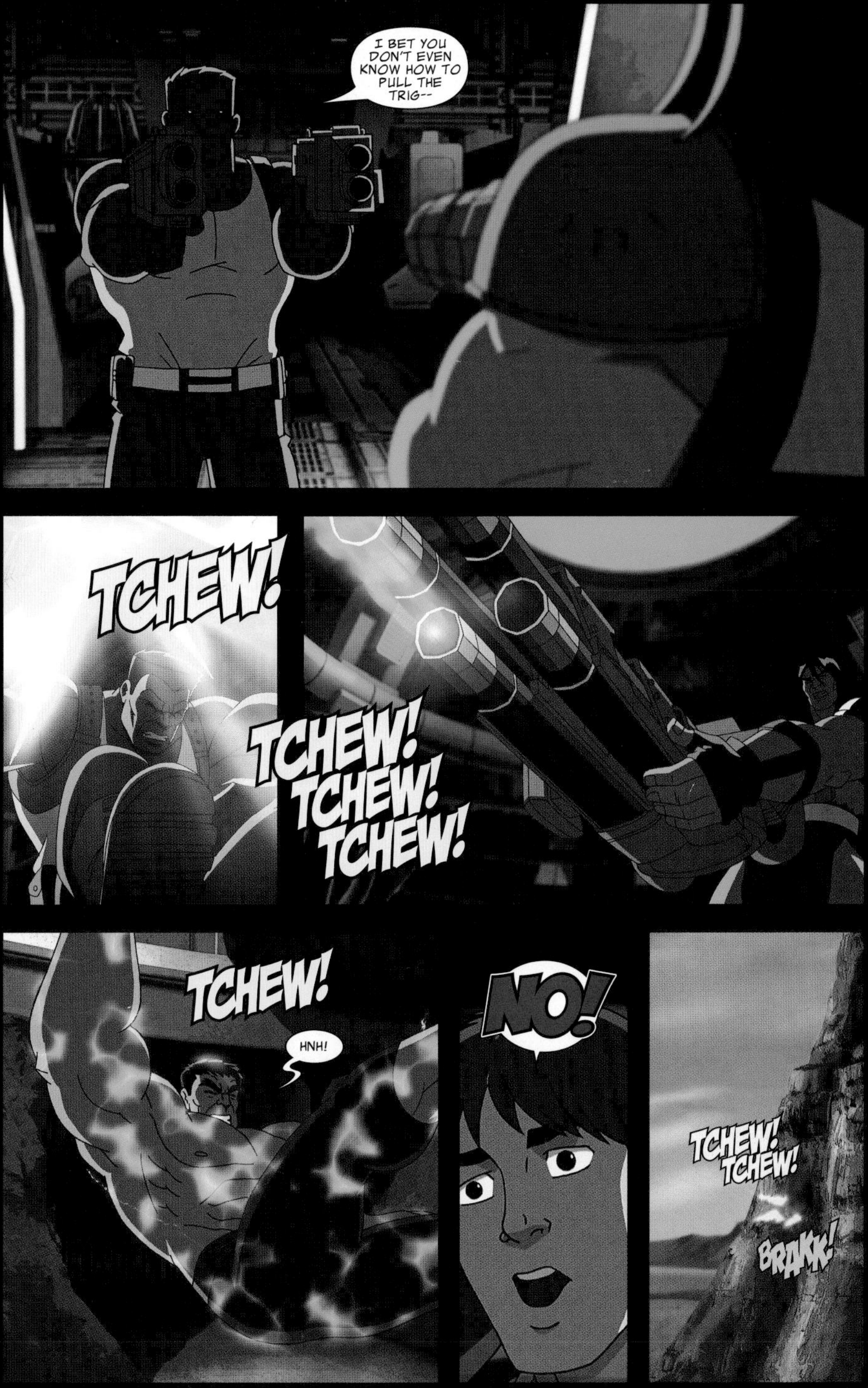
I BET YOU DON'T EVEN KNOW HOW TO PULL THE TRIG--
TCHEW!
TCHEW! TCHEW! TCHEW!
TCHEW!
HNH!
NO!
TCHEW! TCHEW!
BRAKK!

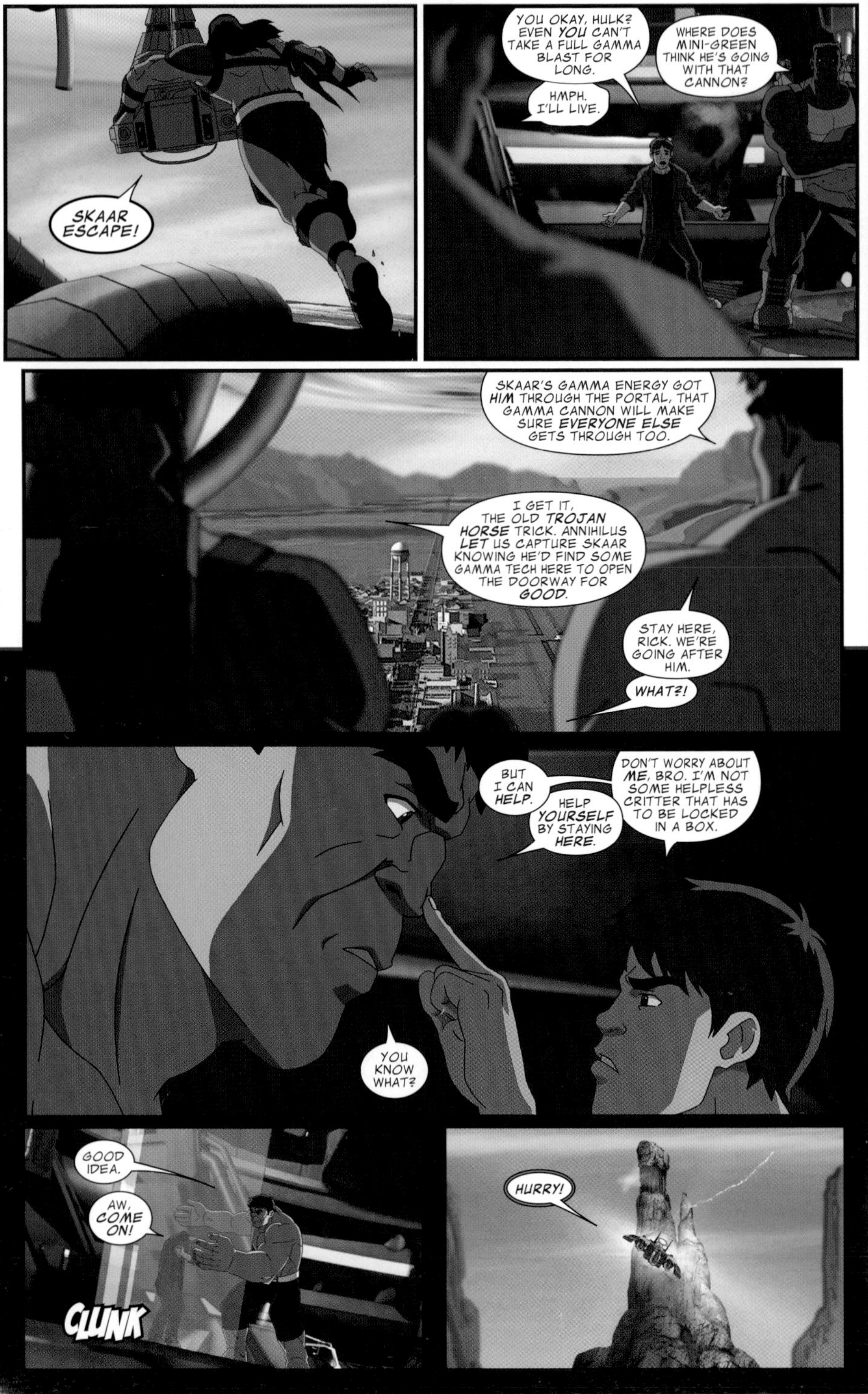
SKAAR ESCAPE!
YOU OKAY, HULK? EVEN YOU CAN'T TAKE A FULL GAMMA BLAST FOR LONG.
HMPH. I'LL LIVE.
WHERE DOES MINI-GREEN THINK HE'S GOING WITH THAT CANNON?
SKAAR'S GAMMA ENERGY GOT HIM THROUGH THE PORTAL, THAT GAMMA CANNON WILL MAKE SURE EVERYONE ELSE GETS THROUGH TOO.
I GET IT, THE OLD TROJAN HORSE TRICK. ANNIHILUS LET US CAPTURE SKAAR KNOWING HE'D FIND SOME GAMMA TECH HERE TO OPEN THE DOORWAY FOR GOOD.
STAY HERE, RICK. WE'RE GOING AFTER HIM.
WHAT?!
BUT I CAN HELP.
HELP YOURSELF BY STAYING HERE.
DON'T WORRY ABOUT ME, BRO. I'M NOT SOME HELPLESS CRITTER THAT HAS TO BE LOCKED IN A BOX.
YOU KNOW WHAT?
GOOD IDEA.
AW, COME ON!
CLUNK
HURRY!

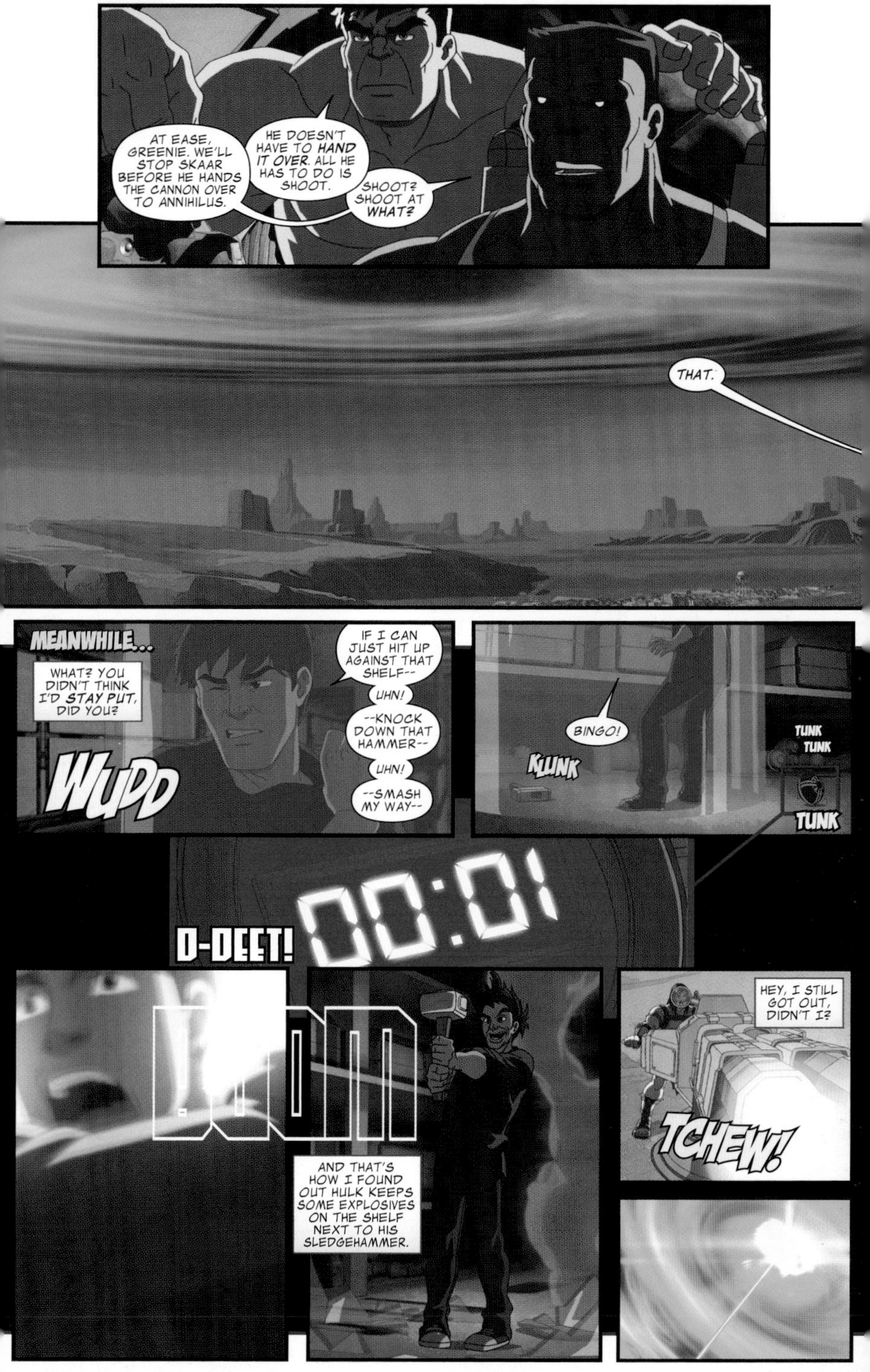
AT EASE, GREENIE. WE'LL STOP SKAAR BEFORE HE HANDS THE CANNON OVER TO ANNIHILUS.
HE DOESN'T HAVE TO HAND IT OVER. ALL HE HAS TO DO IS SHOOT.
SHOOT? SHOOT AT WHAT?
THAT.
MEANWHILE...
WHAT? YOU DIDN'T THINK I'D STAY PUT, DID YOU?
WUDD
IF I CAN JUST HIT UP AGAINST THAT SHELF--
UHN!
--KNOCK DOWN THAT HAMMER--
UHN!
--SMASH MY WAY--
BINGO!
KLUNK
TUNK
TUNK
TUNK
00:01
D-DEET!
AND THAT'S HOW I FOUND OUT HULK KEEPS SOME EXPLOSIVES ON THE SHELF NEXT TO HIS SLEDGEHAMMER.
HEY, I STILL GOT OUT, DIDN'T I?
TCHEW!

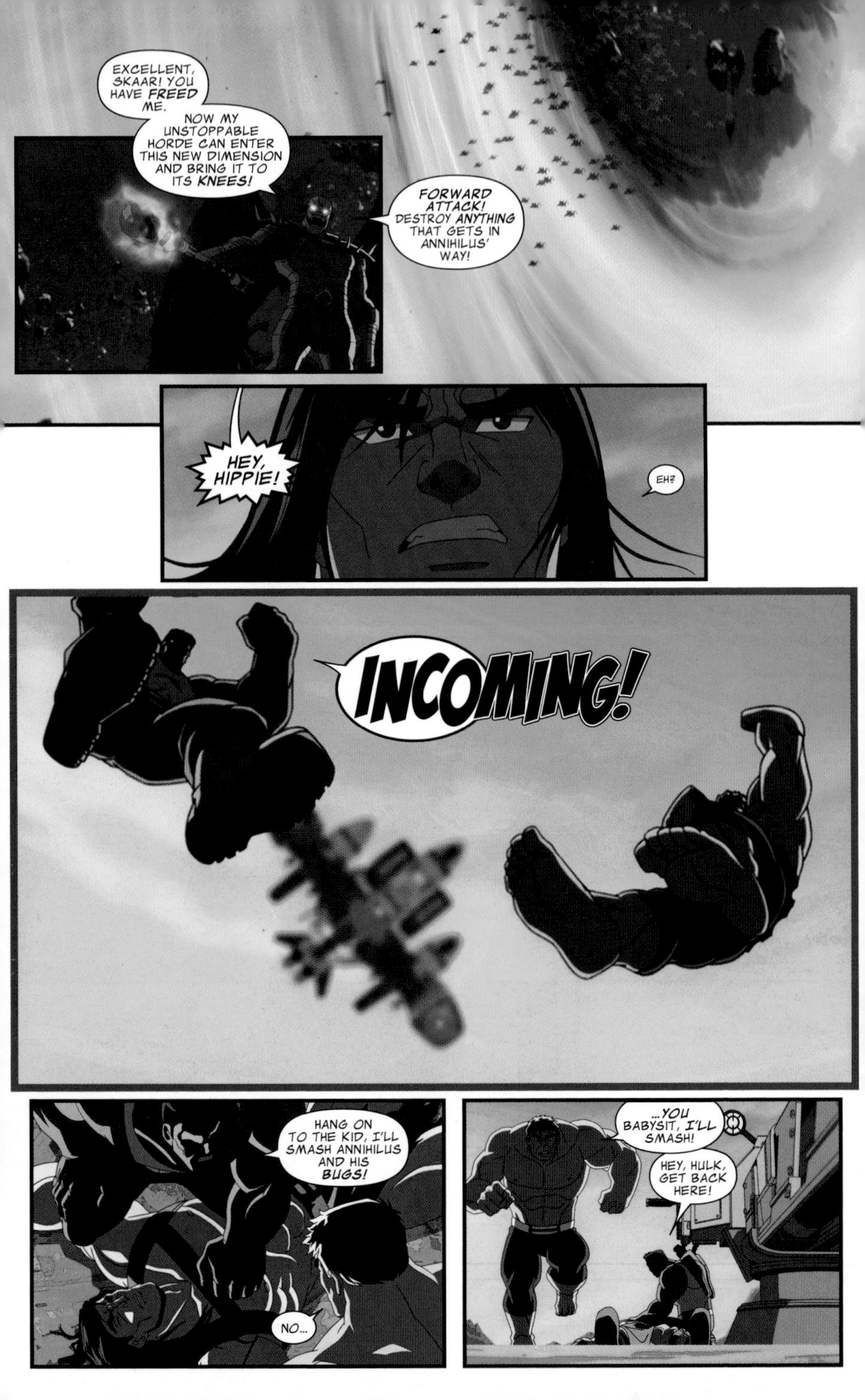
EXCELLENT, SKAAR! YOU HAVE FREED ME.
NOW MY UNSTOPPABLE HORDE CAN ENTER THIS NEW DIMENSION AND BRING IT TO ITS KNEES!
FORWARD ATTACK! DESTROY ANYTHING THAT GETS IN ANNIHILUS' WAY!
HEY, HIPPIE!
EH?
INCOMING!
HANG ON TO THE KID, I'LL SMASH ANNIHILUS AND HIS BUGS!
NO...
...YOU BABYSIT, I'LL SMASH!
HEY, HULK, GET BACK HERE!

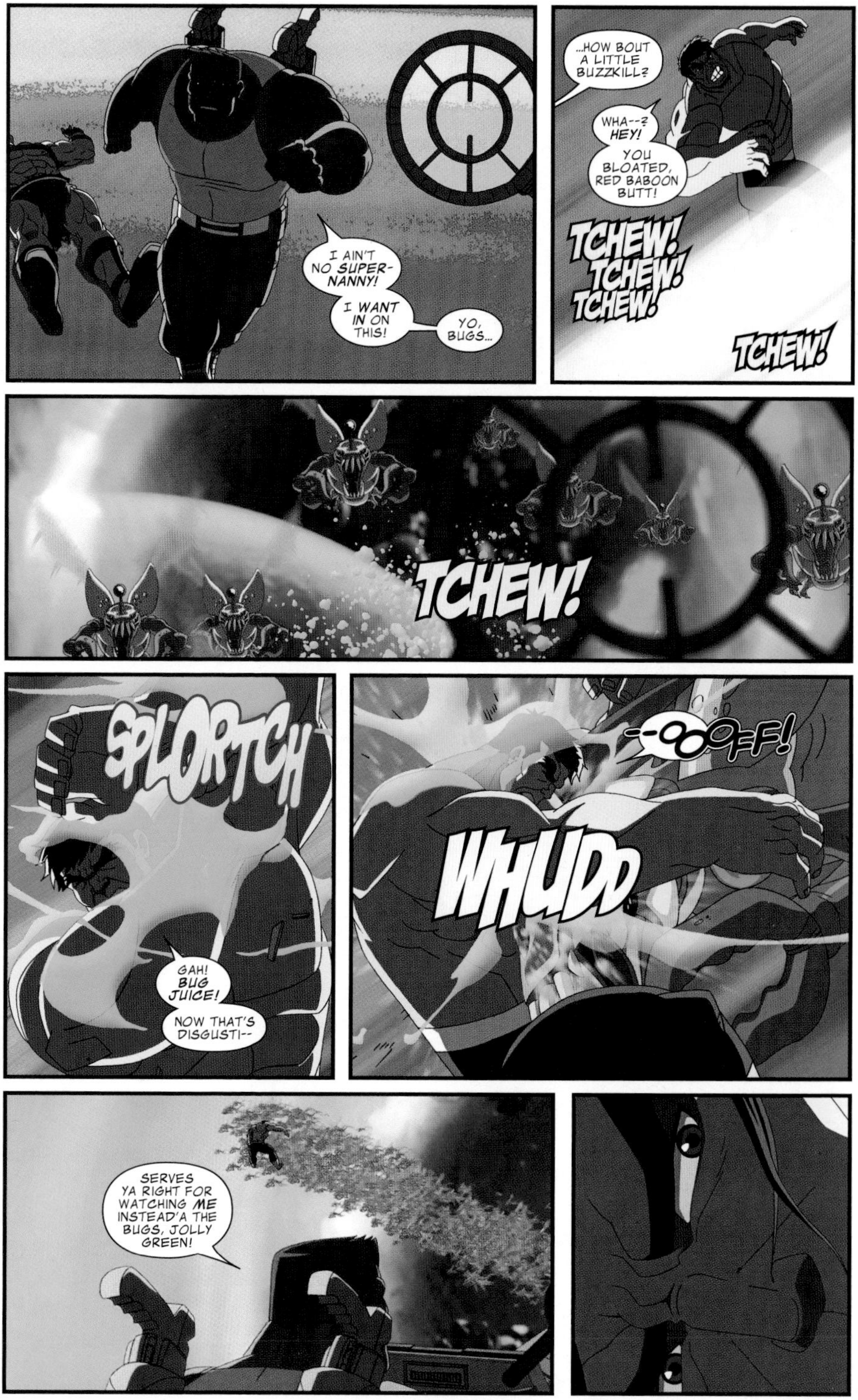
I AIN'T NO SUPER-NANNY!
I WANT IN ON THIS!
YO, BUGS...
...HOW BOUT A LITTLE BUZZKILL?
WHA--? HEY!
YOU BLOATED, RED BABOON BUTT!
TCHEW! TCHEW! TCHEW!
TCHEW!
TCHEW!
SPLORTCH
GAH! BUG JUICE!
NOW THAT'S DISGUSTI--
--OOOFF!
WHUDD
SERVES YA RIGHT FOR WATCHING ME INSTEAD'A THE BUGS, JOLLY GREEN!

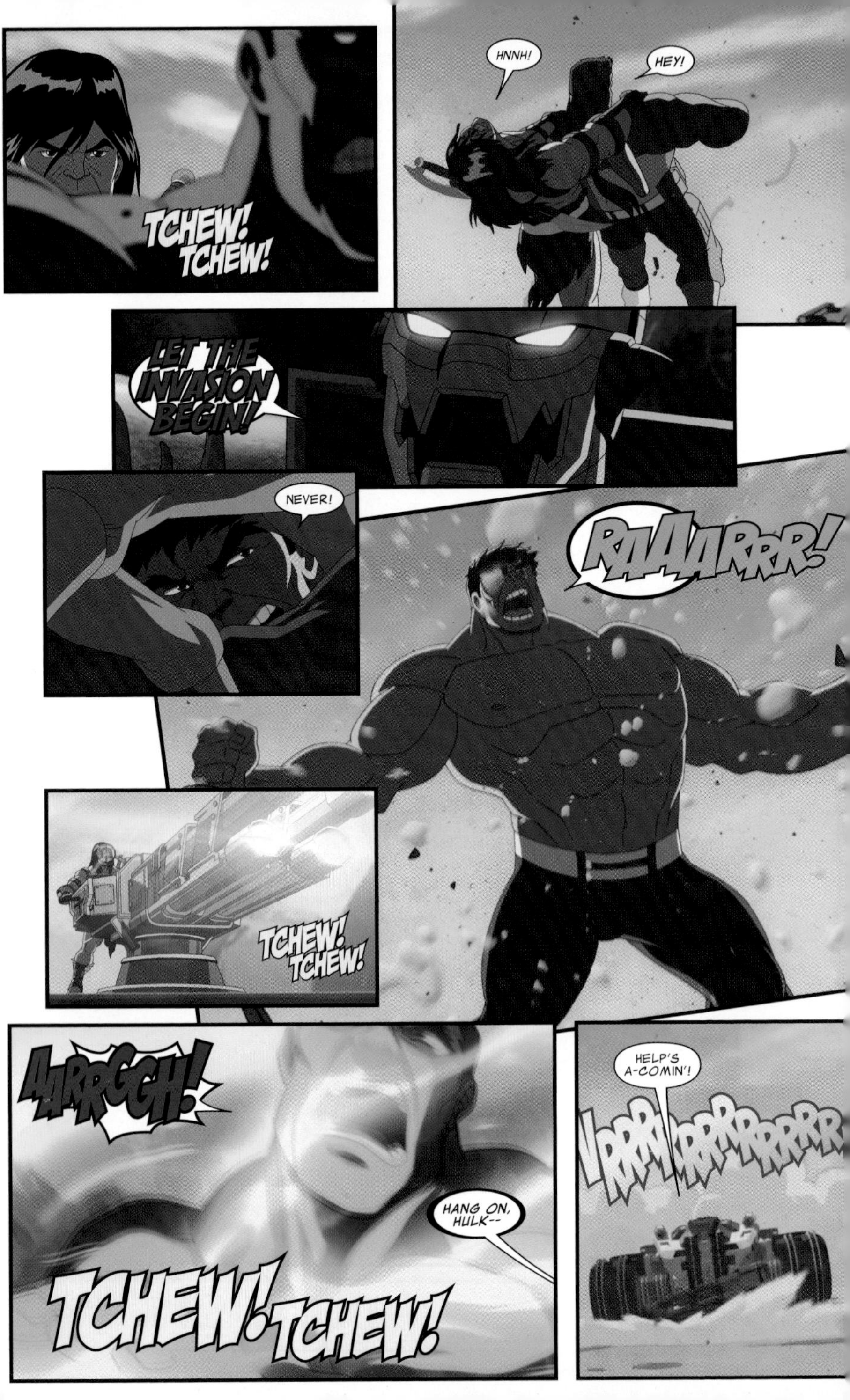
TCHEW! TCHEW!
HNNH!
HEY!
LET THE INVASION BEGIN!
NEVER!
RAAAARRRR!
TCHEW! TCHEW!
AARRGGH!
HANG ON, HULK--
TCHEW! TCHEW!
HELP'S A-COMIN'!
VRRRRRRRRRRRRRRR

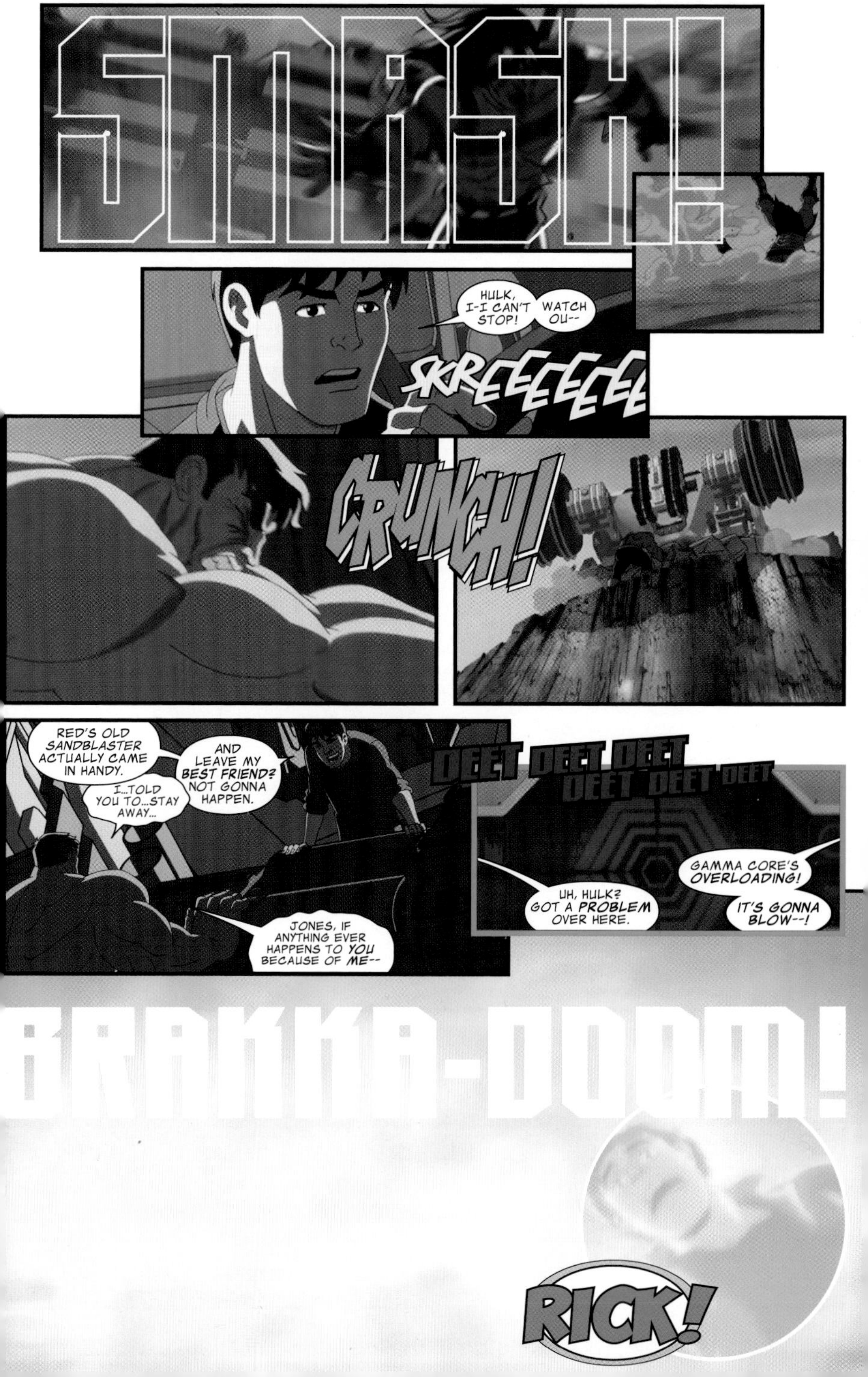
SMASH!
HULK, I-I CAN'T STOP!
WATCH OU--
SKREEEEEEEEE
CRUNCH!
RED'S OLD SANDBLASTER ACTUALLY CAME IN HANDY.
I...TOLD YOU TO...STAY AWAY...
AND LEAVE MY BEST FRIEND? NOT GONNA HAPPEN.
JONES, IF ANYTHING EVER HAPPENS TO YOU BECAUSE OF ME--
DEET DEET DEET
DEET DEET DEET
UH, HULK? GOT A PROBLEM OVER HERE.
GAMMA CORE'S OVERLOADING!
IT'S GONNA BLOW--!
BRAKKA-DOOM!
RICK!

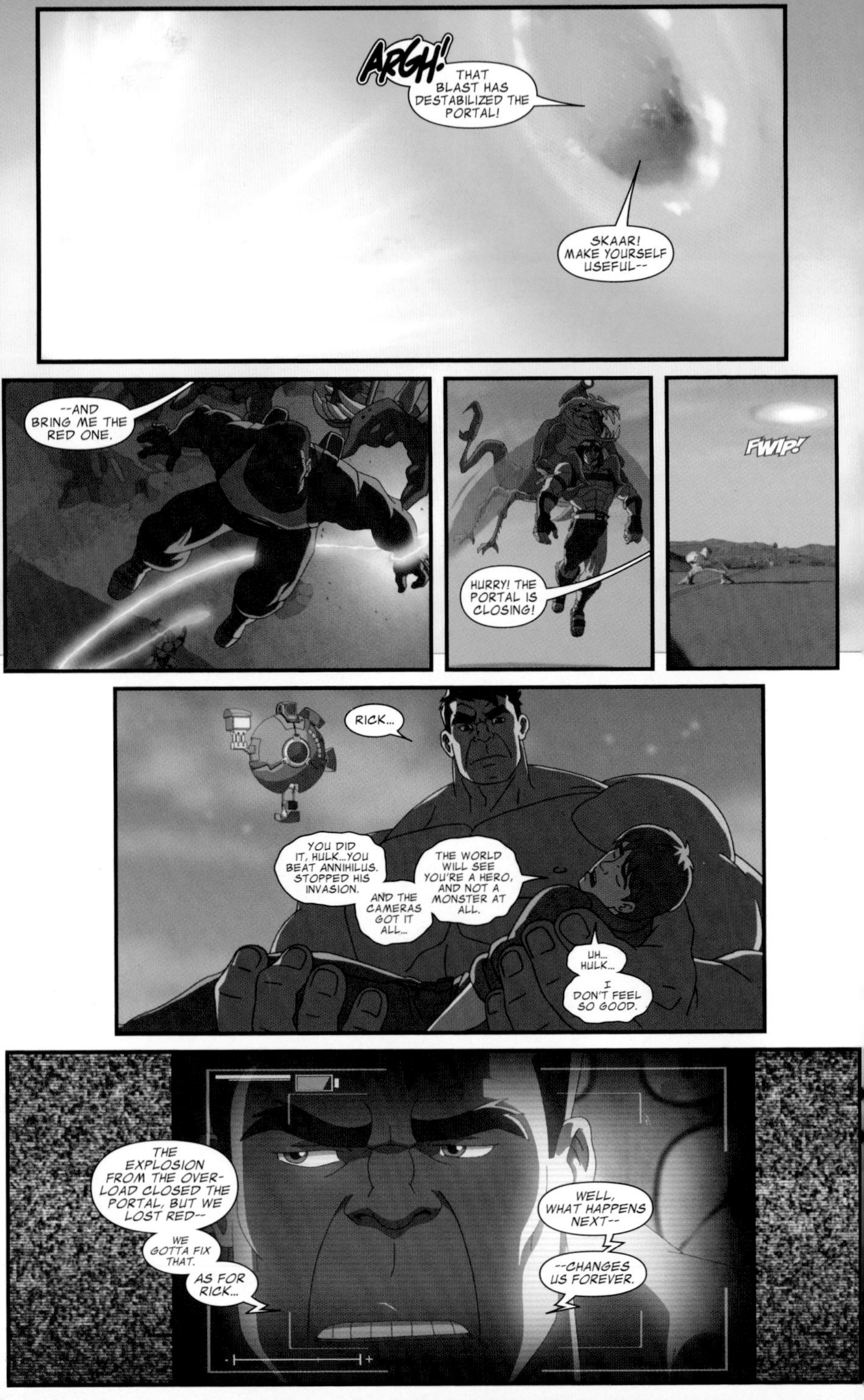
ARGH!
THAT BLAST HAS DESTABILIZED THE PORTAL!
SKAAR! MAKE YOURSELF USEFUL--
--AND BRING ME THE RED ONE.
HURRY! THE PORTAL IS CLOSING!
FWIP!
RICK...
YOU DID IT, HULK...YOU BEAT ANNIHILUS. STOPPED HIS INVASION.
AND THE CAMERAS GOT IT ALL...
THE WORLD WILL SEE YOU'RE A HERO, AND NOT A MONSTER AT ALL.
UH... HULK...
I DON'T FEEL SO GOOD.
THE EXPLOSION FROM THE OVER-LOAD CLOSED THE PORTAL, BUT WE LOST RED--
WE GOTTA FIX THAT.
AS FOR RICK...
WELL, WHAT HAPPENS NEXT--
--CHANGES US FOREVER.

DOORWAY TO DESTRUCTION PART 2

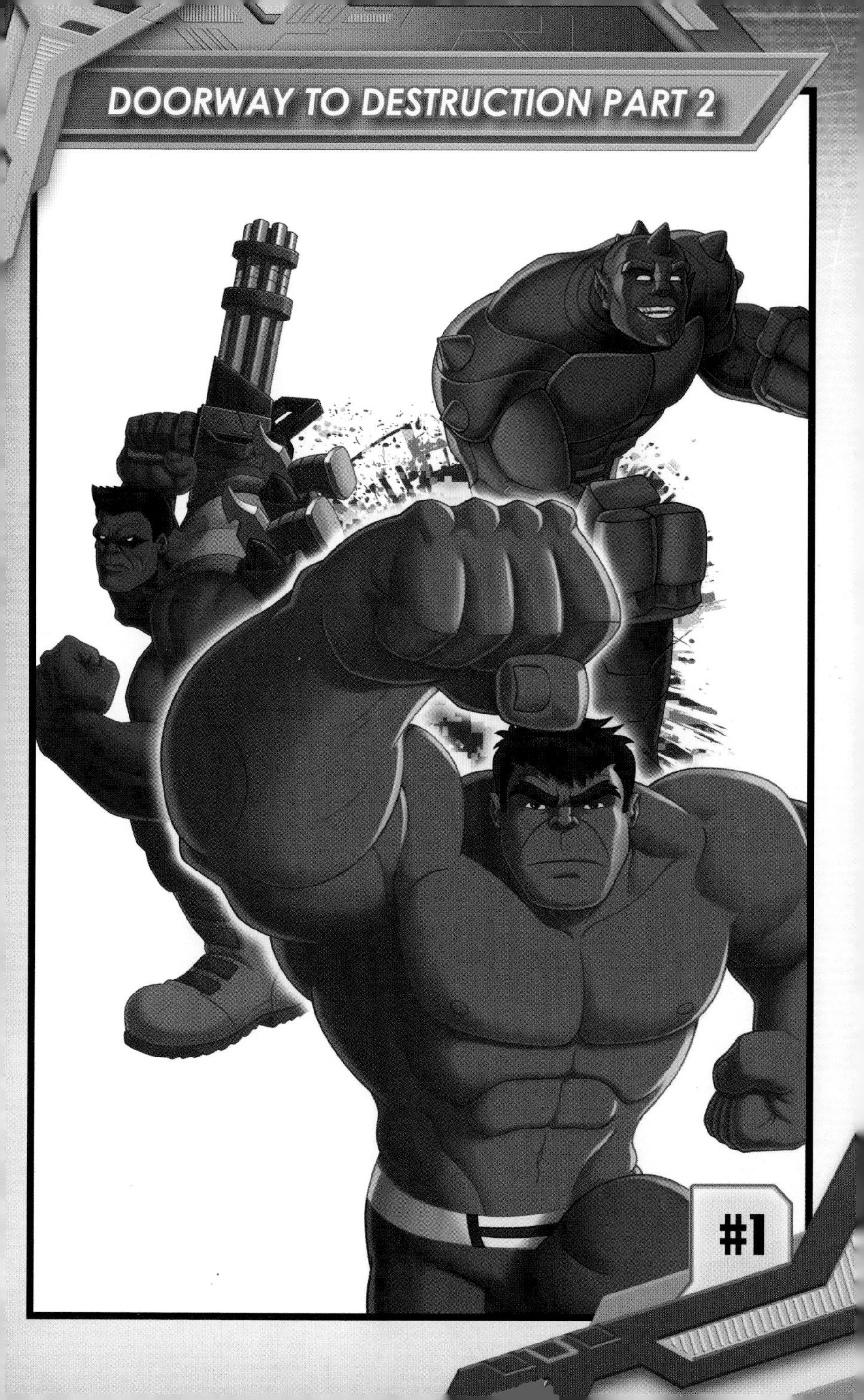

#1

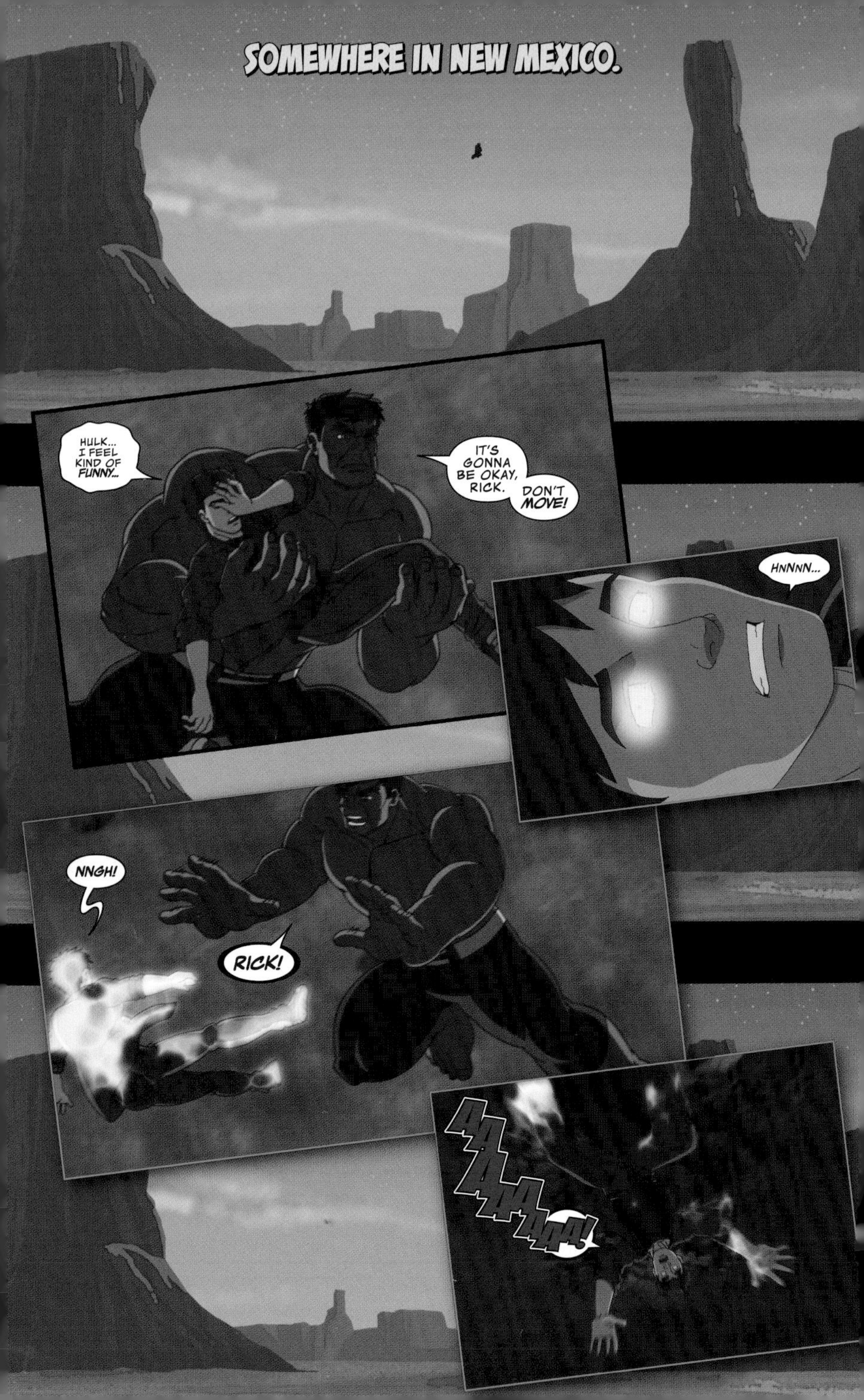
SOMEWHERE IN NEW MEXICO.
HULK... I FEEL KIND OF FUNNY...
IT'S GONNA BE OKAY, RICK.
DON'T MOVE!
HNNNN...
NNGH!
RICK!
AAAAAAAAAA!

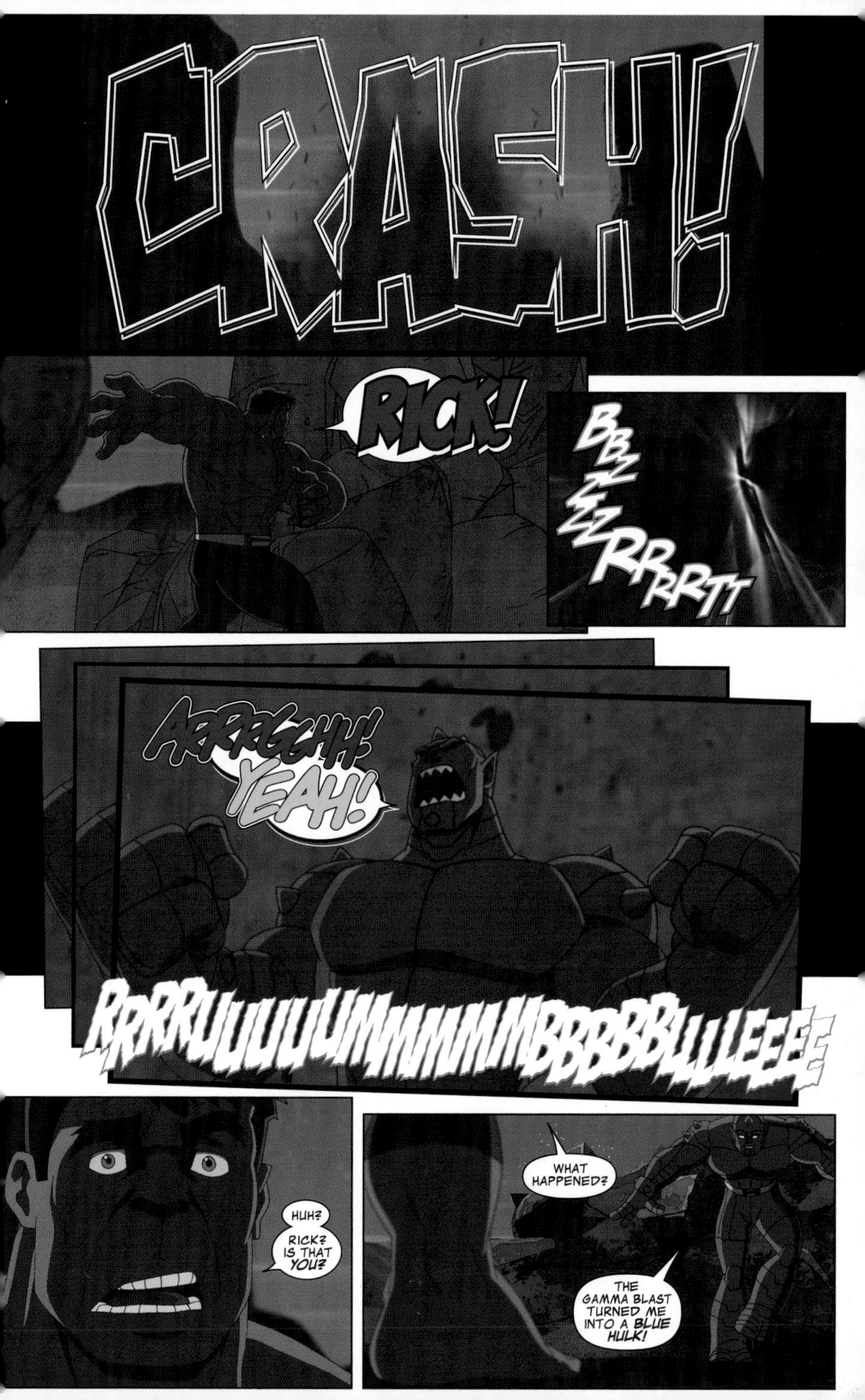

CRASH!
RICK!
BBZZZZRRRRTT
ARRRGGHH!
YEAH!
RRRRUUUUUMMMMMMBBBBBLLLEEEE
HUH?
RICK? IS THAT *YOU?*
WHAT HAPPENED?
THE GAMMA BLAST TURNED ME INTO A ***BLUE HULK!***

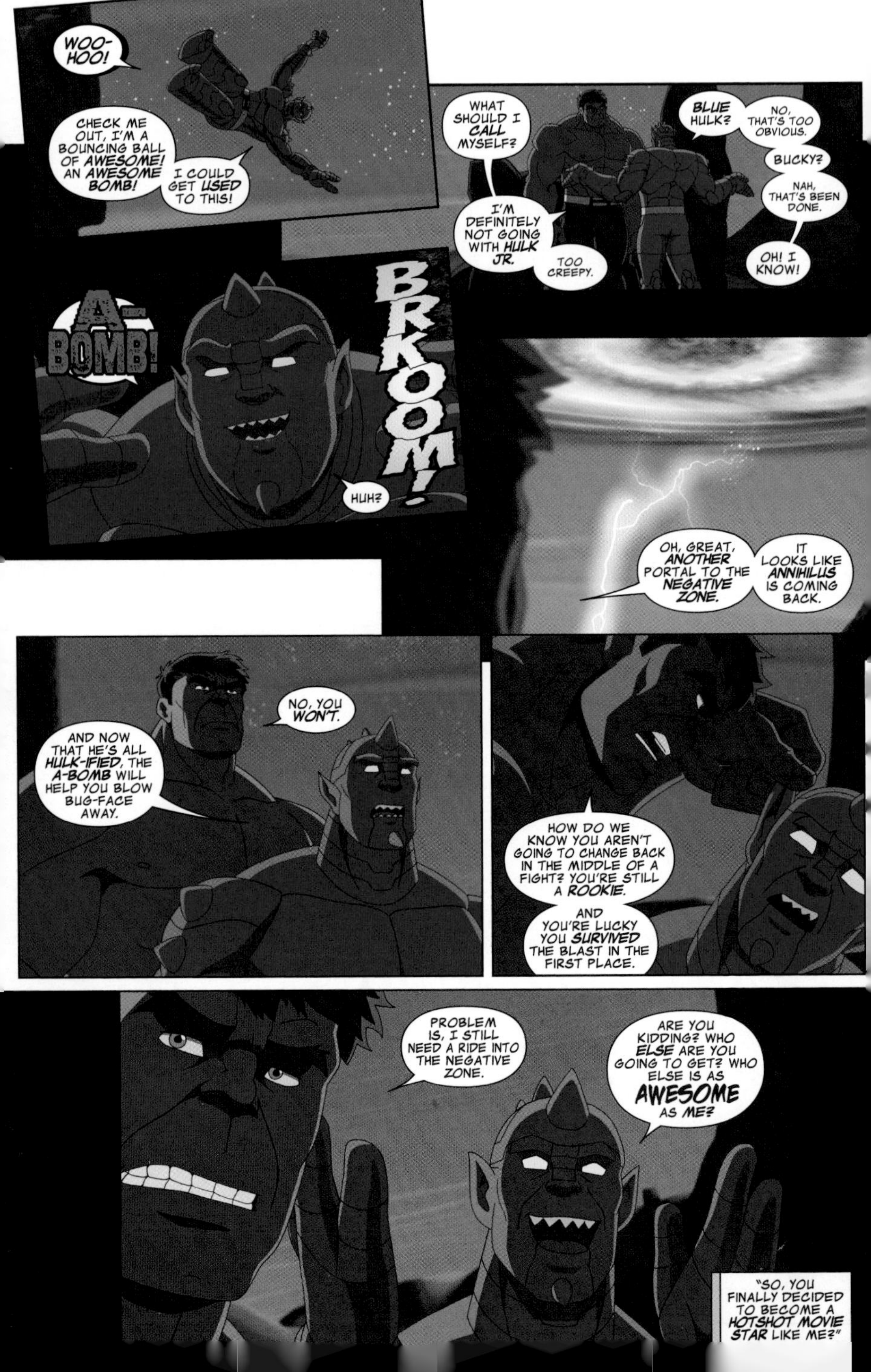
WOO-HOO!
CHECK ME OUT, I'M A BOUNCING BALL OF AWESOME! AN AWESOME BOMB!
I COULD GET USED TO THIS!
WHAT SHOULD I CALL MYSELF?
I'M DEFINITELY NOT GOING WITH HULK JR.
TOO CREEPY.
BLUE HULK?
NO, THAT'S TOO OBVIOUS.
BUCKY?
NAH, THAT'S BEEN DONE.
OH! I KNOW!
A-BOMB!
BRKOOM!
HUH?
OH, GREAT, ANOTHER PORTAL TO THE NEGATIVE ZONE.
IT LOOKS LIKE ANNIHILUS IS COMING BACK.
AND NOW THAT HE'S ALL HULK-IFIED, THE A-BOMB WILL HELP YOU BLOW BUG-FACE AWAY.
NO, YOU WON'T.
HOW DO WE KNOW YOU AREN'T GOING TO CHANGE BACK IN THE MIDDLE OF A FIGHT? YOU'RE STILL A ROOKIE.
AND YOU'RE LUCKY YOU SURVIVED THE BLAST IN THE FIRST PLACE.
PROBLEM IS, I STILL NEED A RIDE INTO THE NEGATIVE ZONE.
ARE YOU KIDDING? WHO ELSE ARE YOU GOING TO GET? WHO ELSE IS AS AWESOME AS ME?
"SO, YOU FINALLY DECIDED TO BECOME A HOTSHOT MOVIE STAR LIKE ME?"

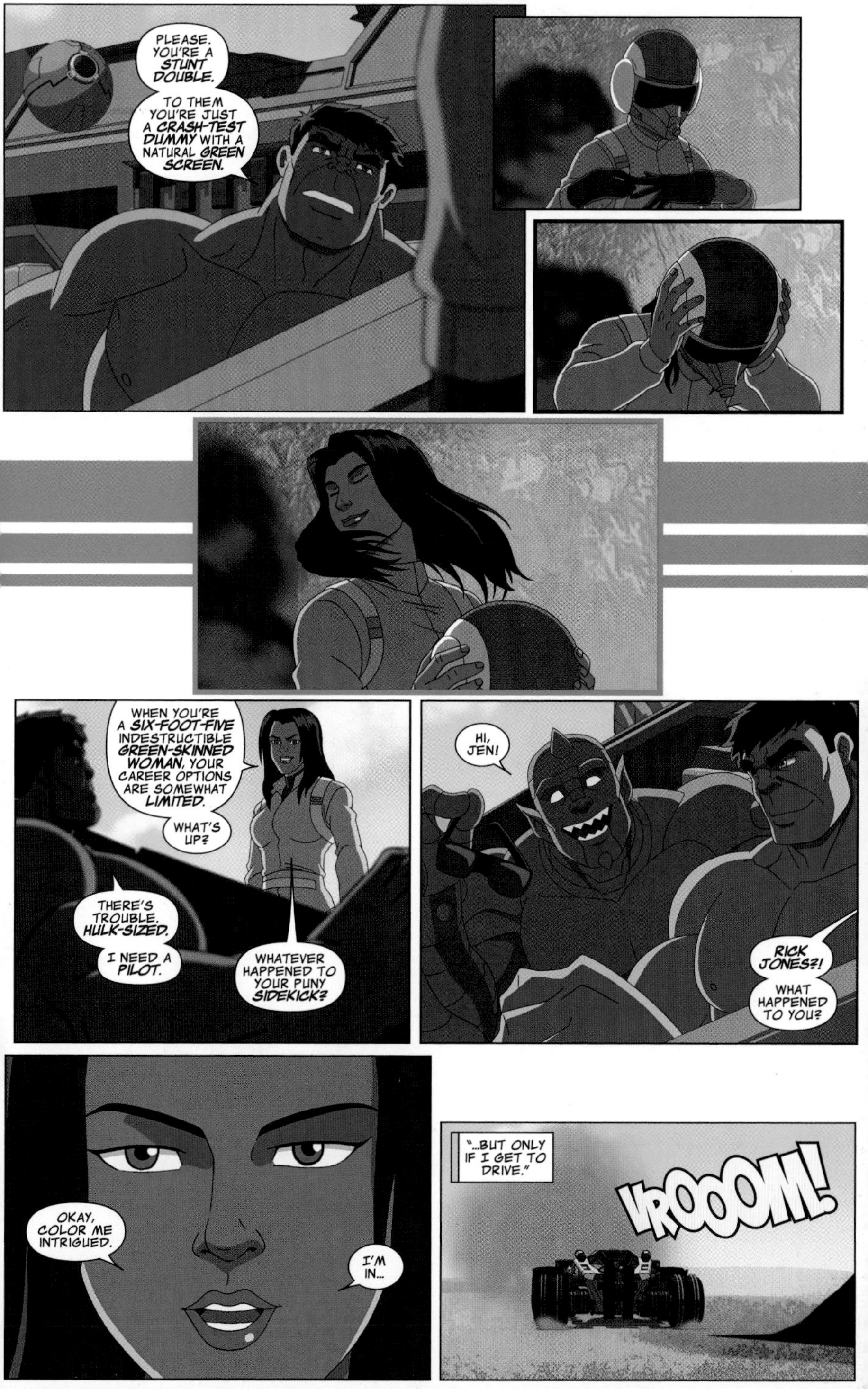
PLEASE. YOU'RE A STUNT DOUBLE.
TO THEM YOU'RE JUST A CRASH-TEST DUMMY WITH A NATURAL GREEN SCREEN.
WHEN YOU'RE A SIX-FOOT-FIVE INDESTRUCTIBLE GREEN-SKINNED WOMAN, YOUR CAREER OPTIONS ARE SOMEWHAT LIMITED.
WHAT'S UP?
THERE'S TROUBLE. HULK-SIZED.
I NEED A PILOT.
WHATEVER HAPPENED TO YOUR PUNY SIDEKICK?
HI, JEN!
RICK JONES?!
WHAT HAPPENED TO YOU?
OKAY, COLOR ME INTRIGUED.
I'M IN...
"...BUT ONLY IF I GET TO DRIVE."
VROOOM!

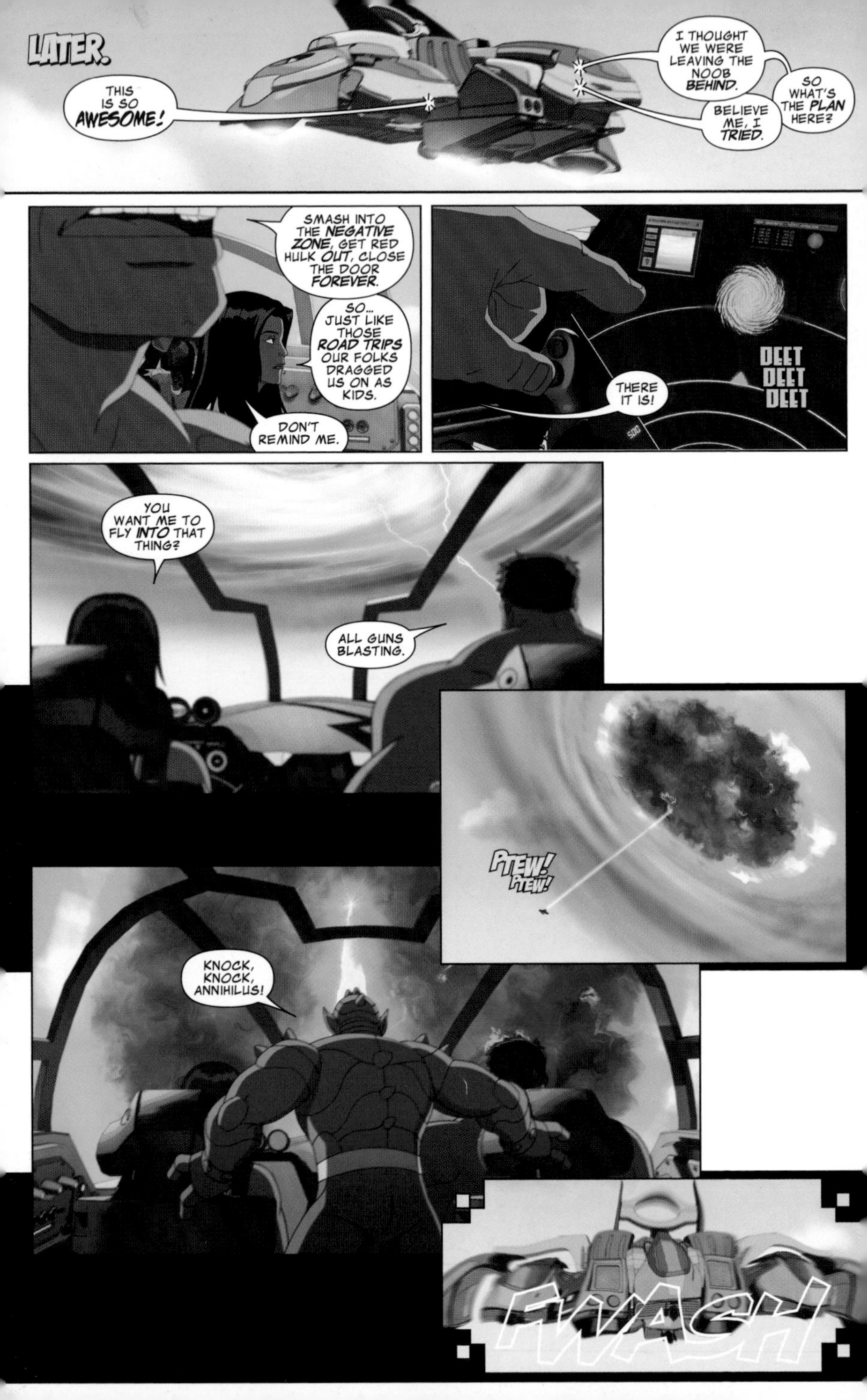
LATER.
THIS IS SO AWESOME!
I THOUGHT WE WERE LEAVING THE NOOB BEHIND.
BELIEVE ME, I TRIED.
SO WHAT'S THE PLAN HERE?
SMASH INTO THE NEGATIVE ZONE, GET RED HULK OUT, CLOSE THE DOOR FOREVER.
SO... JUST LIKE THOSE ROAD TRIPS OUR FOLKS DRAGGED US ON AS KIDS.
DON'T REMIND ME.
THERE IT IS!
DEET DEET DEET
YOU WANT ME TO FLY INTO THAT THING?
ALL GUNS BLASTING.
PTEW! PTEW!
KNOCK, KNOCK, ANNIHILUS!
FWASH

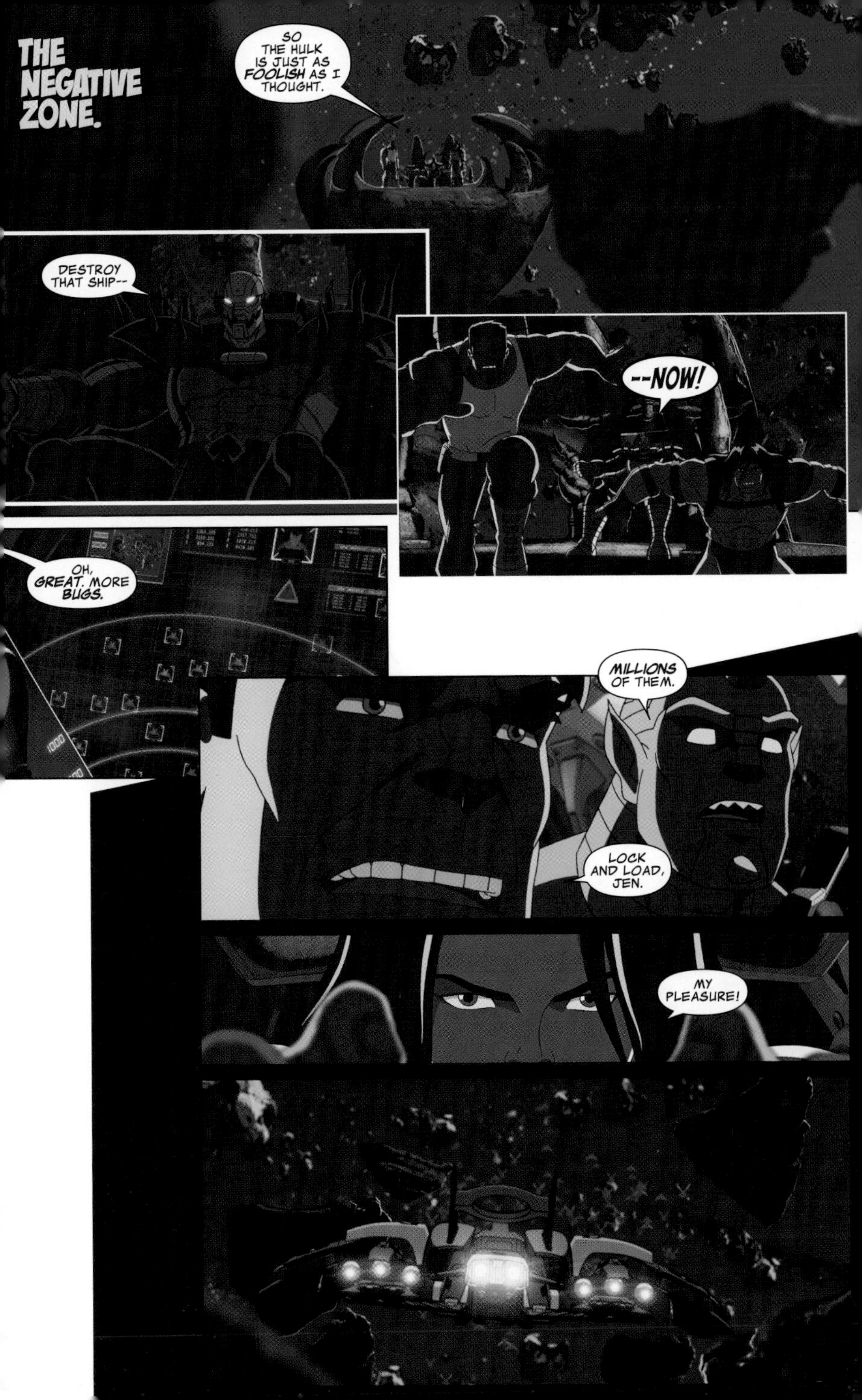
THE NEGATIVE ZONE.
SO THE HULK IS JUST AS FOOLISH AS I THOUGHT.
DESTROY THAT SHIP--
--NOW!
OH, GREAT. MORE BUGS.
MILLIONS OF THEM.
LOCK AND LOAD, JEN.
MY PLEASURE!

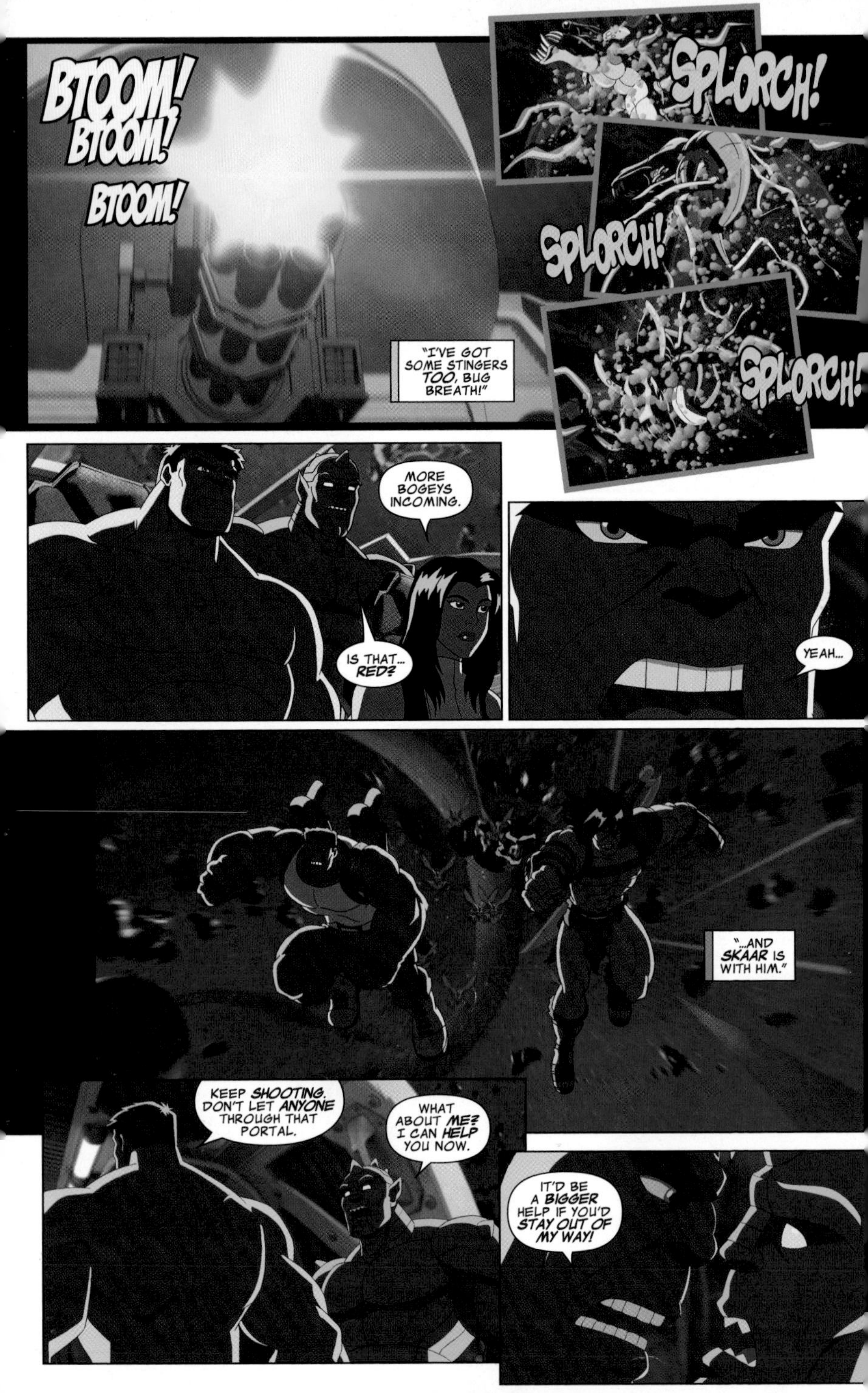
BTOOM!
BTOOM!
BTOOM!
"I'VE GOT SOME STINGERS TOO, BUG BREATH!"
SPLORCH!
SPLORCH!
SPLORCH!
MORE BOGEYS INCOMING.
IS THAT... RED?
YEAH...
"...AND SKAAR IS WITH HIM."
KEEP SHOOTING. DON'T LET ANYONE THROUGH THAT PORTAL.
WHAT ABOUT ME? I CAN HELP YOU NOW.
IT'D BE A BIGGER HELP IF YOU'D STAY OUT OF MY WAY!

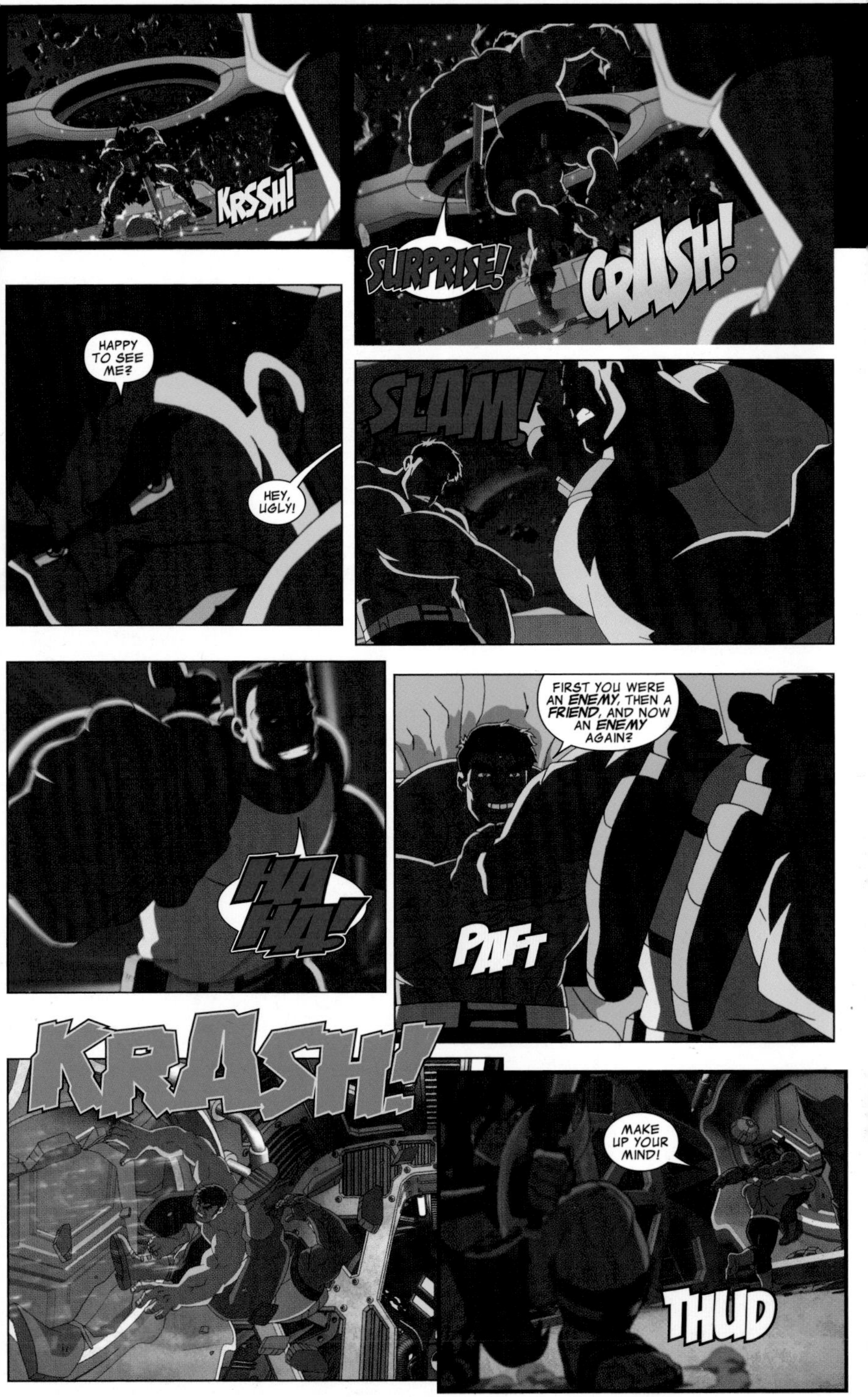

KRSSH!
SURPRISE!
CRASH!
HAPPY TO SEE ME?
HEY, UGLY!
SLAM!
HA HA!
FIRST YOU WERE AN ENEMY, THEN A FRIEND, AND NOW AN ENEMY AGAIN?
PAFT
KRASH!
MAKE UP YOUR MIND!
THUD

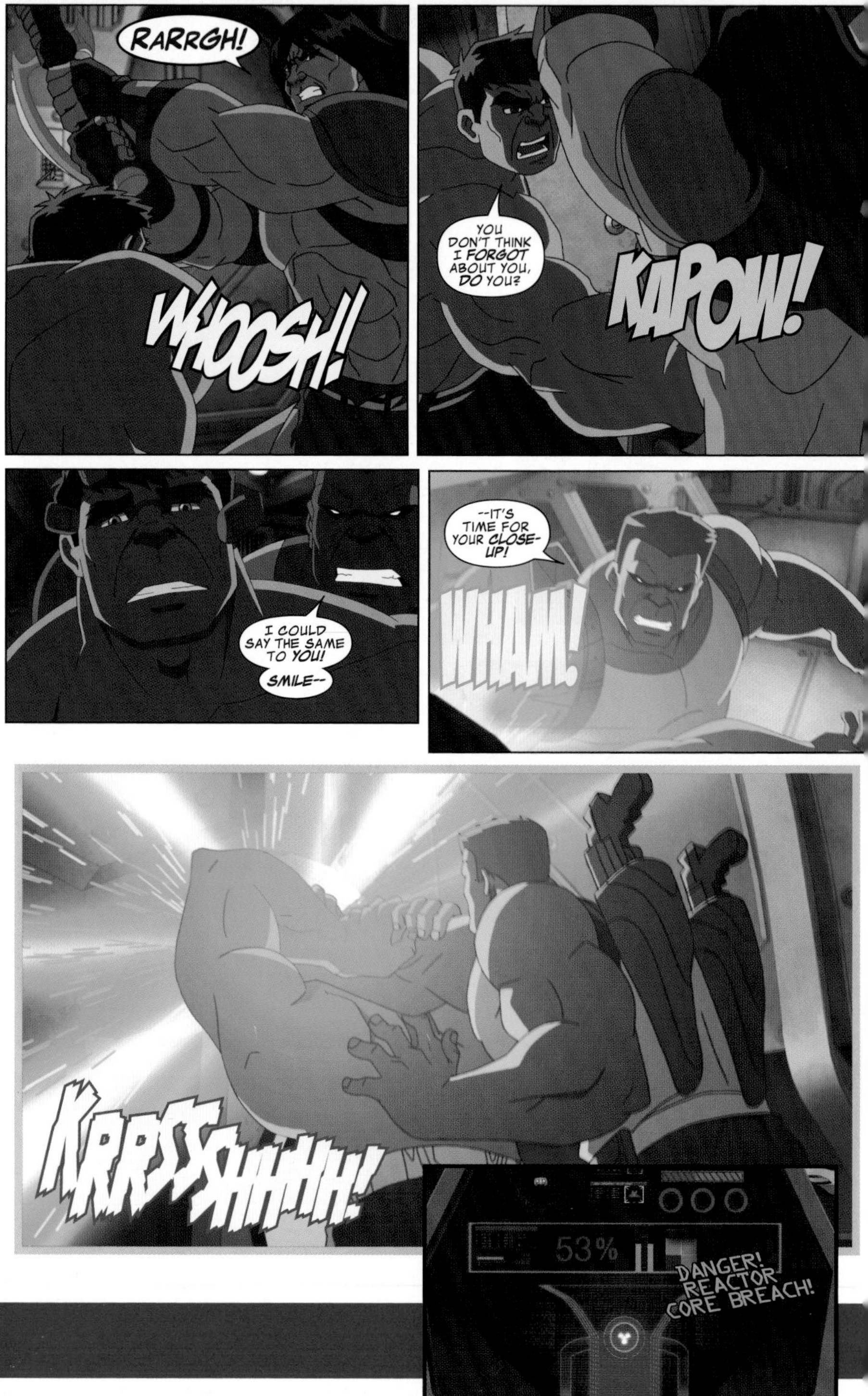
RARRGH!
WHOOSH!
YOU DON'T THINK I FORGOT ABOUT YOU, DO YOU?
KAPOW!
I COULD SAY THE SAME TO YOU!
SMILE--
--IT'S TIME FOR YOUR CLOSE-UP!
WHAM!
KRRSSHHHHH!
53%
DANGER! REACTOR CORE BREACH!

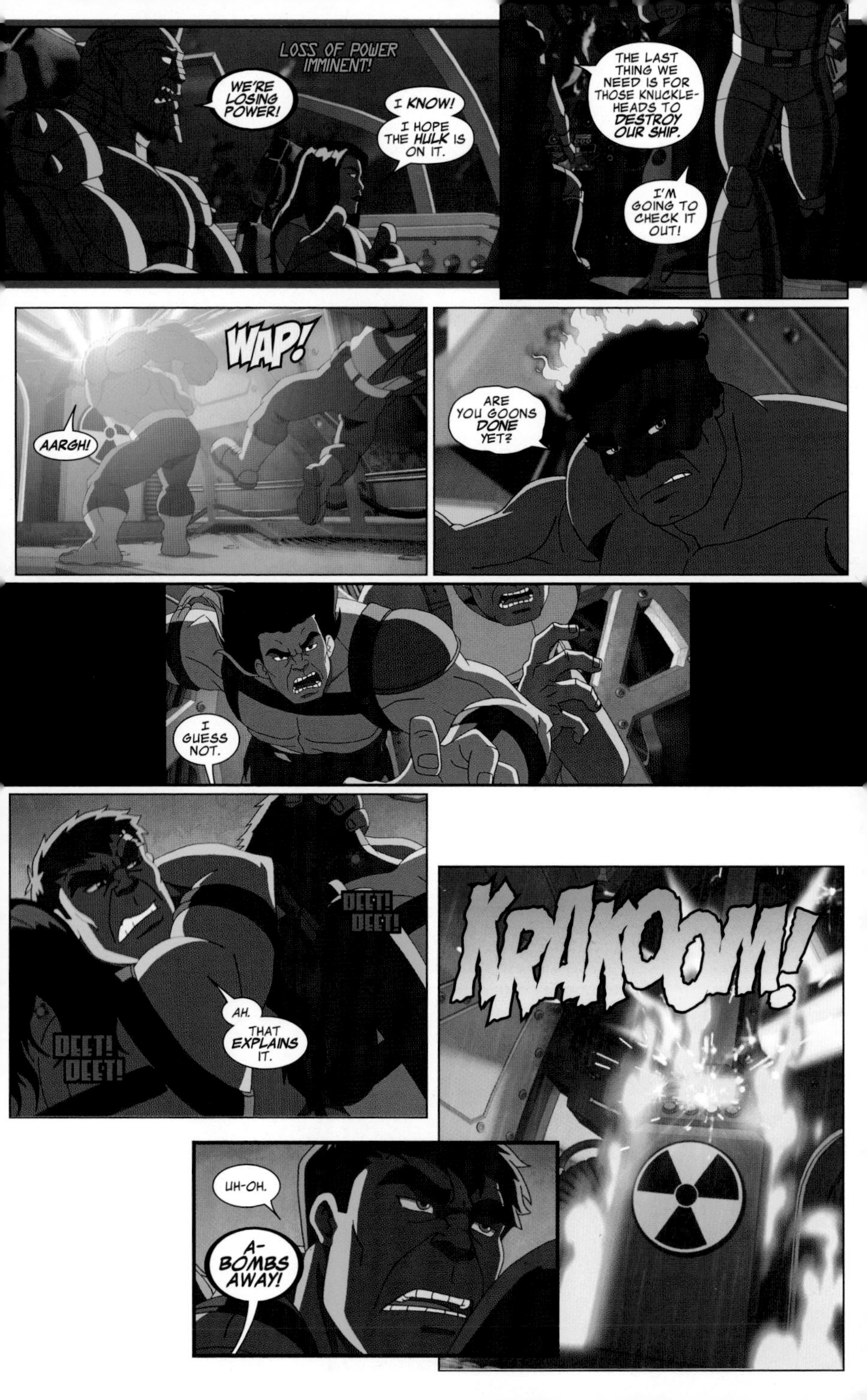
LOSS OF POWER IMMINENT!
WE'RE LOSING POWER!
I KNOW!
I HOPE THE HULK IS ON IT.
THE LAST THING WE NEED IS FOR THOSE KNUCKLE-HEADS TO DESTROY OUR SHIP.
I'M GOING TO CHECK IT OUT!
WAP!
AARGH!
ARE YOU GOONS DONE YET?
I GUESS NOT.
DEET! DEET!
AH. THAT EXPLAINS IT.
DEET! DEET!
KRAKOOM!
UH-OH.
A-BOMBS AWAY!

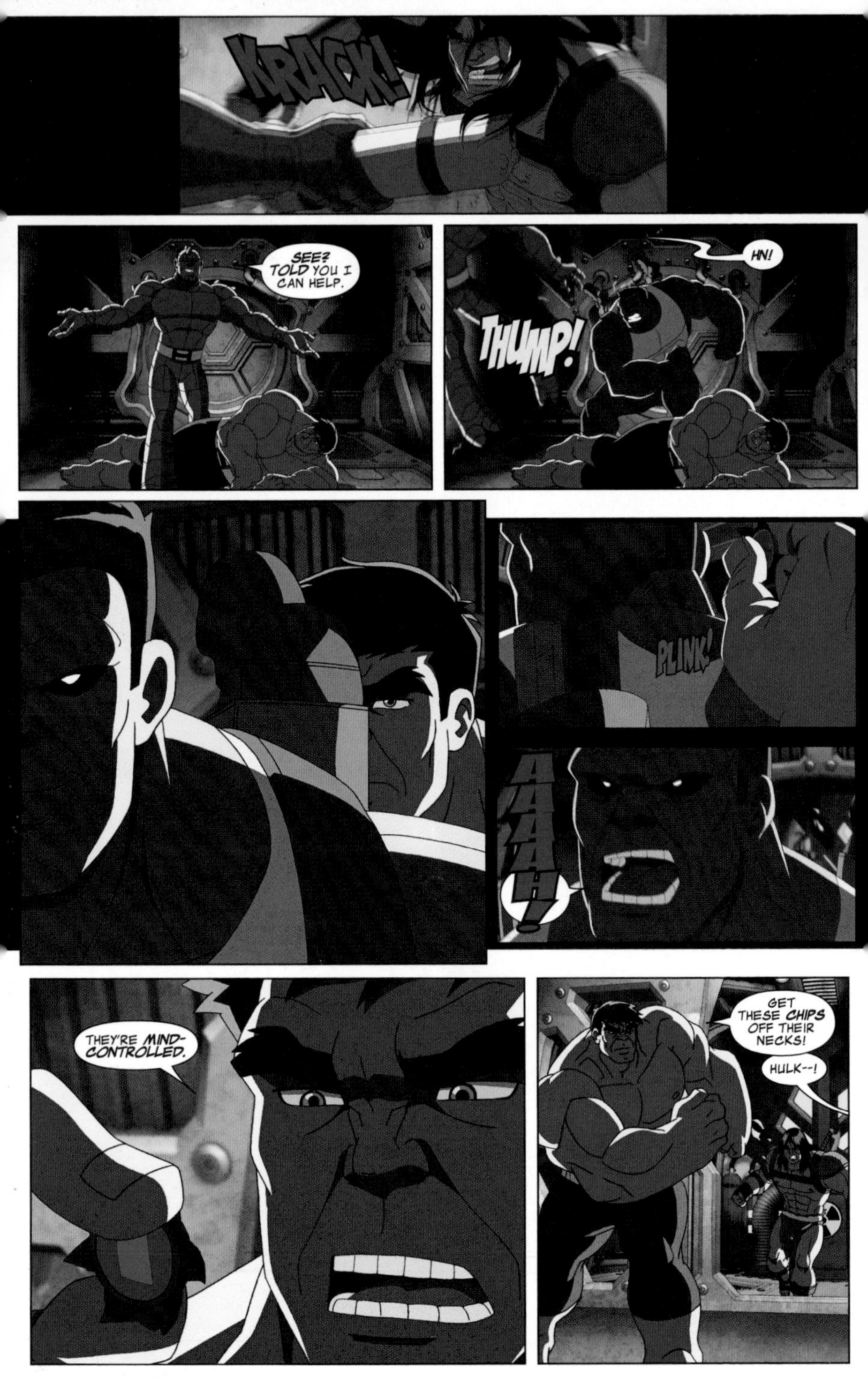
KRACK!
SEE? TOLD YOU I CAN HELP.
HN!
THUMP!
PLINK!
AAAAH!
THEY'RE MIND-CONTROLLED.
GET THESE CHIPS OFF THEIR NECKS!
HULK--!

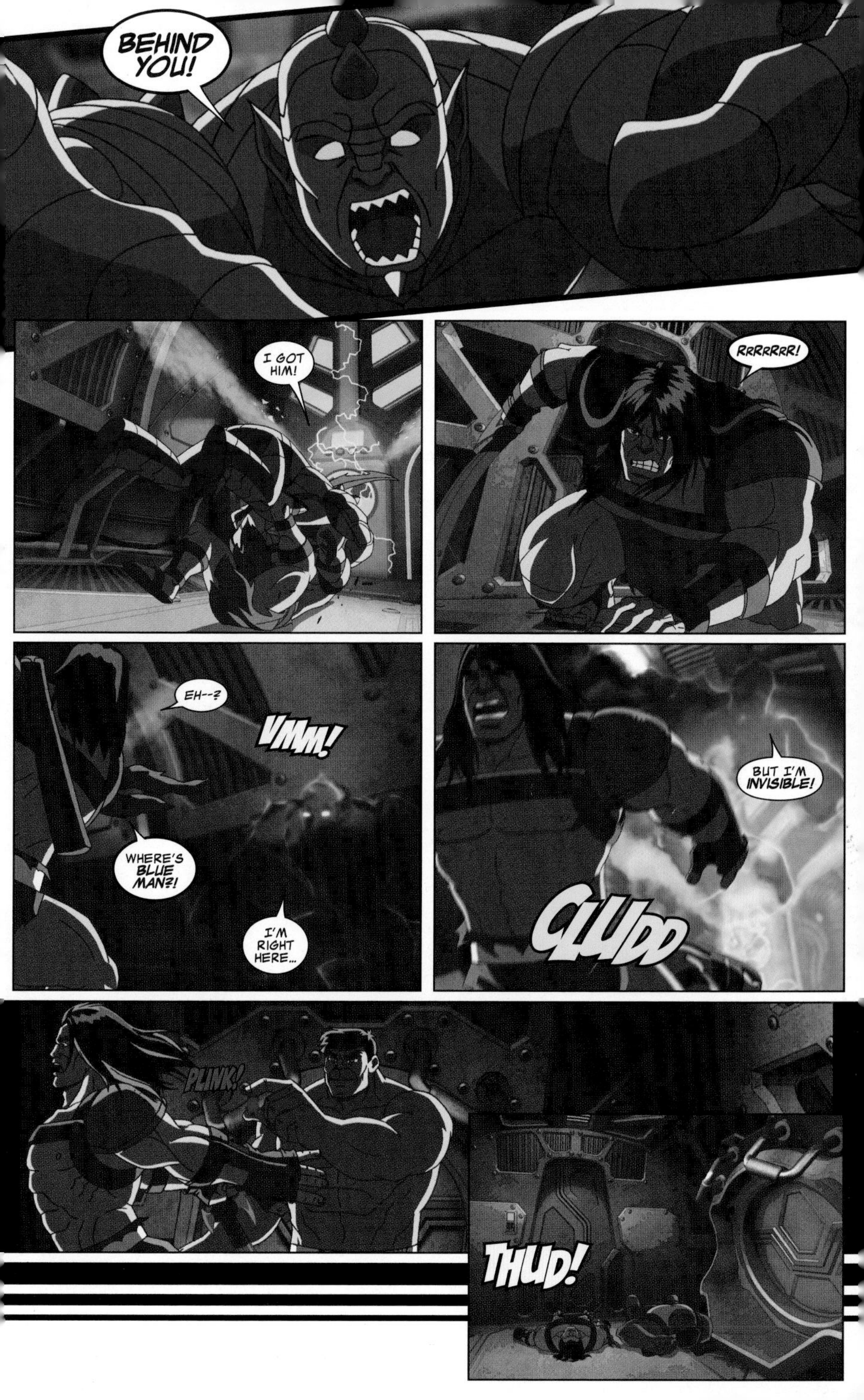
BEHIND YOU!
I GOT HIM!
RRRRRRR!
EH--?
VMM!
WHERE'S BLUE MAN?!
I'M RIGHT HERE...
BUT I'M INVISIBLE!
CLUDD
PLINK!
THUD!

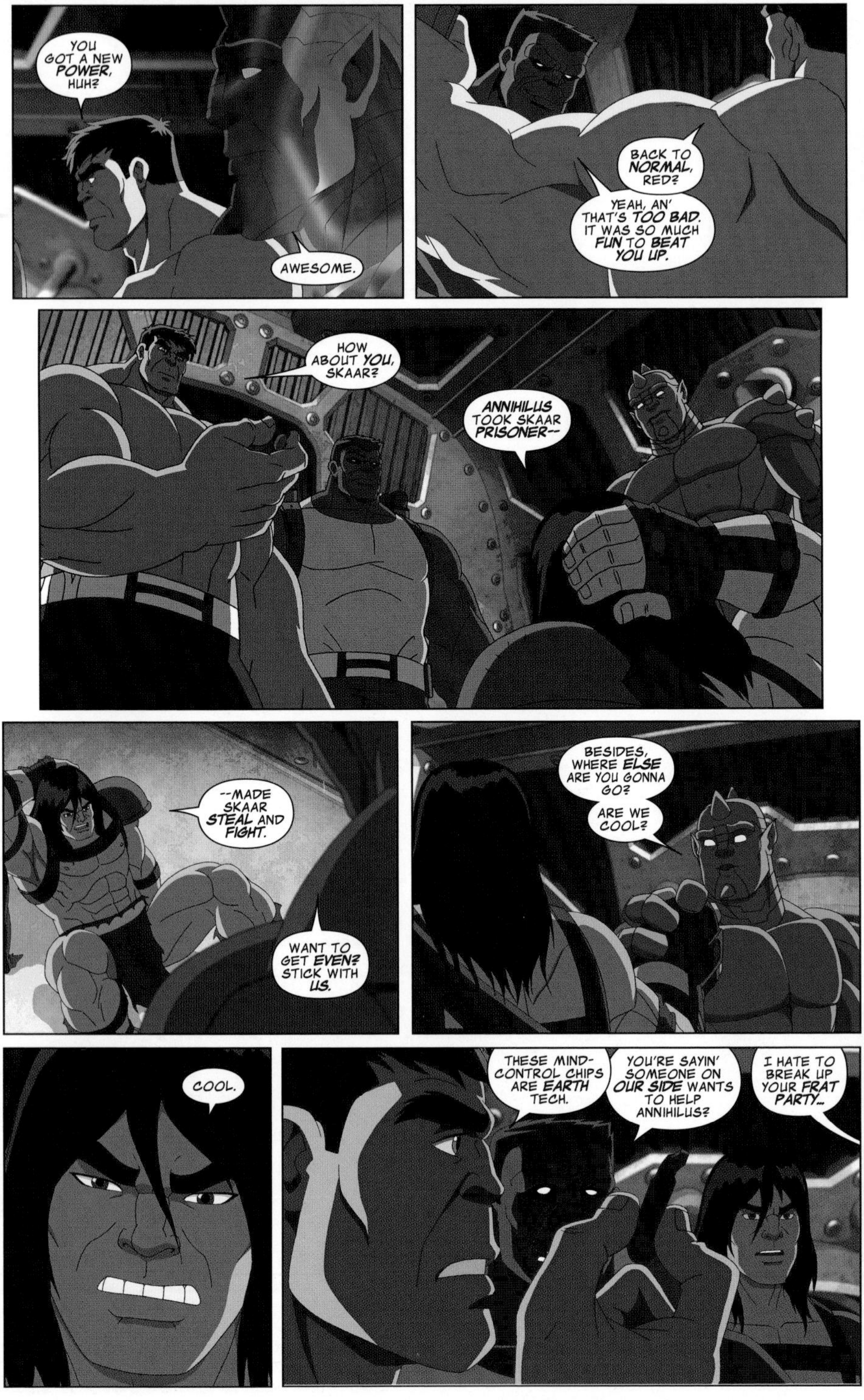
YOU GOT A NEW POWER, HUH?
AWESOME.
BACK TO NORMAL, RED?
YEAH, AN' THAT'S TOO BAD. IT WAS SO MUCH FUN TO BEAT YOU UP.
HOW ABOUT YOU, SKAAR?
ANNIHILUS TOOK SKAAR PRISONER--
--MADE SKAAR STEAL AND FIGHT.
WANT TO GET EVEN? STICK WITH US.
BESIDES, WHERE ELSE ARE YOU GONNA GO?
ARE WE COOL?
COOL.
THESE MIND-CONTROL CHIPS ARE EARTH TECH.
YOU'RE SAYIN' SOMEONE ON OUR SIDE WANTS TO HELP ANNIHILUS?
I HATE TO BREAK UP YOUR FRAT PARTY...

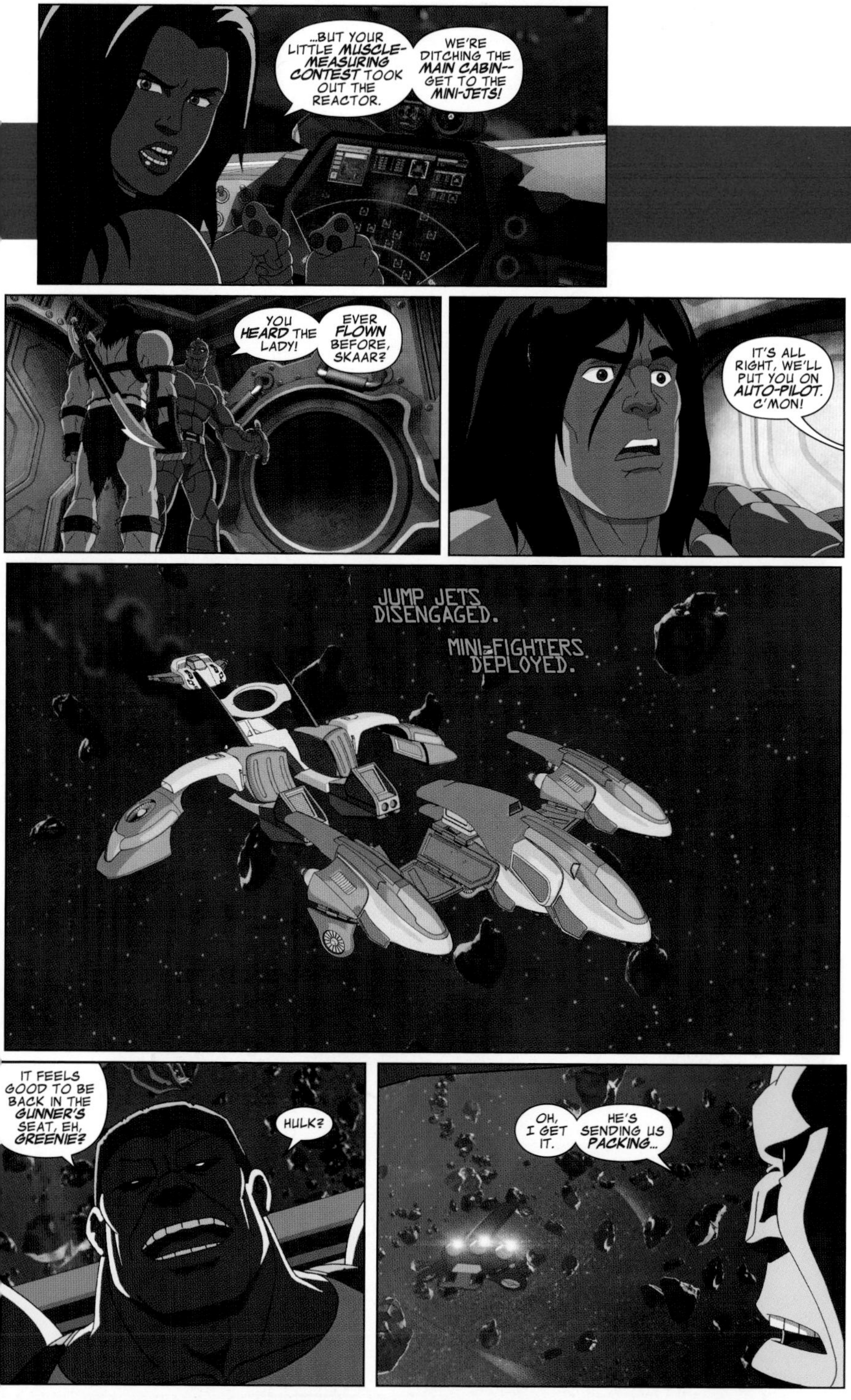
...BUT YOUR LITTLE MUSCLE-MEASURING CONTEST TOOK OUT THE REACTOR.
WE'RE DITCHING THE MAIN CABIN-- GET TO THE MINI-JETS!
YOU HEARD THE LADY!
EVER FLOWN BEFORE, SKAAR?
IT'S ALL RIGHT, WE'LL PUT YOU ON AUTO-PILOT. C'MON!
JUMP JETS DISENGAGED.
MINI-FIGHTERS DEPLOYED.
IT FEELS GOOD TO BE BACK IN THE GUNNER'S SEAT, EH, GREENIE?
HULK?
OH, I GET IT.
HE'S SENDING US PACKING...

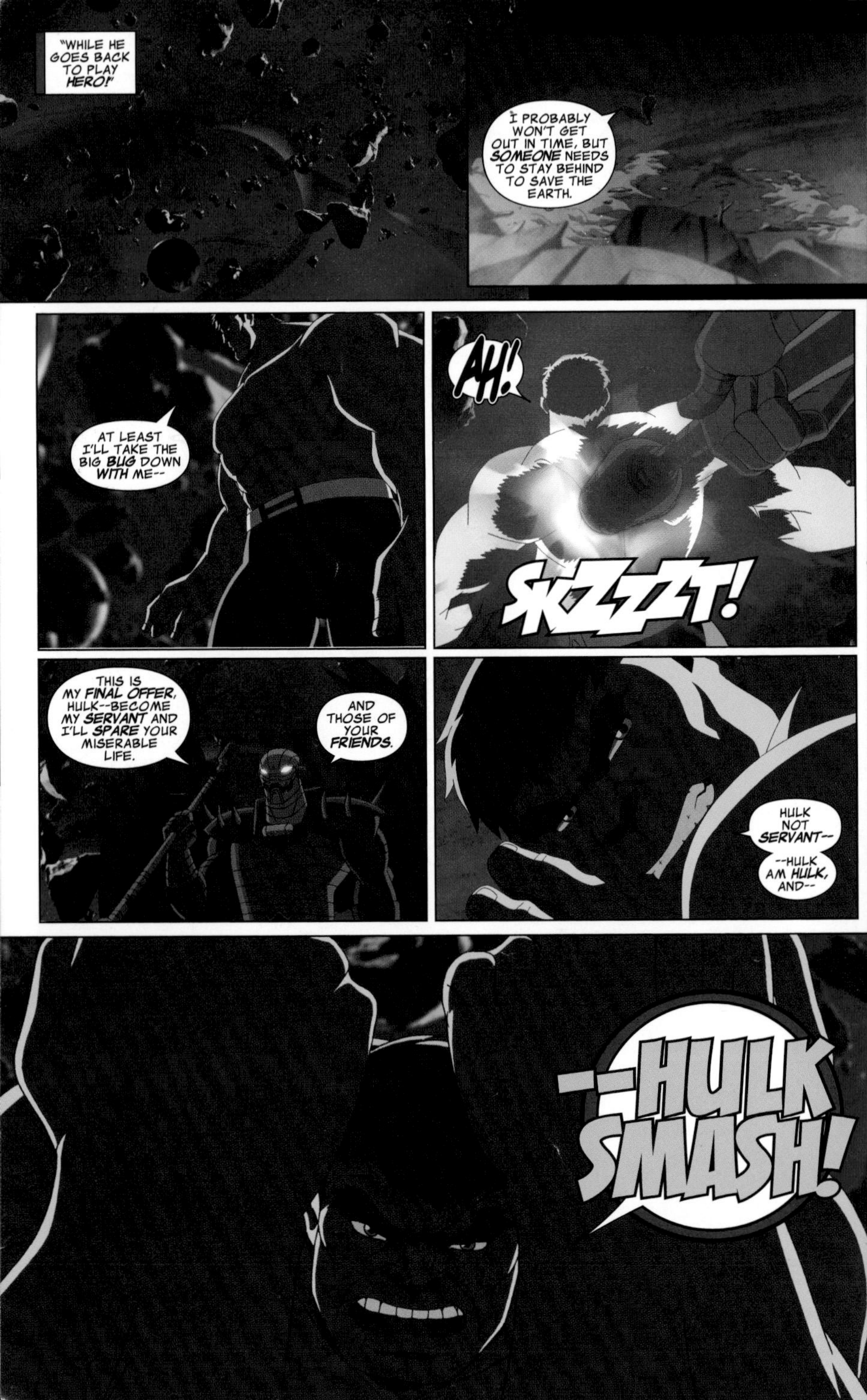
"WHILE HE GOES BACK TO PLAY HERO!"
I PROBABLY WON'T GET OUT IN TIME, BUT SOMEONE NEEDS TO STAY BEHIND TO SAVE THE EARTH.
AT LEAST I'LL TAKE THE BIG BUG DOWN WITH ME--
AH!
SKZZZT!
THIS IS MY FINAL OFFER, HULK--BECOME MY SERVANT AND I'LL SPARE YOUR MISERABLE LIFE.
AND THOSE OF YOUR FRIENDS.
HULK NOT SERVANT--
--HULK AM HULK, AND--
--HULK SMASH!

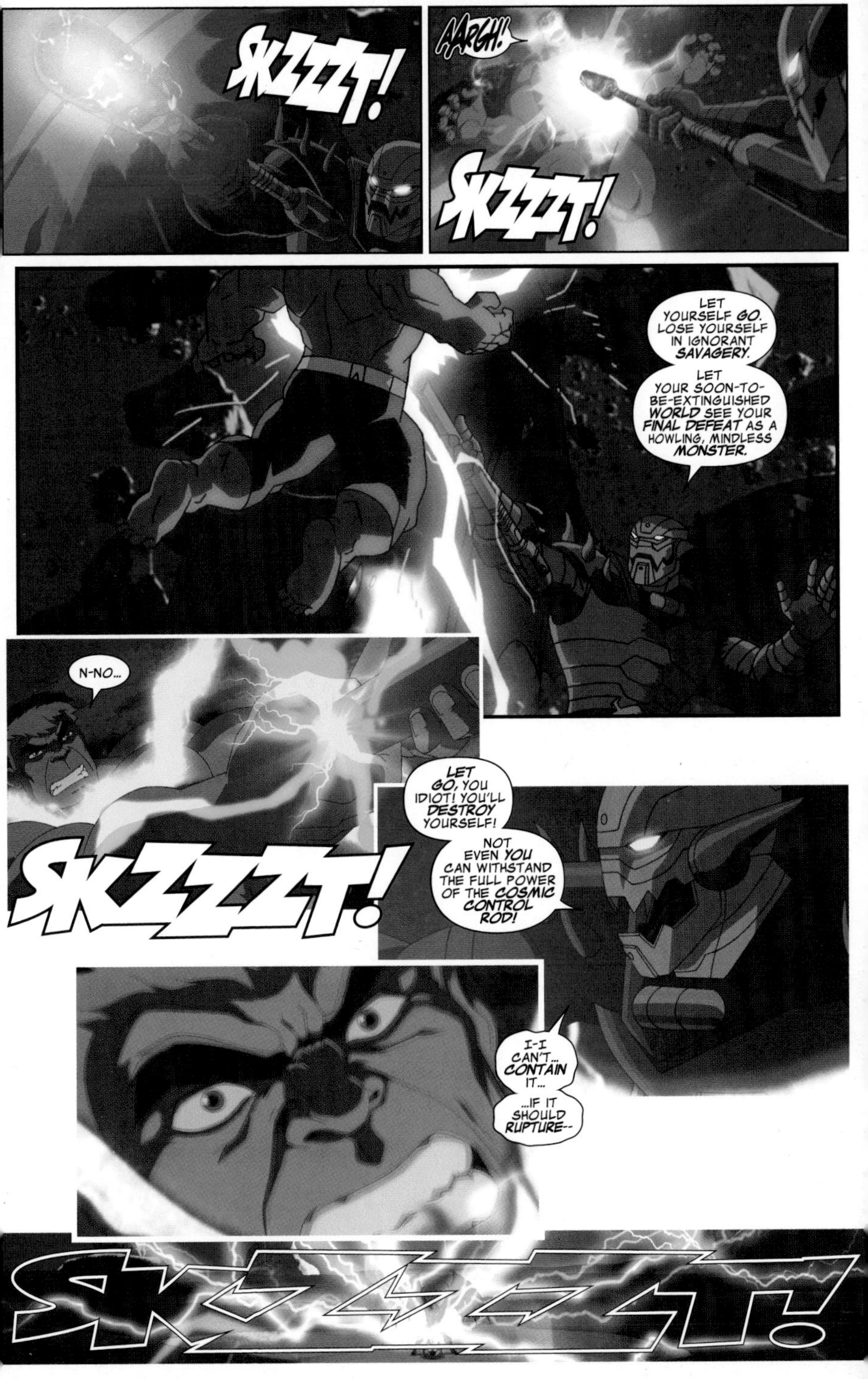
SKZZZT!
AARGH!
SKZZZT!
LET YOURSELF GO. LOSE YOURSELF IN IGNORANT SAVAGERY.
LET YOUR SOON-TO-BE-EXTINGUISHED WORLD SEE YOUR FINAL DEFEAT AS A HOWLING, MINDLESS MONSTER.
N-NO...
SKZZZT!
LET GO, YOU IDIOT! YOU'LL DESTROY YOURSELF!
NOT EVEN YOU CAN WITHSTAND THE FULL POWER OF THE COSMIC CONTROL ROD!
I-I CAN'T... CONTAIN IT...
...IF IT SHOULD RUPTURE--
SKZZZT!

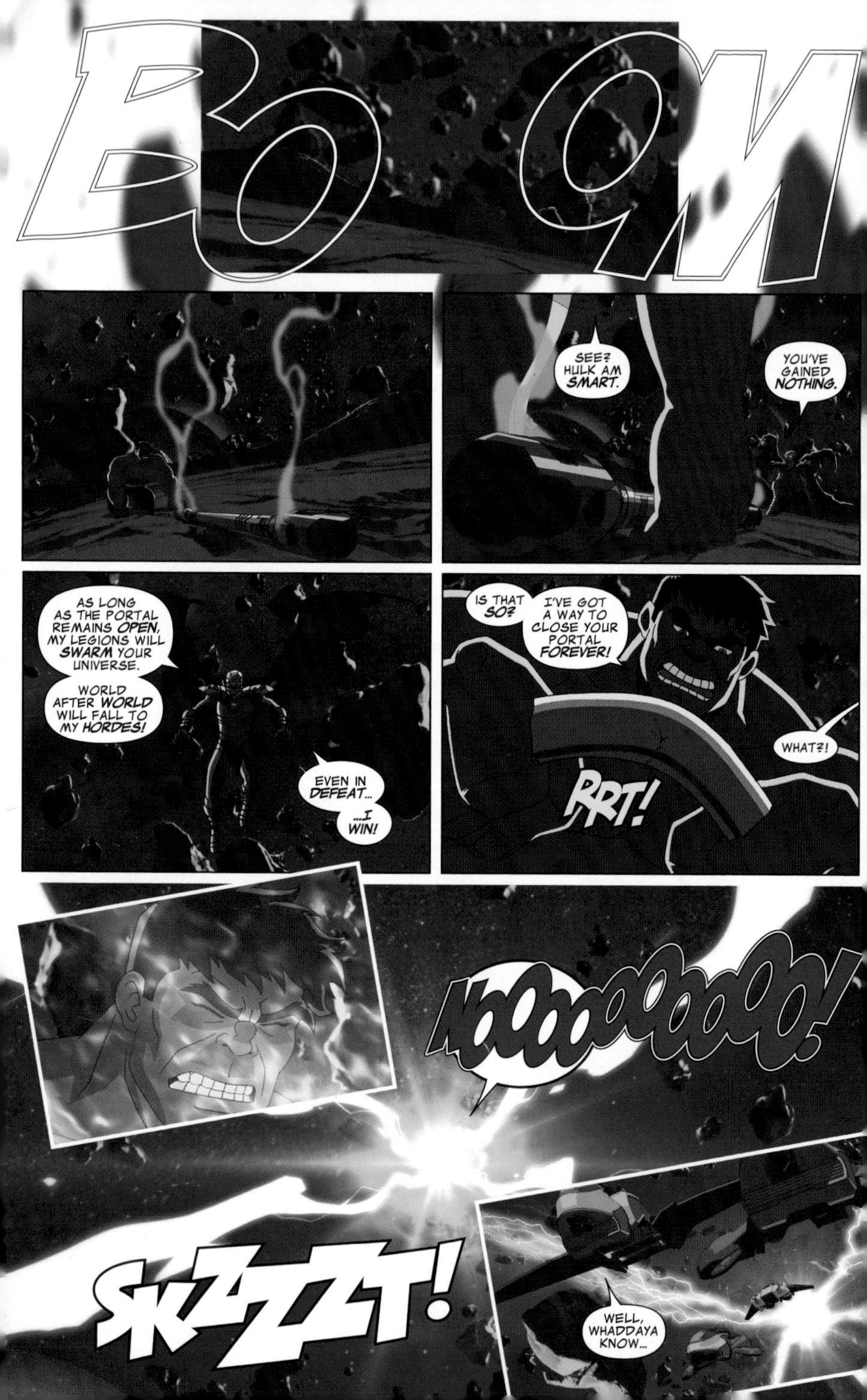
BOOM
SEE? HULK AM SMART.
YOU'VE GAINED NOTHING.
AS LONG AS THE PORTAL REMAINS OPEN, MY LEGIONS WILL SWARM YOUR UNIVERSE.
WORLD AFTER WORLD WILL FALL TO MY HORDES!
EVEN IN DEFEAT...
...I WIN!
IS THAT SO?
I'VE GOT A WAY TO CLOSE YOUR PORTAL FOREVER!
WHAT?!
RRT!
NOOOOOOOOOO!
SKZZZT!
WELL, WHADDAYA KNOW...

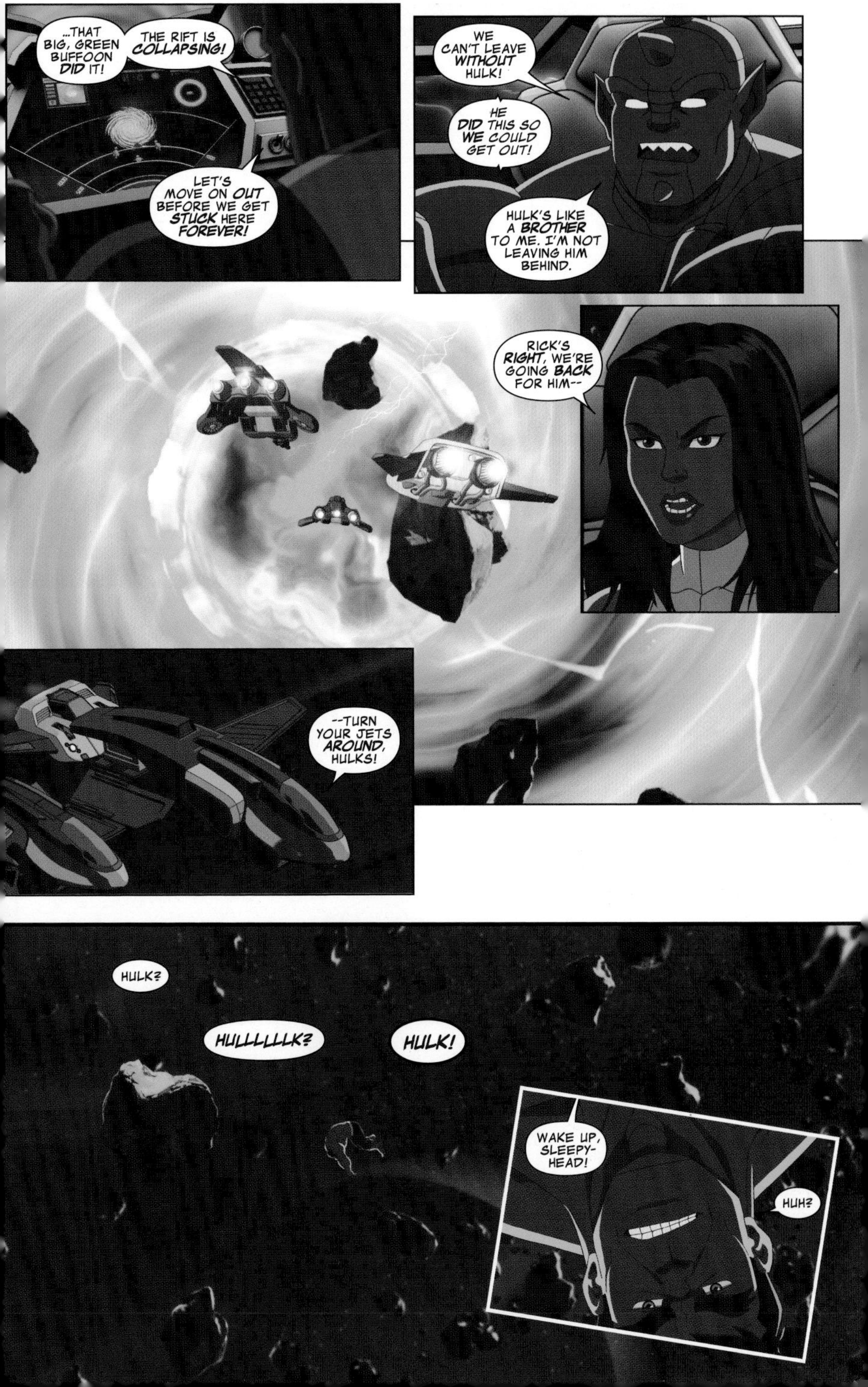
...THAT BIG, GREEN BUFFOON DID IT!
THE RIFT IS COLLAPSING!
LET'S MOVE ON OUT BEFORE WE GET STUCK HERE FOREVER!
WE CAN'T LEAVE WITHOUT HULK!
HE DID THIS SO WE COULD GET OUT!
HULK'S LIKE A BROTHER TO ME. I'M NOT LEAVING HIM BEHIND.
RICK'S RIGHT, WE'RE GOING BACK FOR HIM--
--TURN YOUR JETS AROUND, HULKS!
HULK?
HULLLLLLK?
HULK!
WAKE UP, SLEEPY-HEAD!
HUH?

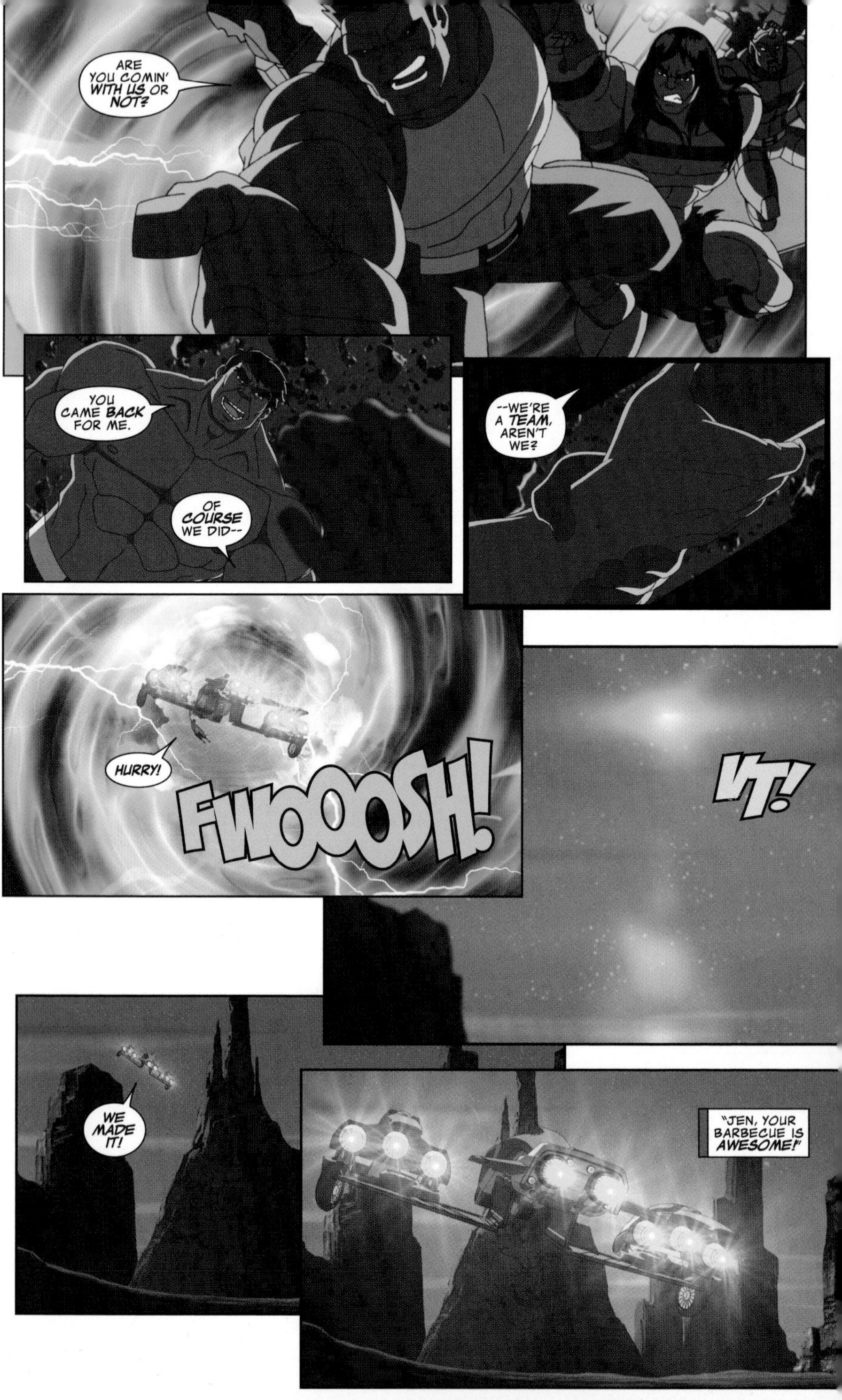
ARE YOU COMIN' WITH US OR NOT?
YOU CAME BACK FOR ME.
OF COURSE WE DID--
--WE'RE A TEAM, AREN'T WE?
HURRY!
FWOOOSH!
VT!
WE MADE IT!
"JEN, YOUR BARBECUE IS AWESOME!"

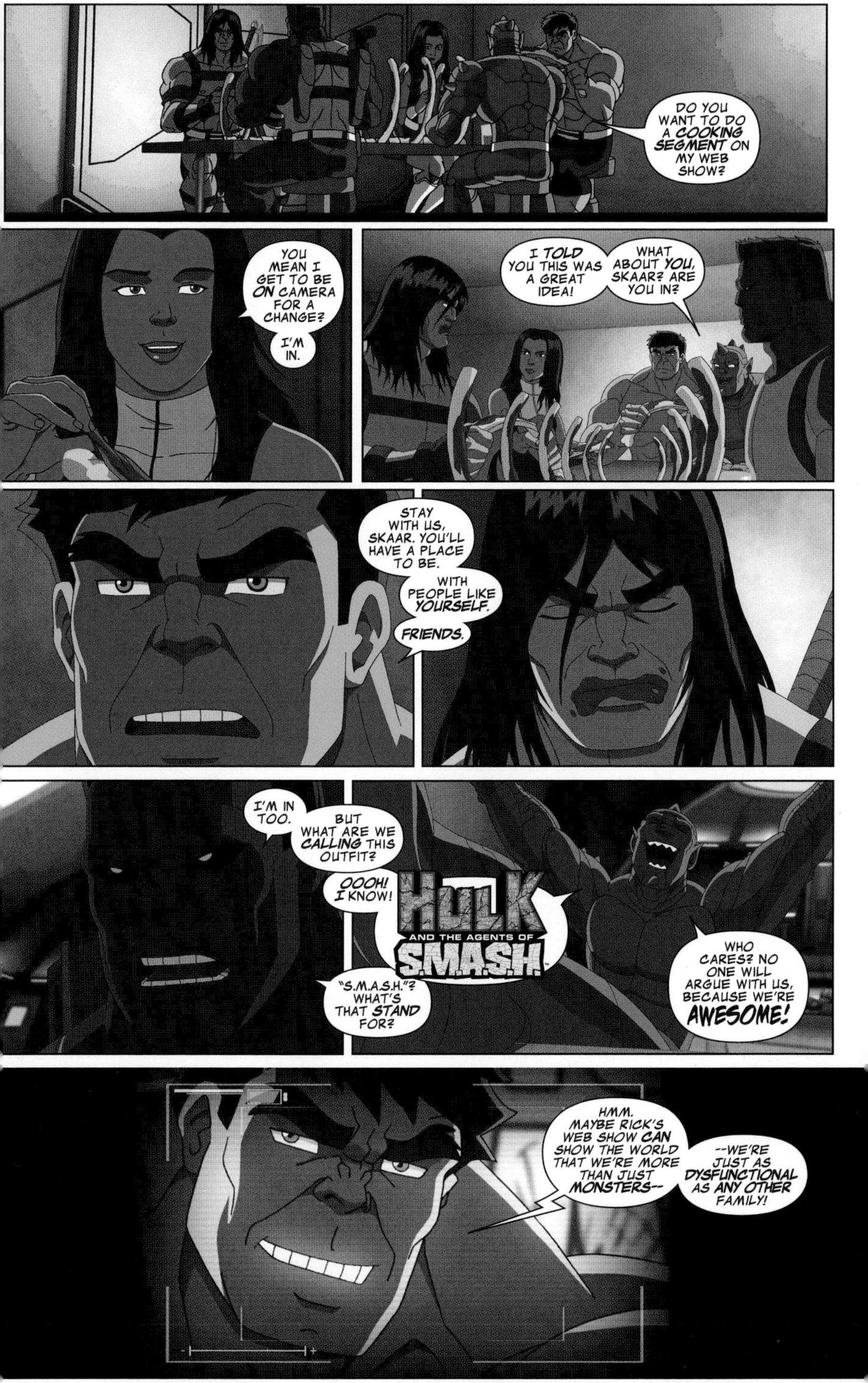

DO YOU WANT TO DO A COOKING SEGMENT ON MY WEB SHOW?
YOU MEAN I GET TO BE ON CAMERA FOR A CHANGE?
I'M IN.
I TOLD YOU THIS WAS A GREAT IDEA!
WHAT ABOUT YOU, SKAAR? ARE YOU IN?
STAY WITH US, SKAAR. YOU'LL HAVE A PLACE TO BE.
WITH PEOPLE LIKE YOURSELF.
FRIENDS.
I'M IN TOO.
BUT WHAT ARE WE CALLING THIS OUTFIT?
OOOH! I KNOW!
HULK AND THE AGENTS OF S.M.A.S.H.
"S.M.A.S.H."? WHAT'S THAT STAND FOR?
WHO CARES? NO ONE WILL ARGUE WITH US, BECAUSE WE'RE AWESOME!
HMM. MAYBE RICK'S WEB SHOW CAN SHOW THE WORLD THAT WE'RE MORE THAN JUST MONSTERS--
--WE'RE JUST AS DYSFUNCTIONAL AS ANY OTHER FAMILY!

HULK BUSTED

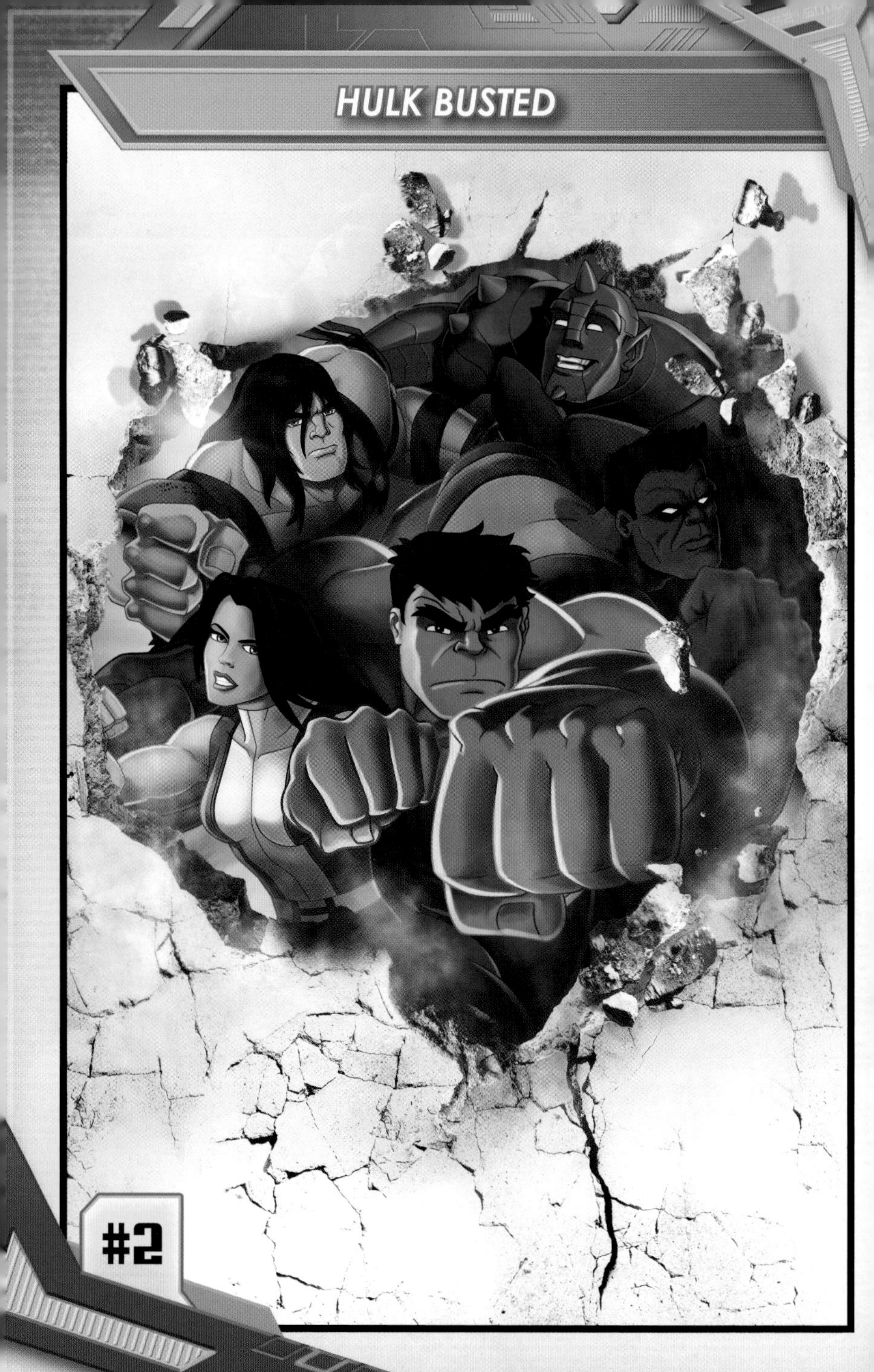

#2

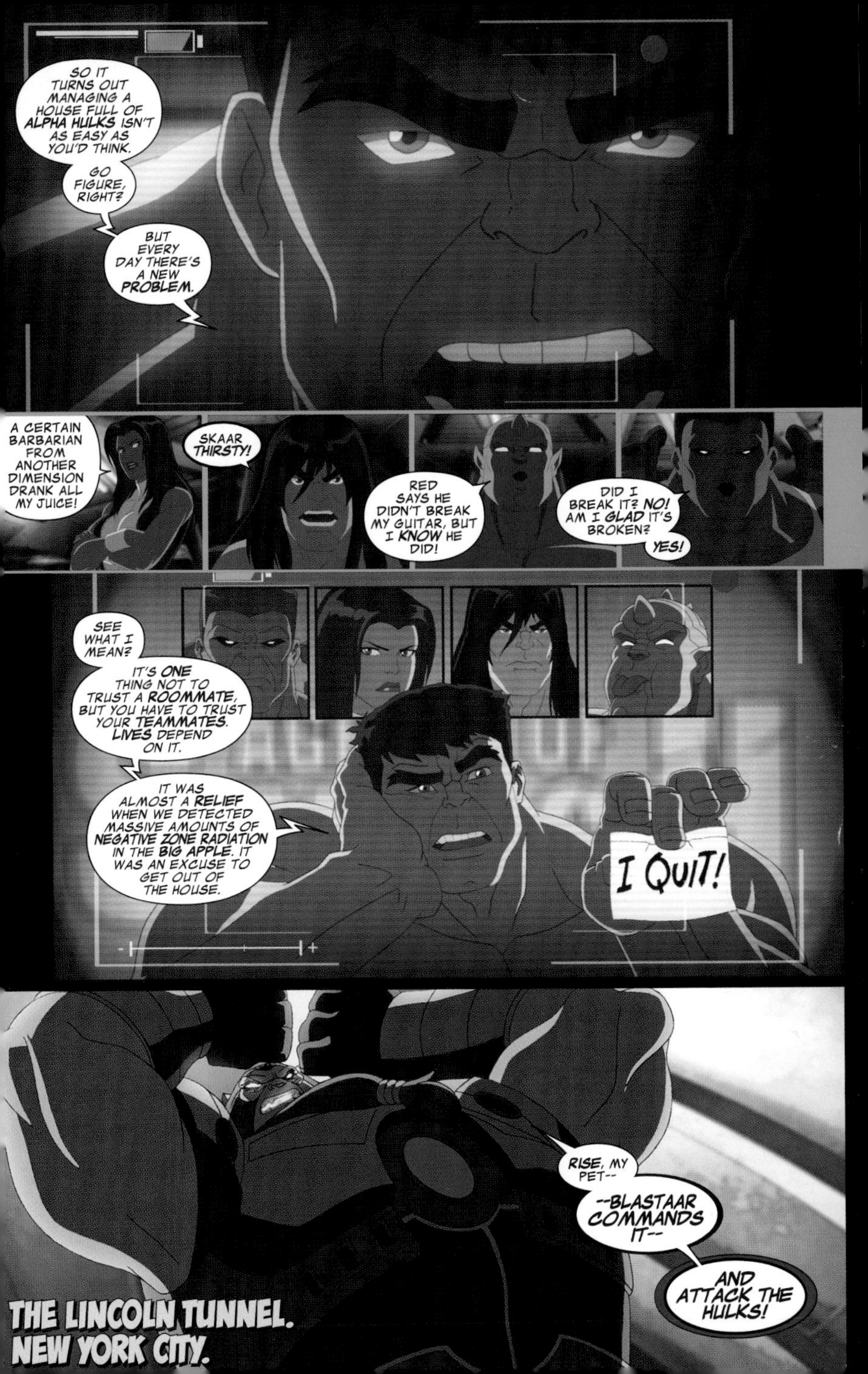
SO IT TURNS OUT MANAGING A HOUSE FULL OF ALPHA HULKS ISN'T AS EASY AS YOU'D THINK.
GO FIGURE, RIGHT?
BUT EVERY DAY THERE'S A NEW PROBLEM.
A CERTAIN BARBARIAN FROM ANOTHER DIMENSION DRANK ALL MY JUICE!
SKAAR THIRSTY!
RED SAYS HE DIDN'T BREAK MY GUITAR, BUT I KNOW HE DID!
DID I BREAK IT? NO! AM I GLAD IT'S BROKEN? YES!
SEE WHAT I MEAN?
IT'S ONE THING NOT TO TRUST A ROOMMATE, BUT YOU HAVE TO TRUST YOUR TEAMMATES. LIVES DEPEND ON IT.
IT WAS ALMOST A RELIEF WHEN WE DETECTED MASSIVE AMOUNTS OF NEGATIVE ZONE RADIATION IN THE BIG APPLE. IT WAS AN EXCUSE TO GET OUT OF THE HOUSE.
I QUIT!
THE LINCOLN TUNNEL. NEW YORK CITY.
RISE, MY PET--
--BLASTAAR COMMANDS IT--
AND ATTACK THE HULKS!

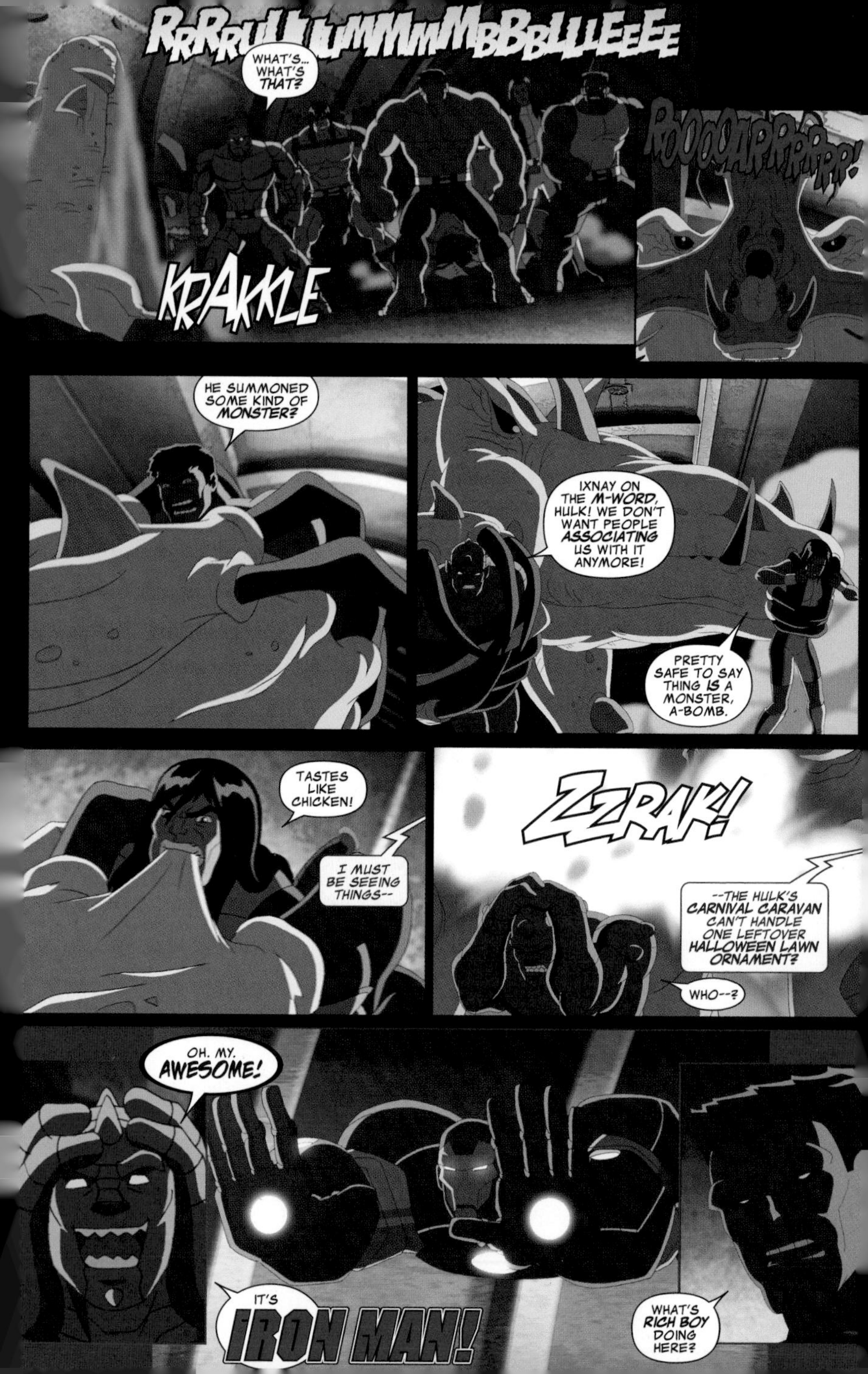
RRRRRUUUMMMMMBBBLLLEEEEE
WHAT'S... WHAT'S THAT?
ROOOOARRRRRP!
KRAKKLE
HE SUMMONED SOME KIND OF MONSTER?
IXNAY ON THE M-WORD, HULK! WE DON'T WANT PEOPLE ASSOCIATING US WITH IT ANYMORE!
PRETTY SAFE TO SAY THING IS A MONSTER, A-BOMB.
TASTES LIKE CHICKEN!
I MUST BE SEEING THINGS--
ZZRAK!
--THE HULK'S CARNIVAL CARAVAN CAN'T HANDLE ONE LEFTOVER HALLOWEEN LAWN ORNAMENT?
WHO--?
OH. MY. AWESOME!
IT'S IRON MAN!
WHAT'S RICH BOY DOING HERE?

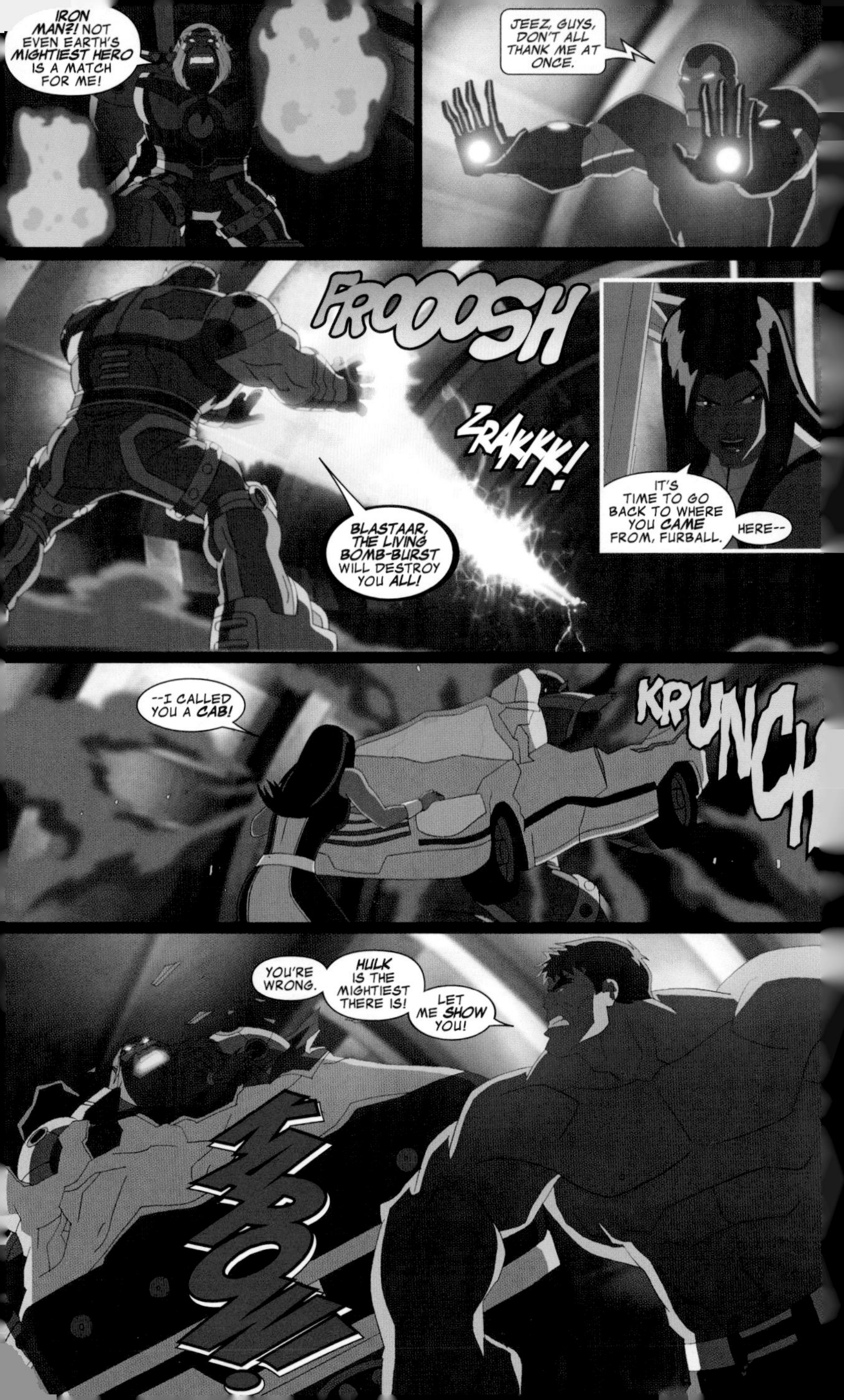
IRON MAN?! NOT EVEN EARTH'S MIGHTIEST HERO IS A MATCH FOR ME!
JEEZ, GUYS, DON'T ALL THANK ME AT ONCE.
FROOOSH
ZRAKKK!
BLASTAAR, THE LIVING BOMB-BURST WILL DESTROY YOU ALL!
IT'S TIME TO GO BACK TO WHERE YOU CAME FROM, FURBALL.
HERE--
--I CALLED YOU A CAB!
KRUNCH
YOU'RE WRONG.
HULK IS THE MIGHTIEST THERE IS!
LET ME SHOW YOU!

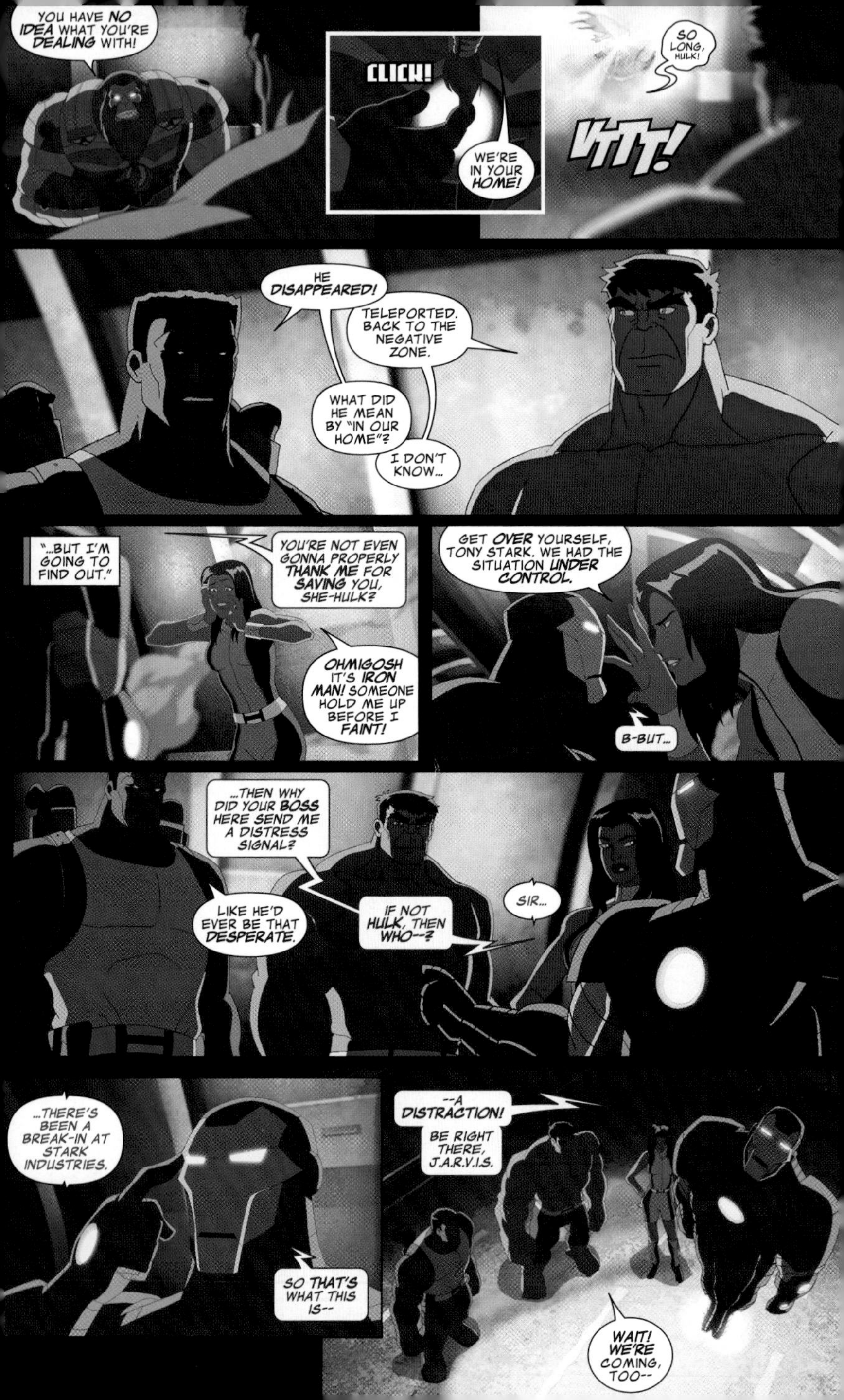
YOU HAVE NO IDEA WHAT YOU'RE DEALING WITH!
CLICK!
WE'RE IN YOUR HOME!
SO LONG, HULK!
VTTT!
HE DISAPPEARED!
TELEPORTED. BACK TO THE NEGATIVE ZONE.
WHAT DID HE MEAN BY "IN OUR HOME"?
I DON'T KNOW...
"...BUT I'M GOING TO FIND OUT."
YOU'RE NOT EVEN GONNA PROPERLY THANK ME FOR SAVING YOU, SHE-HULK?
OHMIGOSH IT'S IRON MAN! SOMEONE HOLD ME UP BEFORE I FAINT!
GET OVER YOURSELF, TONY STARK. WE HAD THE SITUATION UNDER CONTROL.
B-BUT...
...THEN WHY DID YOUR BOSS HERE SEND ME A DISTRESS SIGNAL?
LIKE HE'D EVER BE THAT DESPERATE.
IF NOT HULK, THEN WHO--?
SIR...
...THERE'S BEEN A BREAK-IN AT STARK INDUSTRIES.
SO THAT'S WHAT THIS IS--
--A DISTRACTION!
BE RIGHT THERE, J.A.R.V.I.S.
WAIT! WE'RE COMING, TOO--

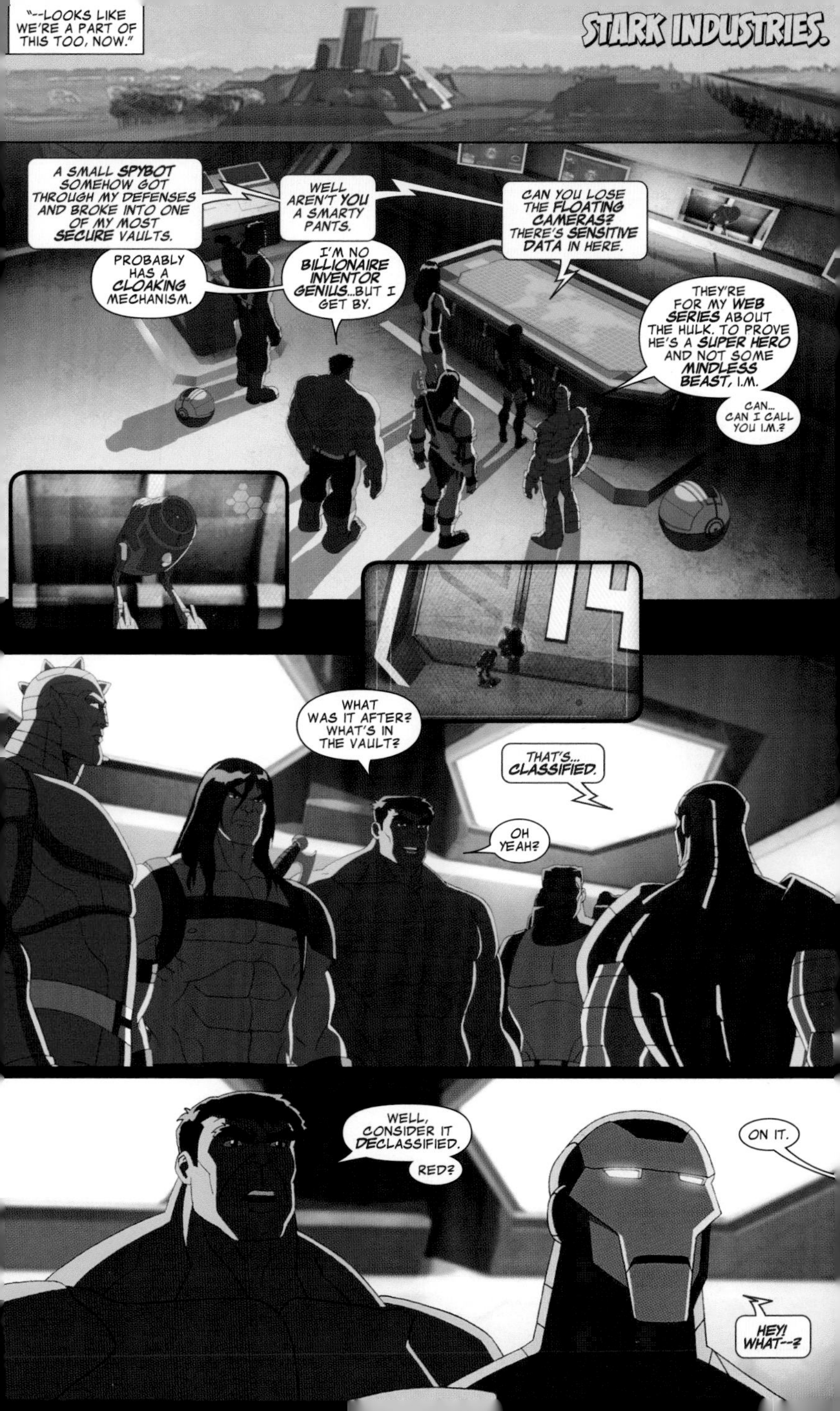
"--LOOKS LIKE WE'RE A PART OF THIS TOO, NOW."
STARK INDUSTRIES.
A SMALL SPYBOT SOMEHOW GOT THROUGH MY DEFENSES AND BROKE INTO ONE OF MY MOST SECURE VAULTS.
WELL AREN'T YOU A SMARTY PANTS.
CAN YOU LOSE THE FLOATING CAMERAS? THERE'S SENSITIVE DATA IN HERE.
PROBABLY HAS A CLOAKING MECHANISM.
I'M NO BILLIONAIRE INVENTOR GENIUS...BUT I GET BY.
THEY'RE FOR MY WEB SERIES ABOUT THE HULK. TO PROVE HE'S A SUPER HERO AND NOT SOME MINDLESS BEAST, I.M.
CAN... CAN I CALL YOU I.M.?
14
WHAT WAS IT AFTER? WHAT'S IN THE VAULT?
THAT'S... CLASSIFIED.
OH YEAH?
WELL, CONSIDER IT DECLASSIFIED.
RED?
ON IT.
HEY! WHAT--?

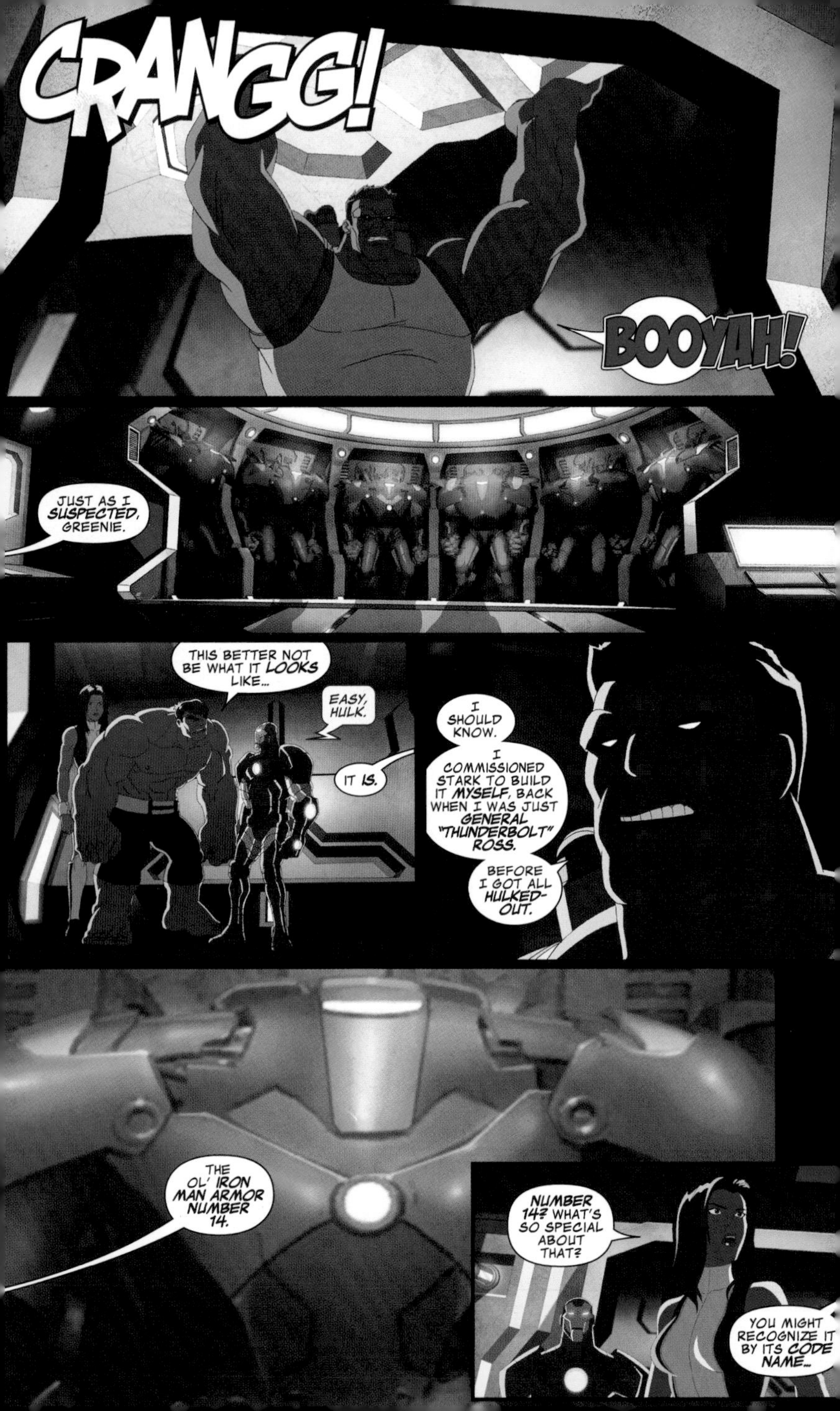
CRANGG!
BOOYAH!
JUST AS I SUSPECTED, GREENIE.
THIS BETTER NOT BE WHAT IT LOOKS LIKE...
EASY, HULK.
IT IS.
I SHOULD KNOW.
I COMMISSIONED STARK TO BUILD IT MYSELF, BACK WHEN I WAS JUST GENERAL "THUNDERBOLT" ROSS.
BEFORE I GOT ALL HULKED-OUT.
THE OL' IRON MAN ARMOR NUMBER 14.
NUMBER 14? WHAT'S SO SPECIAL ABOUT THAT?
YOU MIGHT RECOGNIZE IT BY ITS CODE NAME...

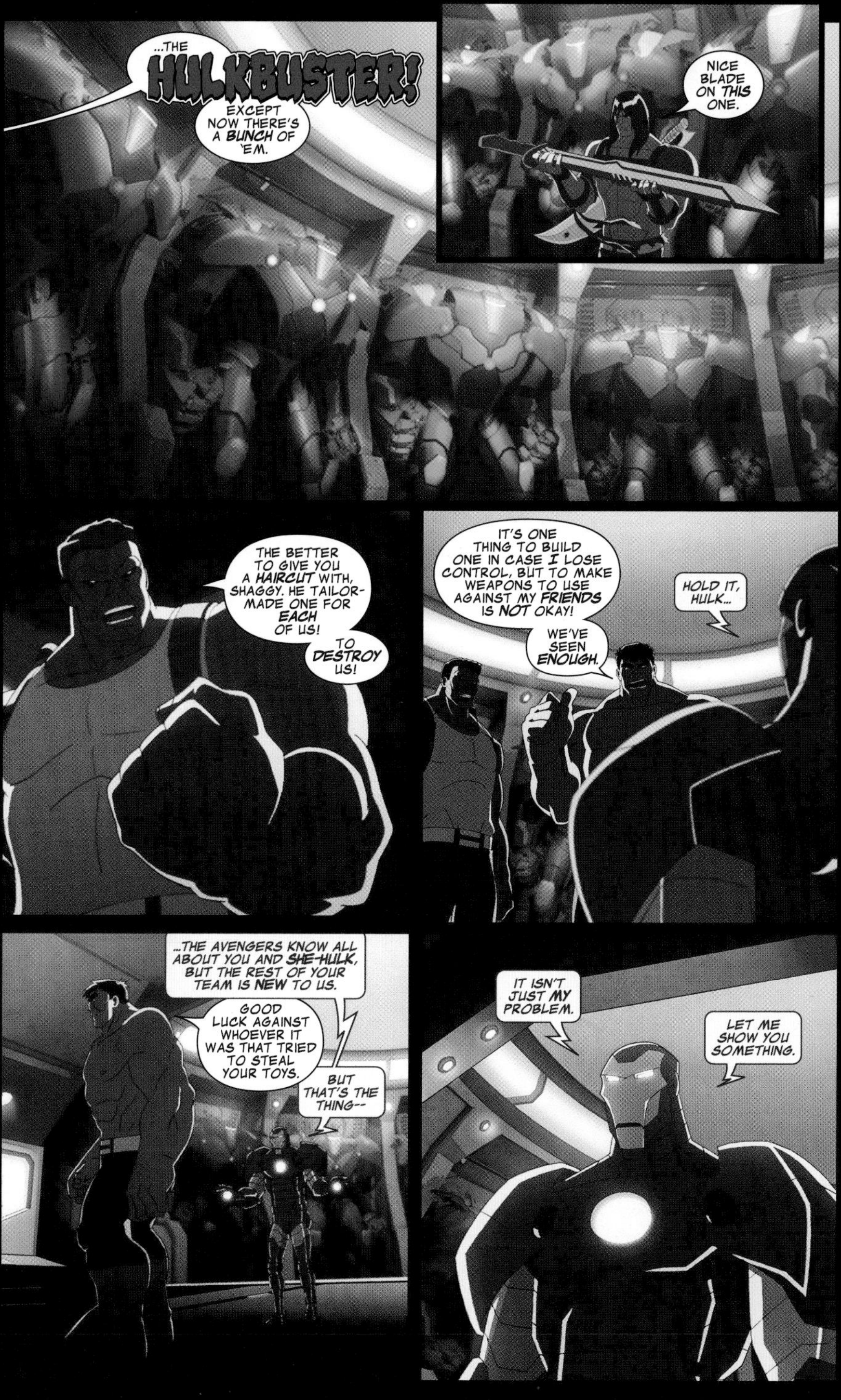
...THE HULKBUSTER!
EXCEPT NOW THERE'S A BUNCH OF 'EM.
NICE BLADE ON THIS ONE.
THE BETTER TO GIVE YOU A HAIRCUT WITH, SHAGGY. HE TAILOR-MADE ONE FOR EACH OF US!
TO DESTROY US!
IT'S ONE THING TO BUILD ONE IN CASE I LOSE CONTROL, BUT TO MAKE WEAPONS TO USE AGAINST MY FRIENDS IS NOT OKAY!
WE'VE SEEN ENOUGH.
HOLD IT, HULK...
...THE AVENGERS KNOW ALL ABOUT YOU AND SHE-HULK, BUT THE REST OF YOUR TEAM IS NEW TO US.
GOOD LUCK AGAINST WHOEVER IT WAS THAT TRIED TO STEAL YOUR TOYS.
BUT THAT'S THE THING--
IT ISN'T JUST MY PROBLEM.
LET ME SHOW YOU SOMETHING.

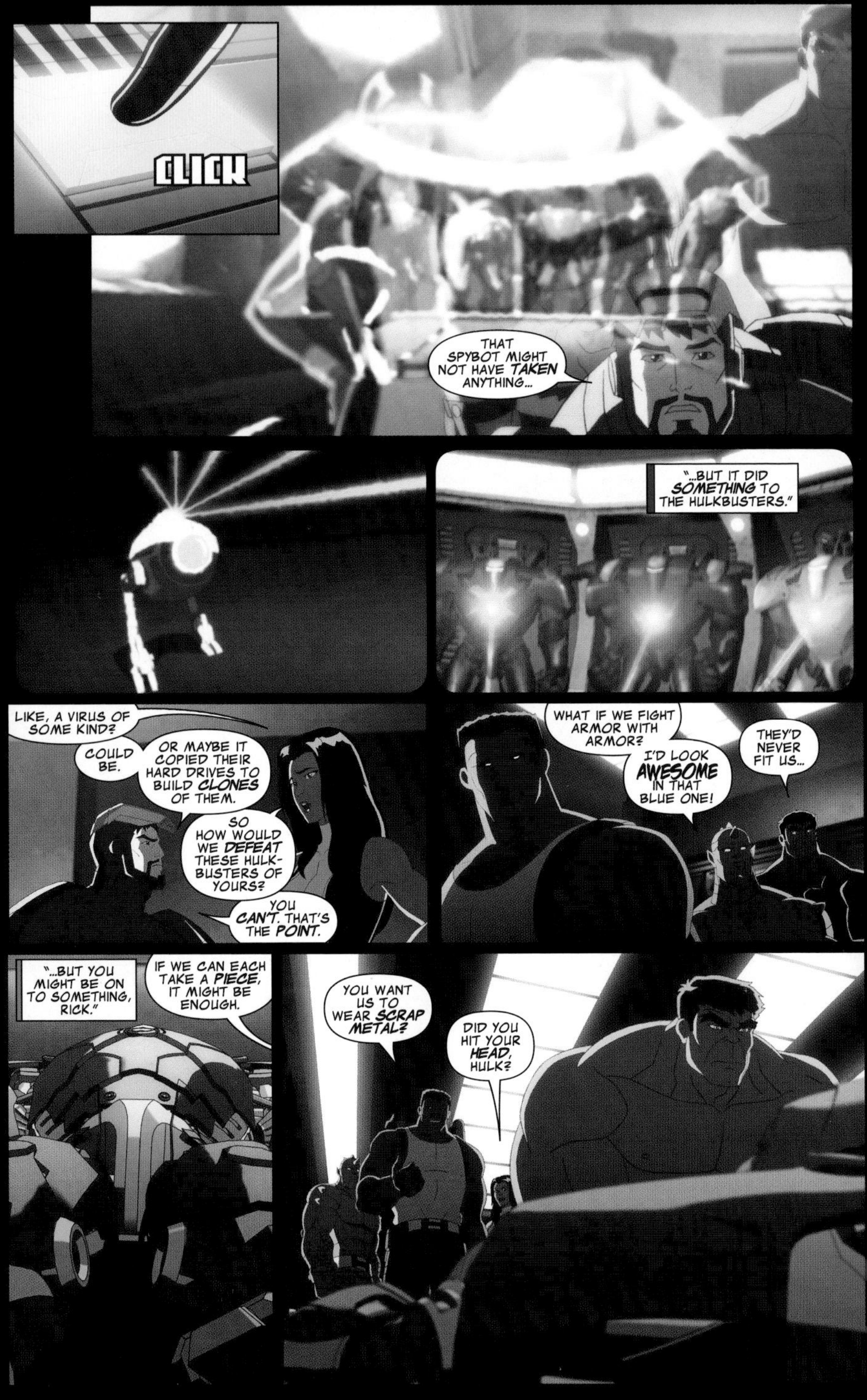
CLICK
THAT SPYBOT MIGHT NOT HAVE TAKEN ANYTHING...
"...BUT IT DID SOMETHING TO THE HULKBUSTERS."
LIKE, A VIRUS OF SOME KIND?
COULD BE.
OR MAYBE IT COPIED THEIR HARD DRIVES TO BUILD CLONES OF THEM.
SO HOW WOULD WE DEFEAT THESE HULK-BUSTERS OF YOURS?
YOU CAN'T. THAT'S THE POINT.
WHAT IF WE FIGHT ARMOR WITH ARMOR?
I'D LOOK AWESOME IN THAT BLUE ONE!
THEY'D NEVER FIT US...
"...BUT YOU MIGHT BE ON TO SOMETHING, RICK."
IF WE CAN EACH TAKE A PIECE, IT MIGHT BE ENOUGH.
YOU WANT US TO WEAR SCRAP METAL?
DID YOU HIT YOUR HEAD, HULK?

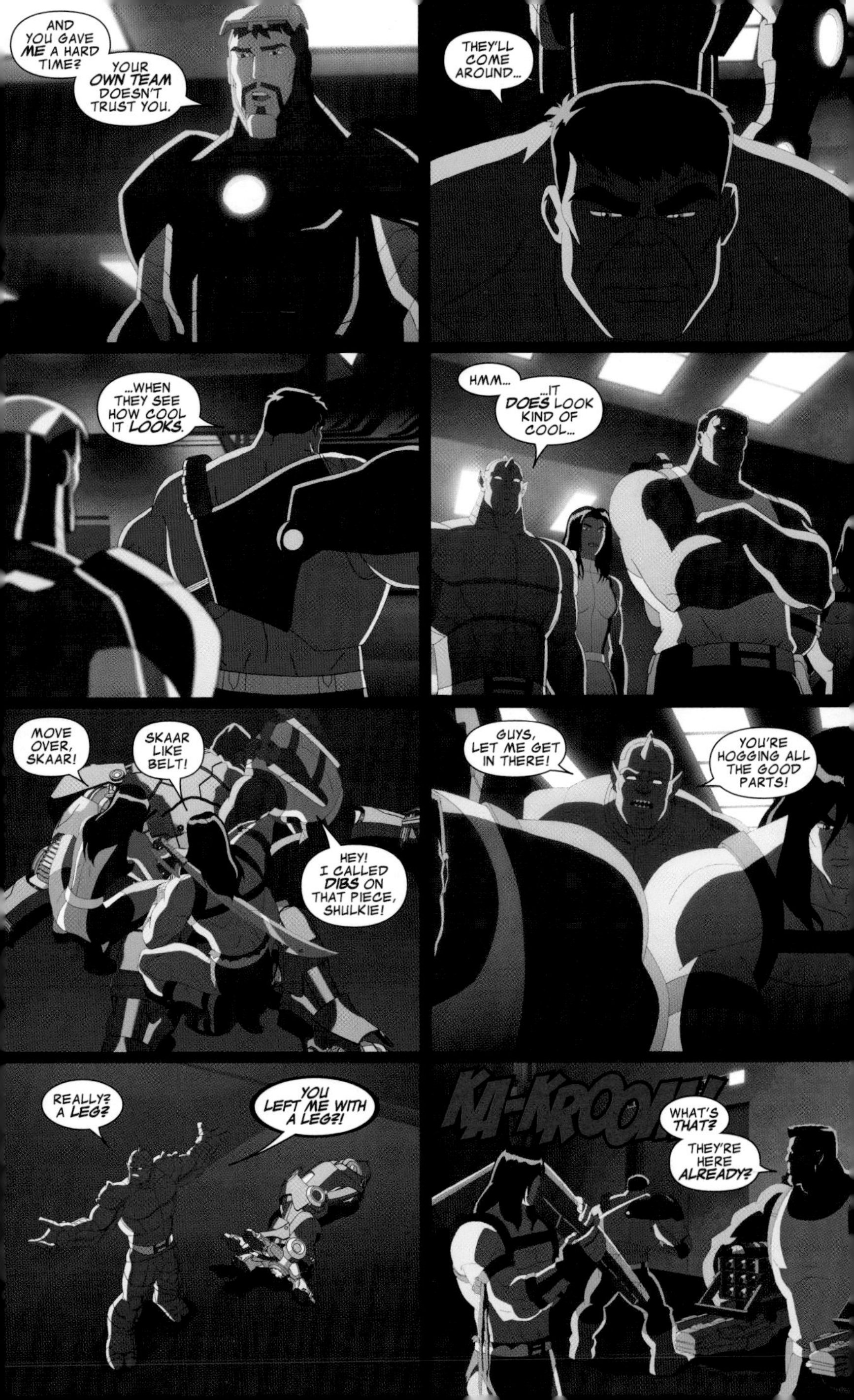
AND YOU GAVE ME A HARD TIME?
YOUR OWN TEAM DOESN'T TRUST YOU.
THEY'LL COME AROUND...
...WHEN THEY SEE HOW COOL IT LOOKS.
HMM...
...IT DOES LOOK KIND OF COOL...
MOVE OVER, SKAAR!
SKAAR LIKE BELT!
HEY! I CALLED DIBS ON THAT PIECE, SHULKIE!
GUYS, LET ME GET IN THERE!
YOU'RE HOGGING ALL THE GOOD PARTS!
REALLY? A LEG?
YOU LEFT ME WITH A LEG?!
KA-KROOM!
WHAT'S THAT?
THEY'RE HERE ALREADY?

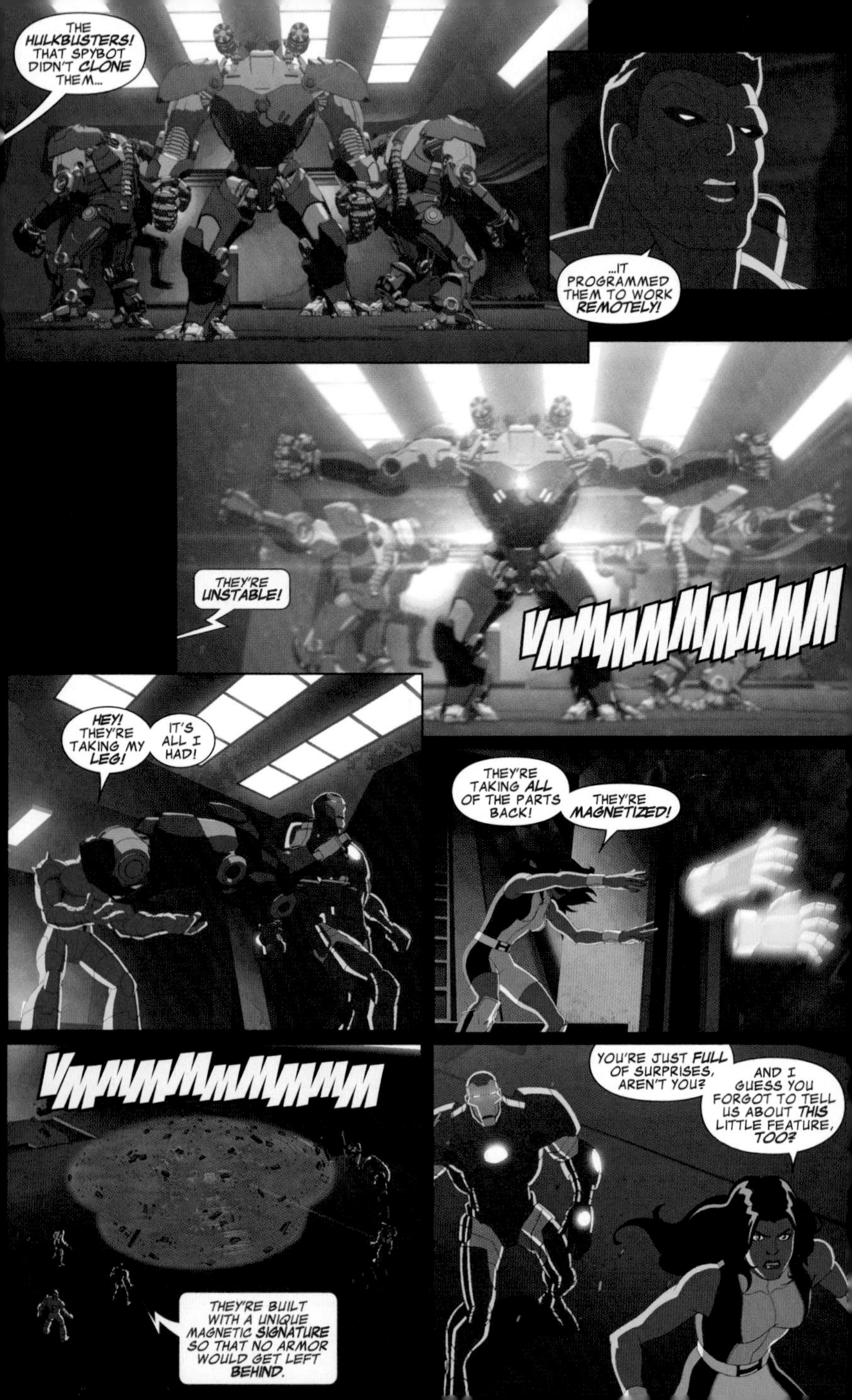

THE HULKBUSTERS! THAT SPYBOT DIDN'T CLONE THEM...
...IT PROGRAMMED THEM TO WORK REMOTELY!
THEY'RE UNSTABLE!
VMMMMMMMMMMM
HEY! THEY'RE TAKING MY LEG!
IT'S ALL I HAD!
THEY'RE TAKING ALL OF THE PARTS BACK!
THEY'RE MAGNETIZED!
VMMMMMMMMMMM
THEY'RE BUILT WITH A UNIQUE MAGNETIC SIGNATURE SO THAT NO ARMOR WOULD GET LEFT BEHIND.
YOU'RE JUST FULL OF SURPRISES, AREN'T YOU?
AND I GUESS YOU FORGOT TO TELL US ABOUT THIS LITTLE FEATURE, TOO?

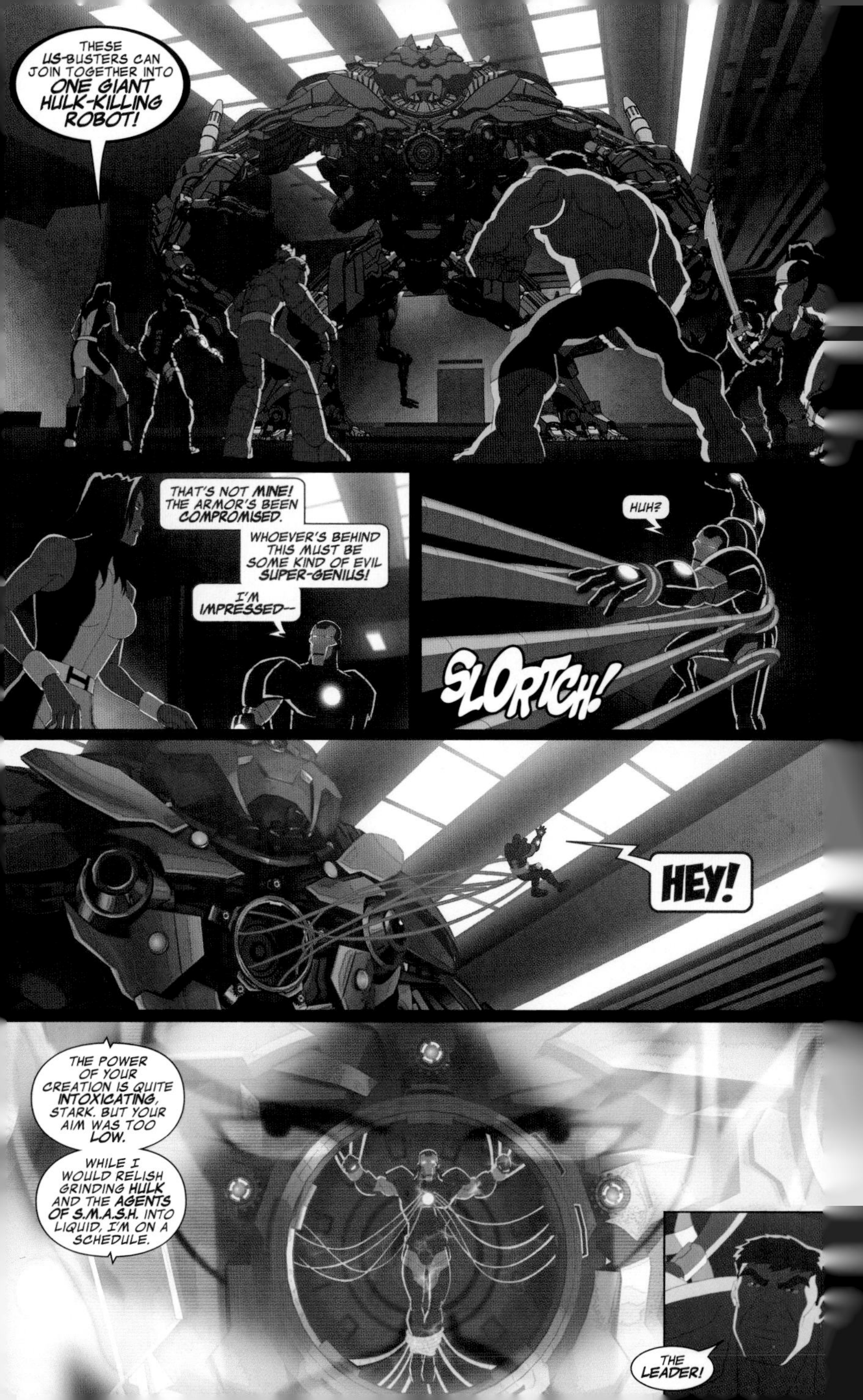
THESE US-BUSTERS CAN JOIN TOGETHER INTO ONE GIANT HULK-KILLING ROBOT!
THAT'S NOT MINE! THE ARMOR'S BEEN COMPROMISED.
WHOEVER'S BEHIND THIS MUST BE SOME KIND OF EVIL SUPER-GENIUS!
I'M IMPRESSED--
HUH?
SLORTCH!
HEY!
THE POWER OF YOUR CREATION IS QUITE INTOXICATING, STARK. BUT YOUR AIM WAS TOO LOW.
WHILE I WOULD RELISH GRINDING HULK AND THE AGENTS OF S.M.A.S.H. INTO LIQUID, I'M ON A SCHEDULE.
THE LEADER!

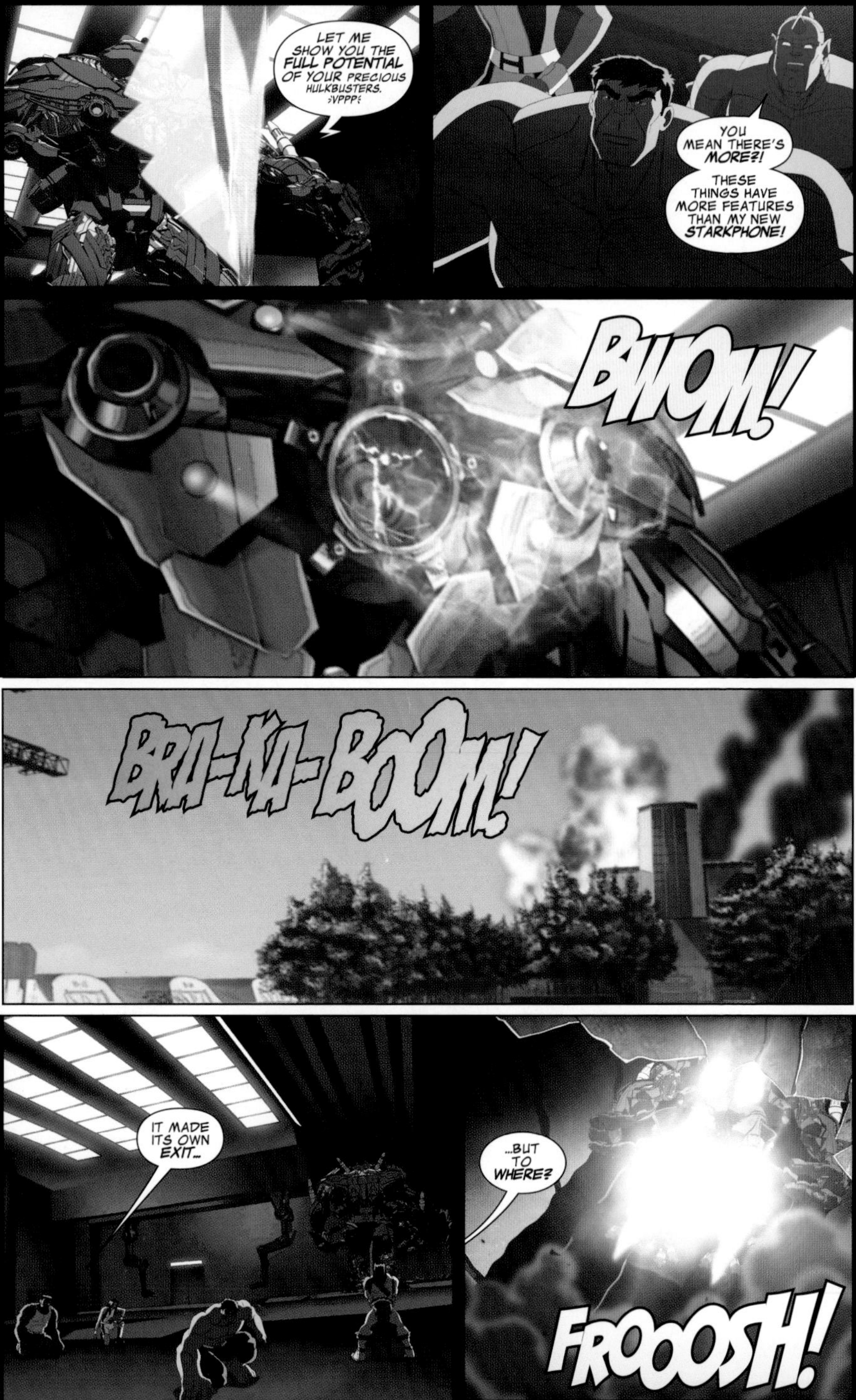
LET ME SHOW YOU THE FULL POTENTIAL OF YOUR PRECIOUS HULKBUSTERS.
›VPPP‹
YOU MEAN THERE'S MORE?!
THESE THINGS HAVE MORE FEATURES THAN MY NEW STARKPHONE!
BWOM!
BRA-KA-BOOM!
IT MADE ITS OWN EXIT...
...BUT TO WHERE?
FROOOSH!

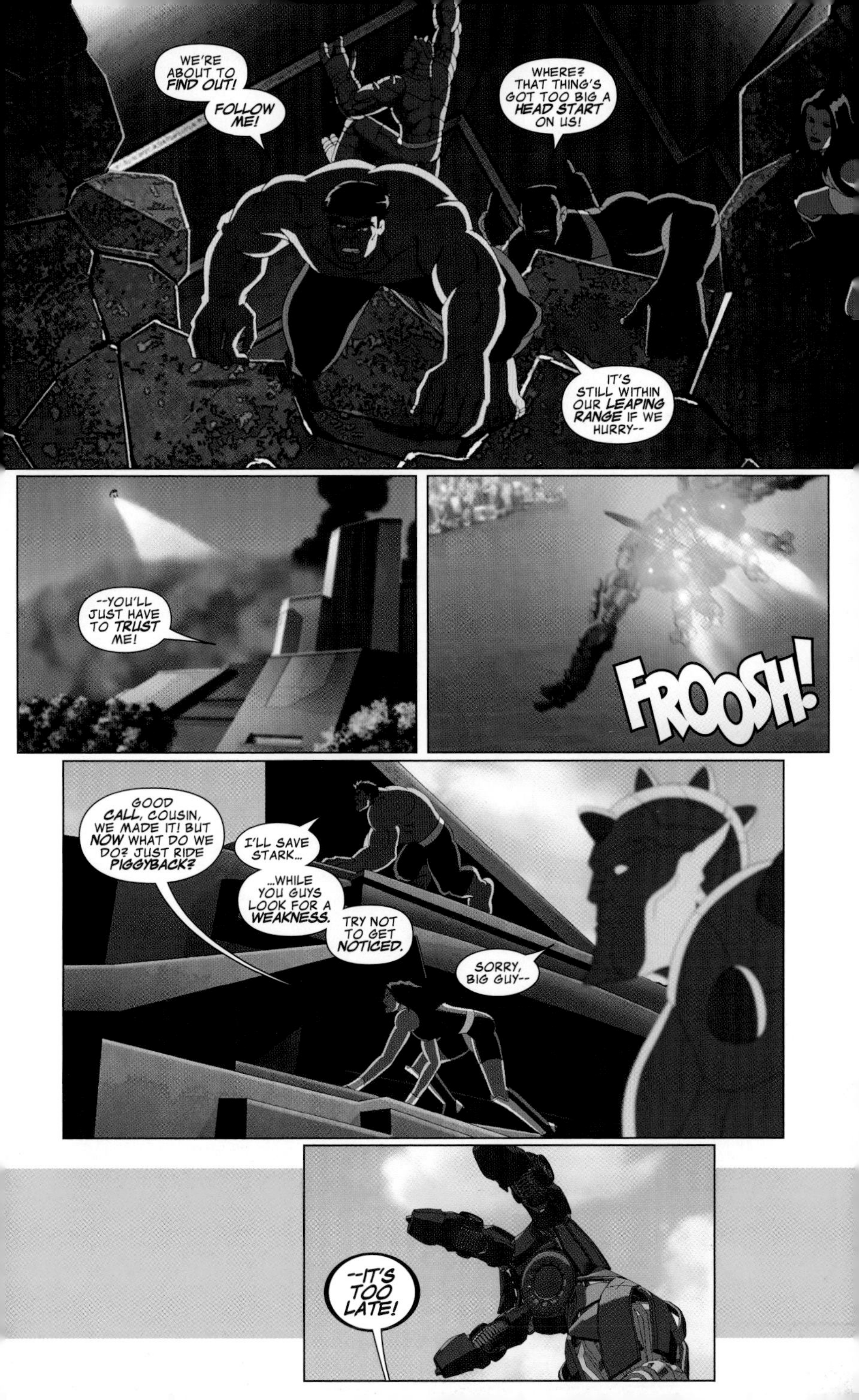
WE'RE ABOUT TO FIND OUT!
FOLLOW ME!
WHERE? THAT THING'S GOT TOO BIG A HEAD START ON US!
IT'S STILL WITHIN OUR LEAPING RANGE IF WE HURRY--
--YOU'LL JUST HAVE TO TRUST ME!
FROOSH!
GOOD CALL, COUSIN, WE MADE IT! BUT NOW WHAT DO WE DO? JUST RIDE PIGGYBACK?
I'LL SAVE STARK...
...WHILE YOU GUYS LOOK FOR A WEAKNESS.
TRY NOT TO GET NOTICED.
SORRY, BIG GUY--
--IT'S TOO LATE!

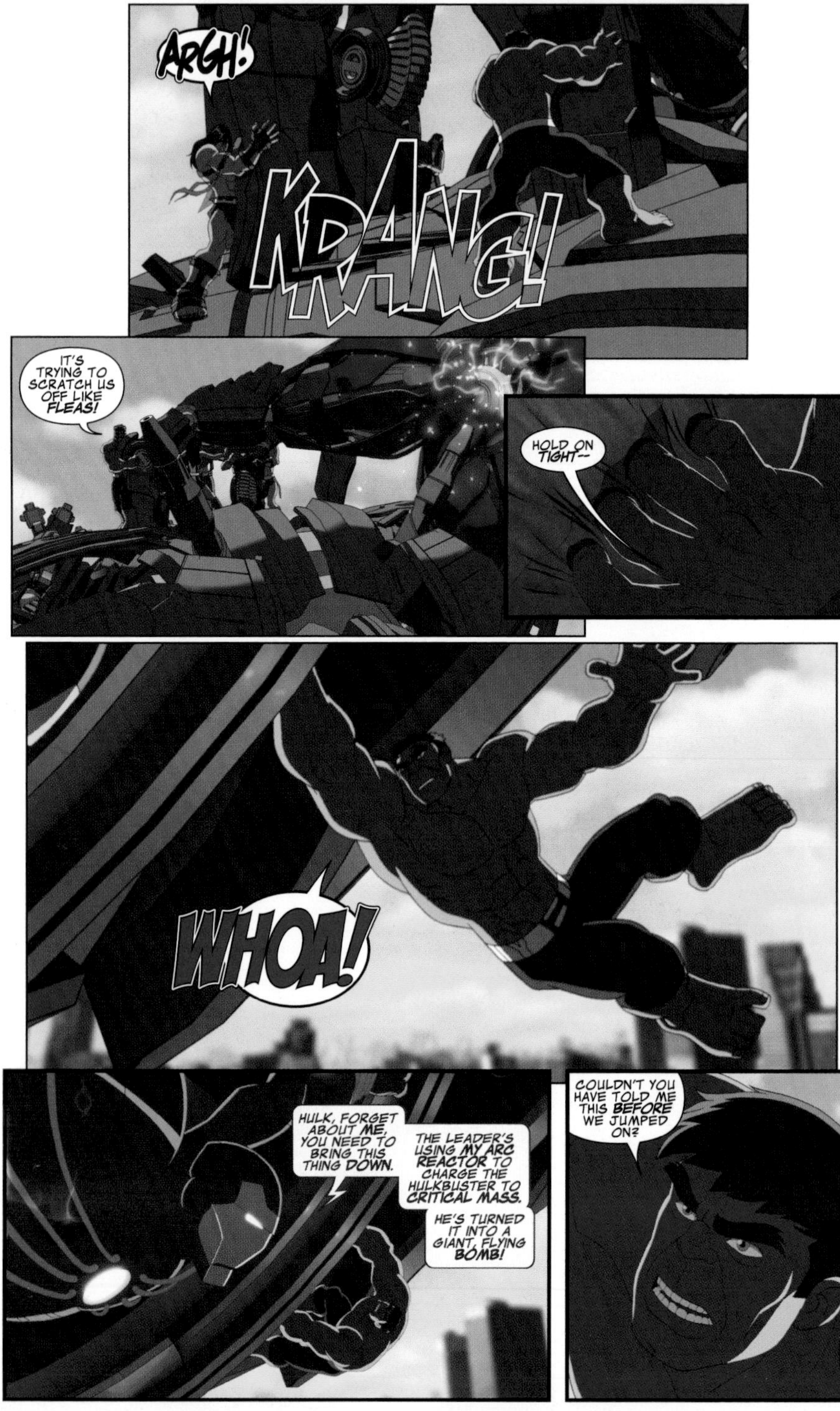
ARGH!
KDANG!
IT'S TRYING TO SCRATCH US OFF LIKE FLEAS!
HOLD ON TIGHT--
WHOA!
HULK, FORGET ABOUT ME, YOU NEED TO BRING THIS THING DOWN.
THE LEADER'S USING MY ARC REACTOR TO CHARGE THE HULKBUSTER TO CRITICAL MASS.
HE'S TURNED IT INTO A GIANT, FLYING BOMB!
COULDN'T YOU HAVE TOLD ME THIS BEFORE WE JUMPED ON?

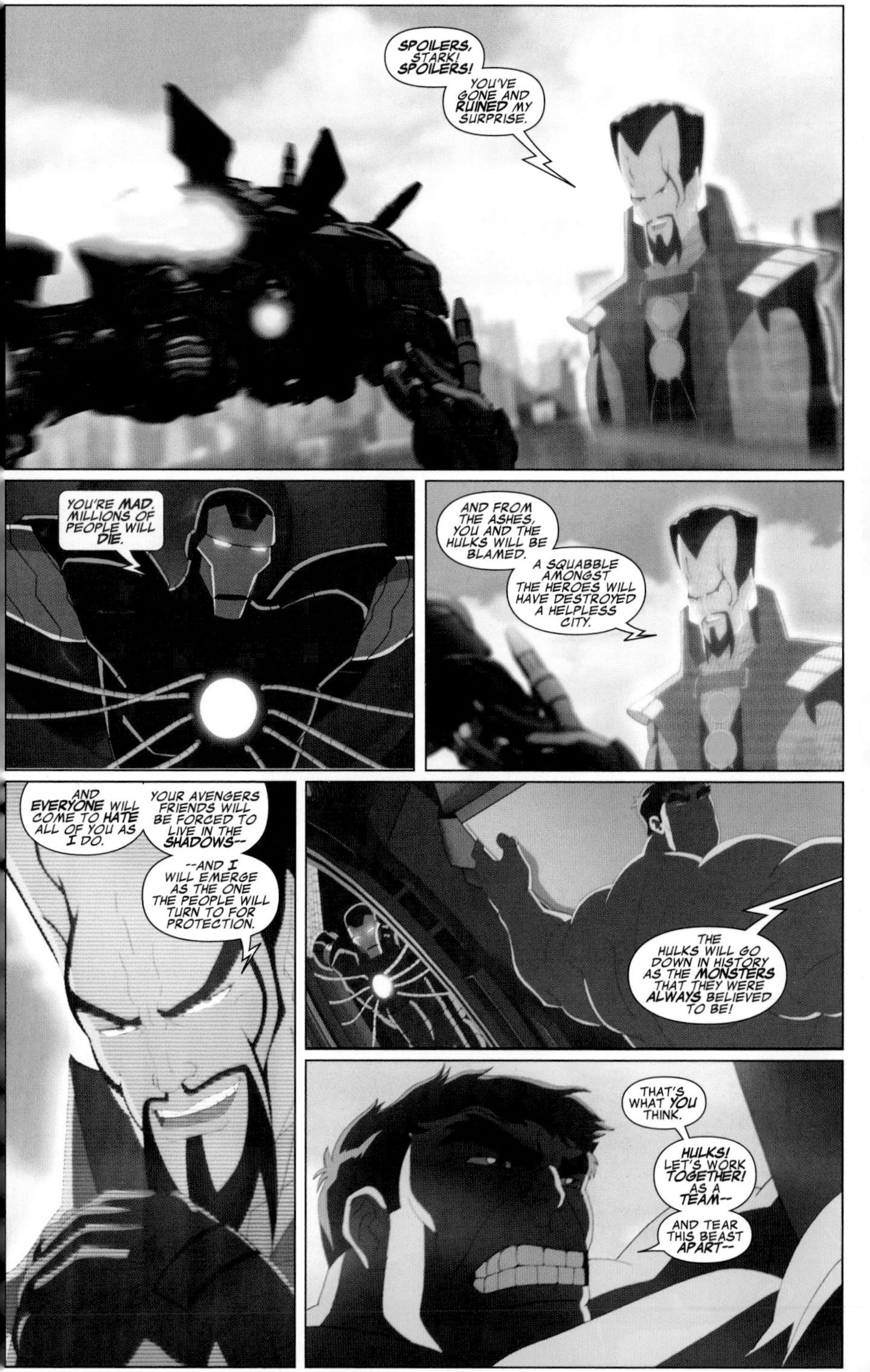
SPOILERS, STARK! SPOILERS!
YOU'VE GONE AND RUINED MY SURPRISE.
YOU'RE MAD. MILLIONS OF PEOPLE WILL DIE.
AND FROM THE ASHES, YOU AND THE HULKS WILL BE BLAMED.
A SQUABBLE AMONGST THE HEROES WILL HAVE DESTROYED A HELPLESS CITY.
AND EVERYONE WILL COME TO HATE ALL OF YOU AS I DO.
YOUR AVENGERS FRIENDS WILL BE FORCED TO LIVE IN THE SHADOWS--
--AND I WILL EMERGE AS THE ONE THE PEOPLE WILL TURN TO FOR PROTECTION.
THE HULKS WILL GO DOWN IN HISTORY AS THE MONSTERS THAT THEY WERE ALWAYS BELIEVED TO BE!
THAT'S WHAT YOU THINK.
HULKS! LET'S WORK TOGETHER! AS A TEAM--
AND TEAR THIS BEAST APART--

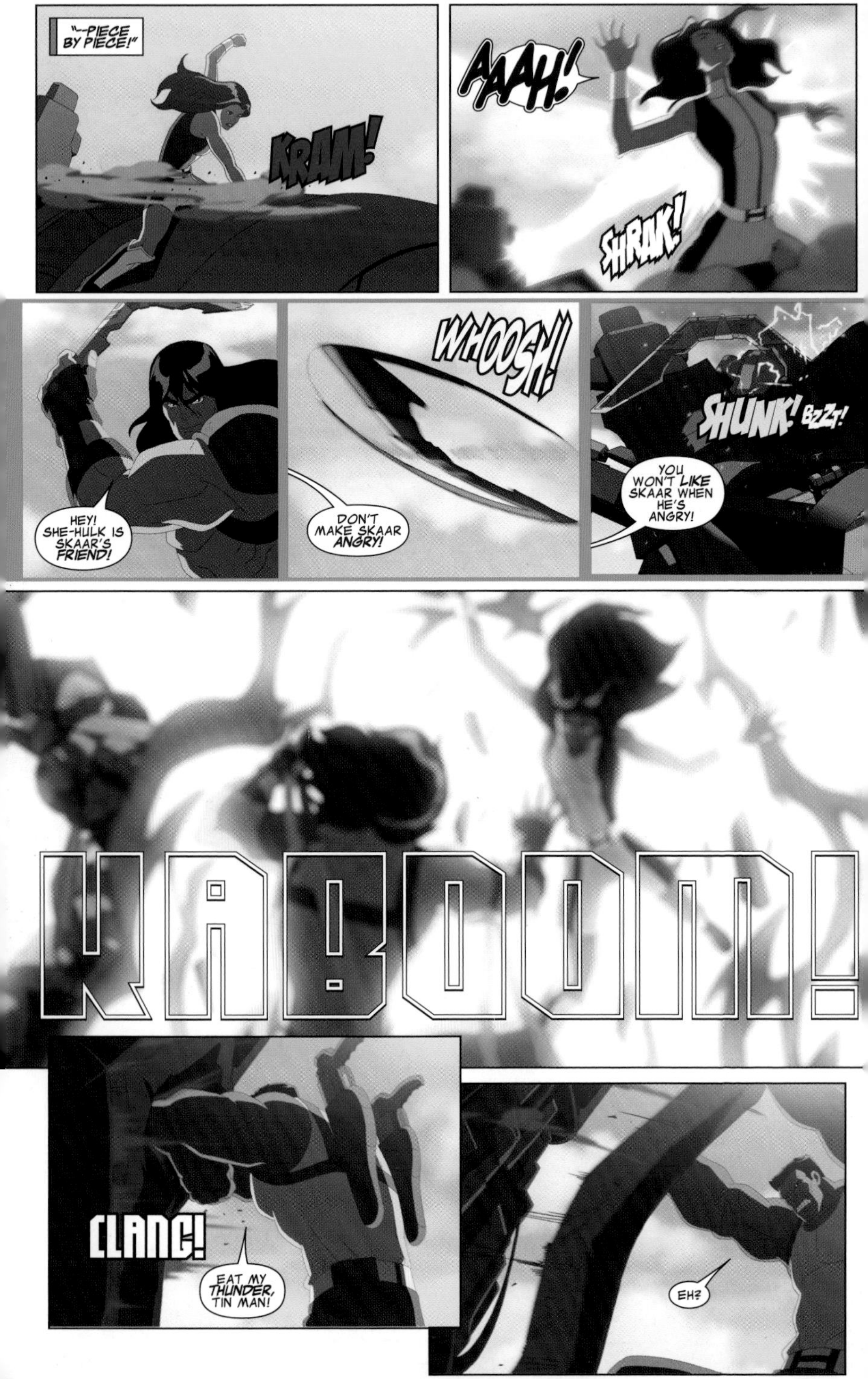
"--PIECE BY PIECE!"
KRAM!
AAAH!
SHRAK!
HEY! SHE-HULK IS SKAAR'S FRIEND!
WHOOSH!
DON'T MAKE SKAAR ANGRY!
SHUNK! BZZT!
YOU WON'T LIKE SKAAR WHEN HE'S ANGRY!
KABOOM!
CLANG!
EAT MY THUNDER, TIN MAN!
EH?

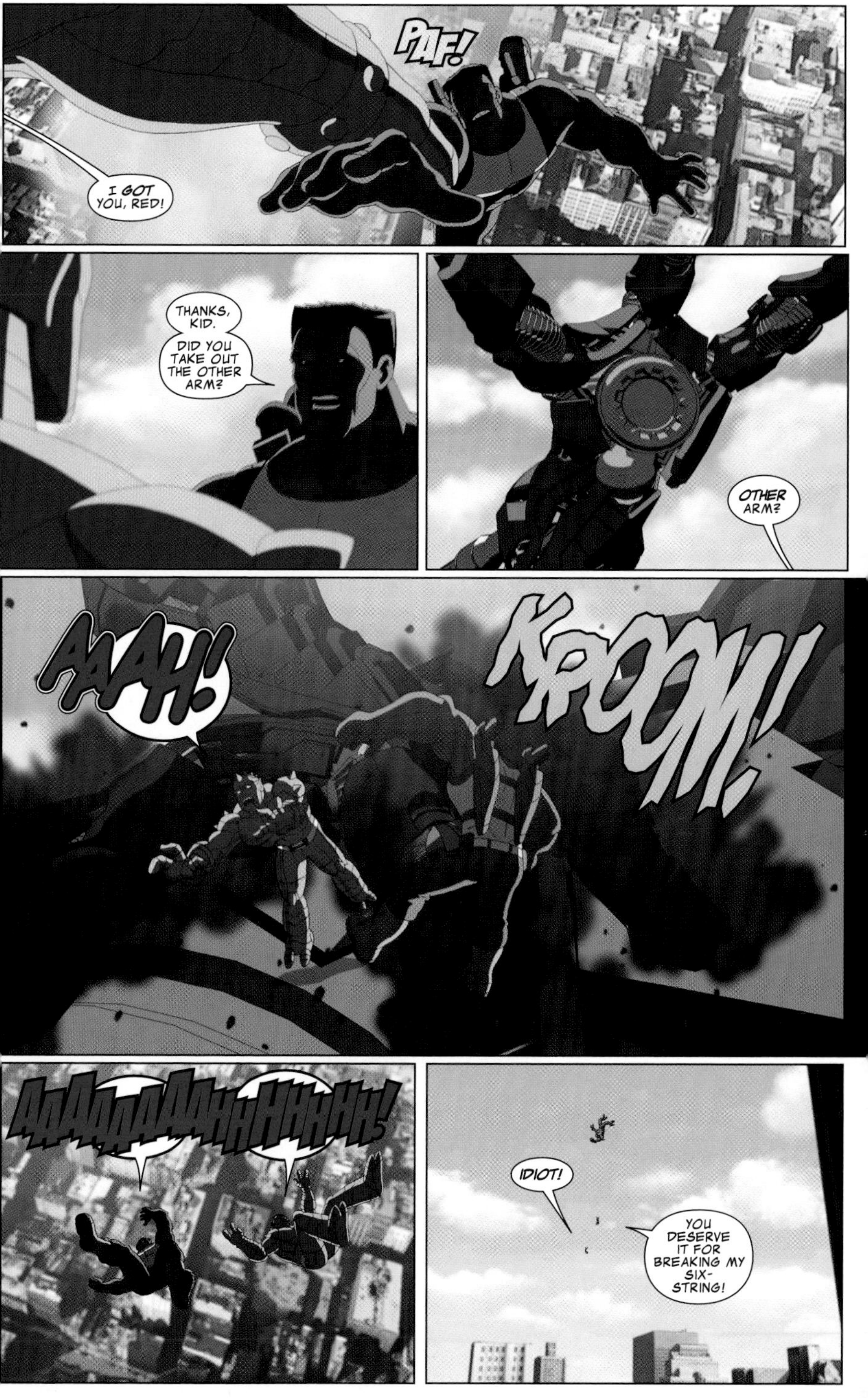
PAF!
I GOT YOU, RED!
THANKS, KID.
DID YOU TAKE OUT THE OTHER ARM?
OTHER ARM?
AAAH!
KROOM!
AAAAAAAAHHHHHHH!
IDIOT!
YOU DESERVE IT FOR BREAKING MY SIX-STRING!

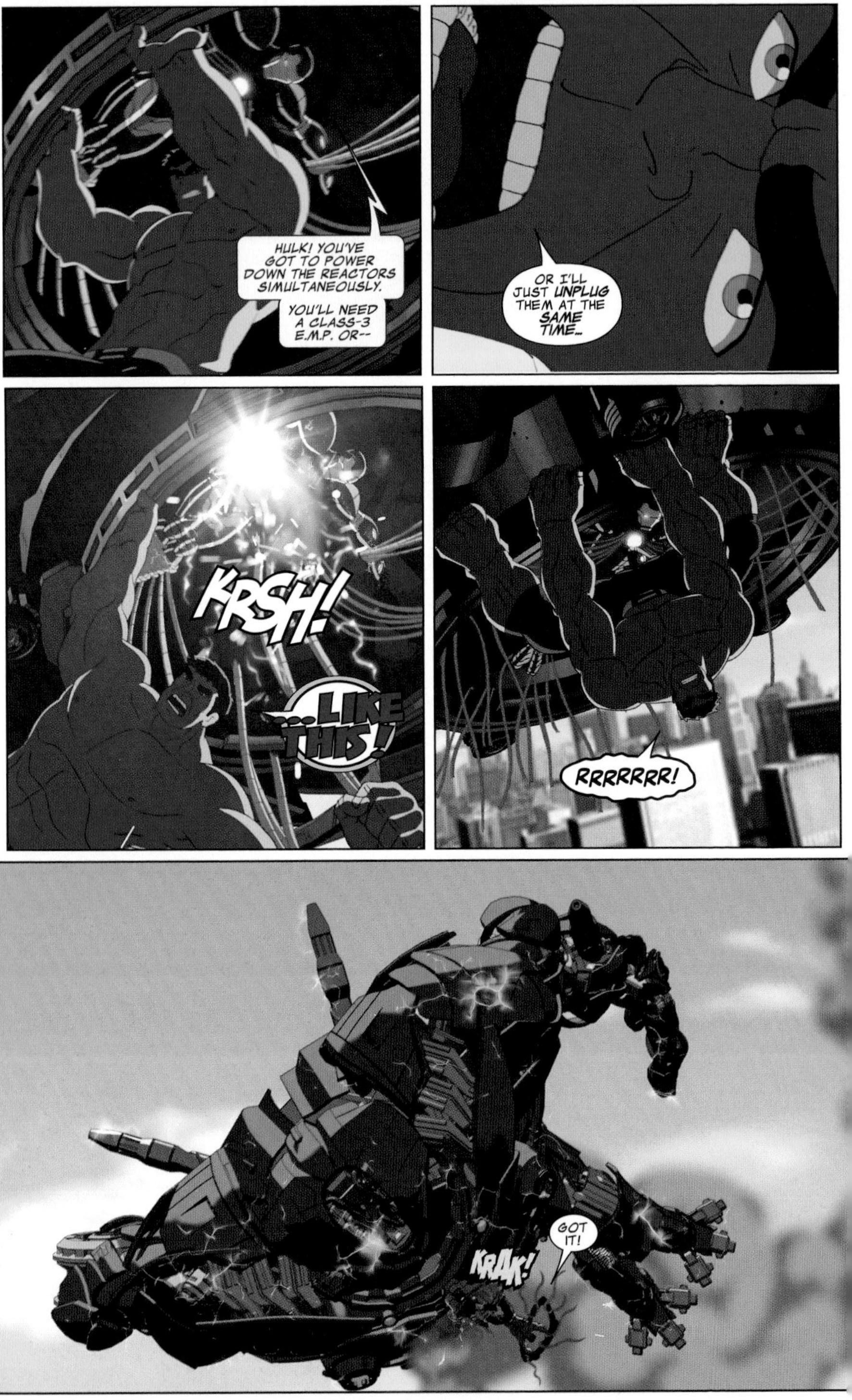
HULK! YOU'VE GOT TO POWER DOWN THE REACTORS SIMULTANEOUSLY.
YOU'LL NEED A CLASS-3 E.M.P. OR--
OR I'LL JUST UNPLUG THEM AT THE SAME TIME...
KRSH!
...LIKE THIS!
RRRRRRR!
KRAK!
GOT IT!

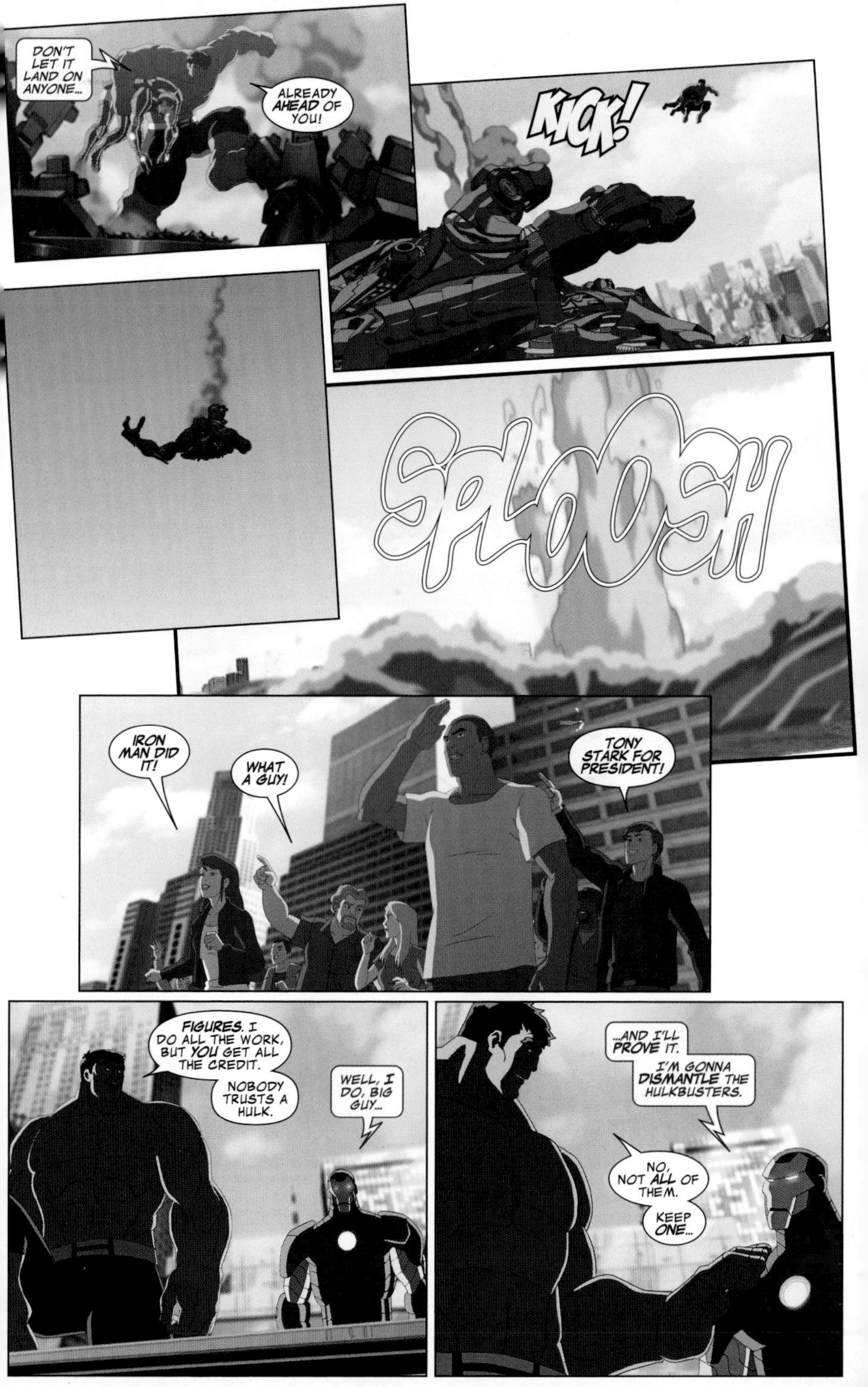
DON'T LET IT LAND ON ANYONE...
ALREADY AHEAD OF YOU!
KICK!
SPLOOSH
IRON MAN DID IT!
WHAT A GUY!
TONY STARK FOR PRESIDENT!
FIGURES. I DO ALL THE WORK, BUT YOU GET ALL THE CREDIT.
NOBODY TRUSTS A HULK.
WELL, I DO, BIG GUY...
...AND I'LL PROVE IT.
I'M GONNA DISMANTLE THE HULKBUSTERS.
NO, NOT ALL OF THEM.
KEEP ONE...

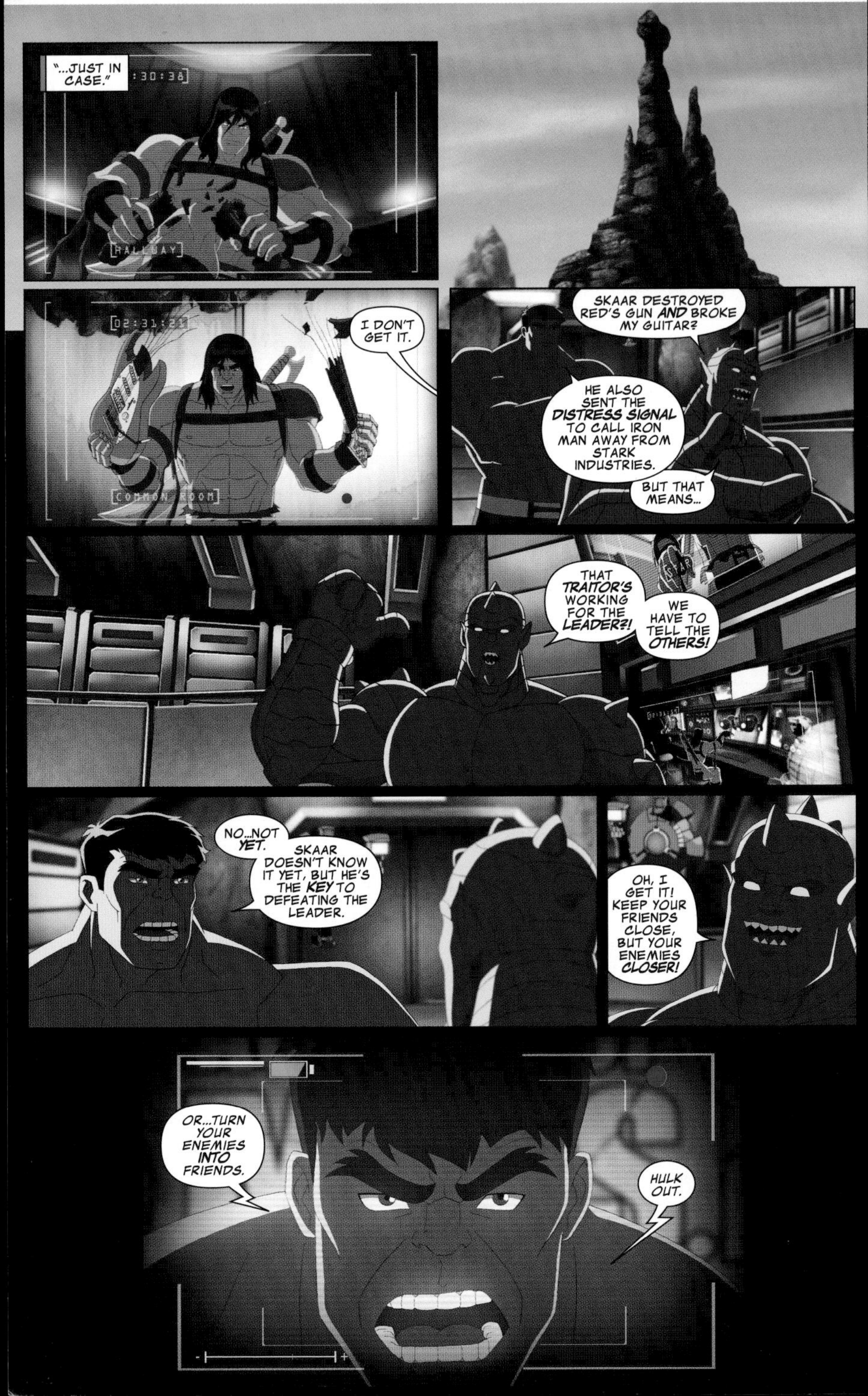
"...JUST IN CASE."
HALLWAY
02:31:21
I DON'T GET IT.
COMMON ROOM
SKAAR DESTROYED RED'S GUN **AND** BROKE MY GUITAR?
HE ALSO SENT THE **DISTRESS SIGNAL** TO CALL IRON MAN AWAY FROM STARK INDUSTRIES.
BUT THAT MEANS...
THAT **TRAITOR'S** WORKING FOR THE **LEADER?!**
WE HAVE TO TELL THE **OTHERS!**
NO...NOT **YET**.
SKAAR DOESN'T KNOW IT YET, BUT HE'S THE **KEY** TO DEFEATING THE LEADER.
OH, I GET IT! KEEP YOUR FRIENDS CLOSE, BUT YOUR ENEMIES **CLOSER!**
OR...TURN YOUR ENEMIES **INTO** FRIENDS.
HULK OUT.

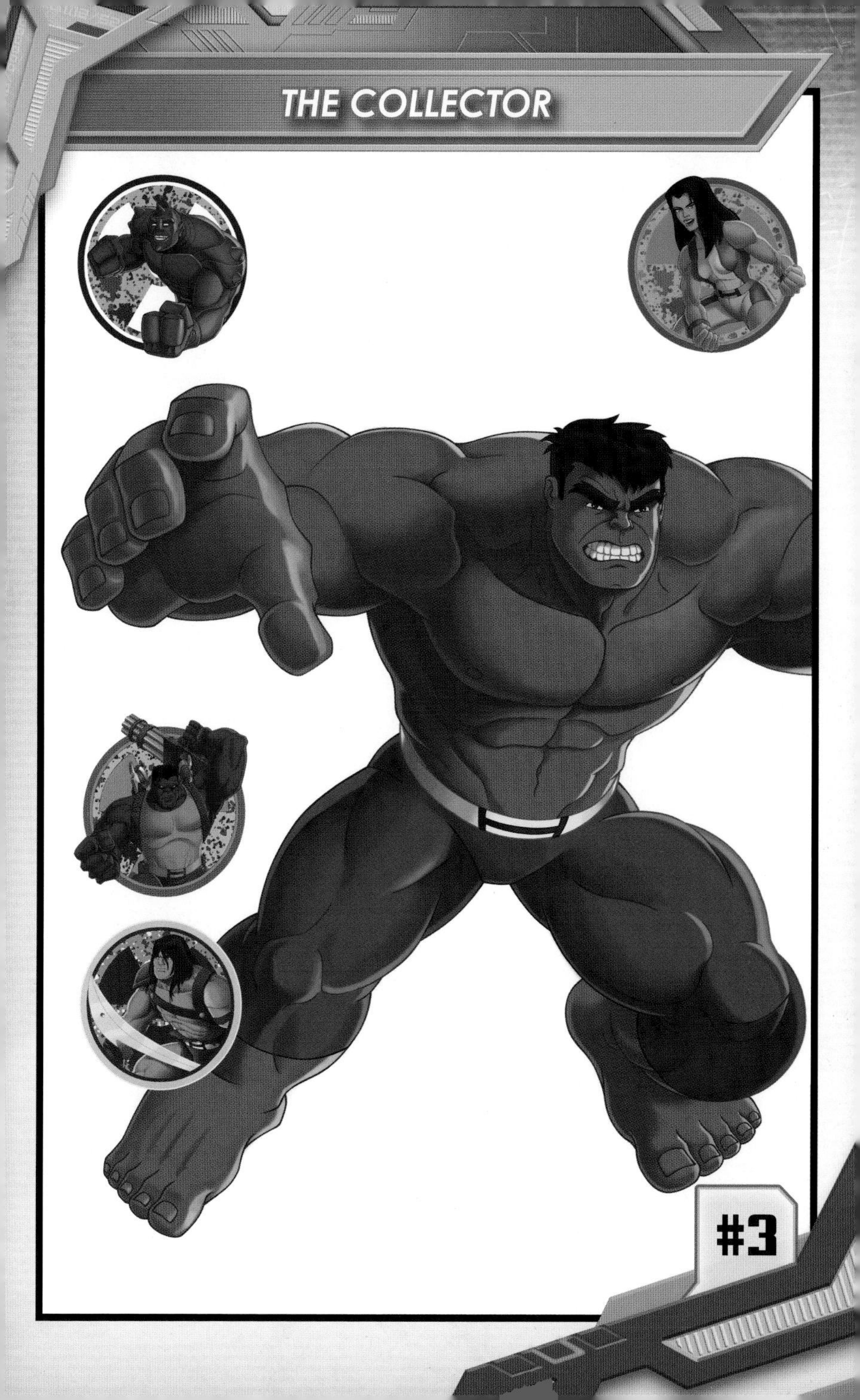
THE COLLECTOR
#3

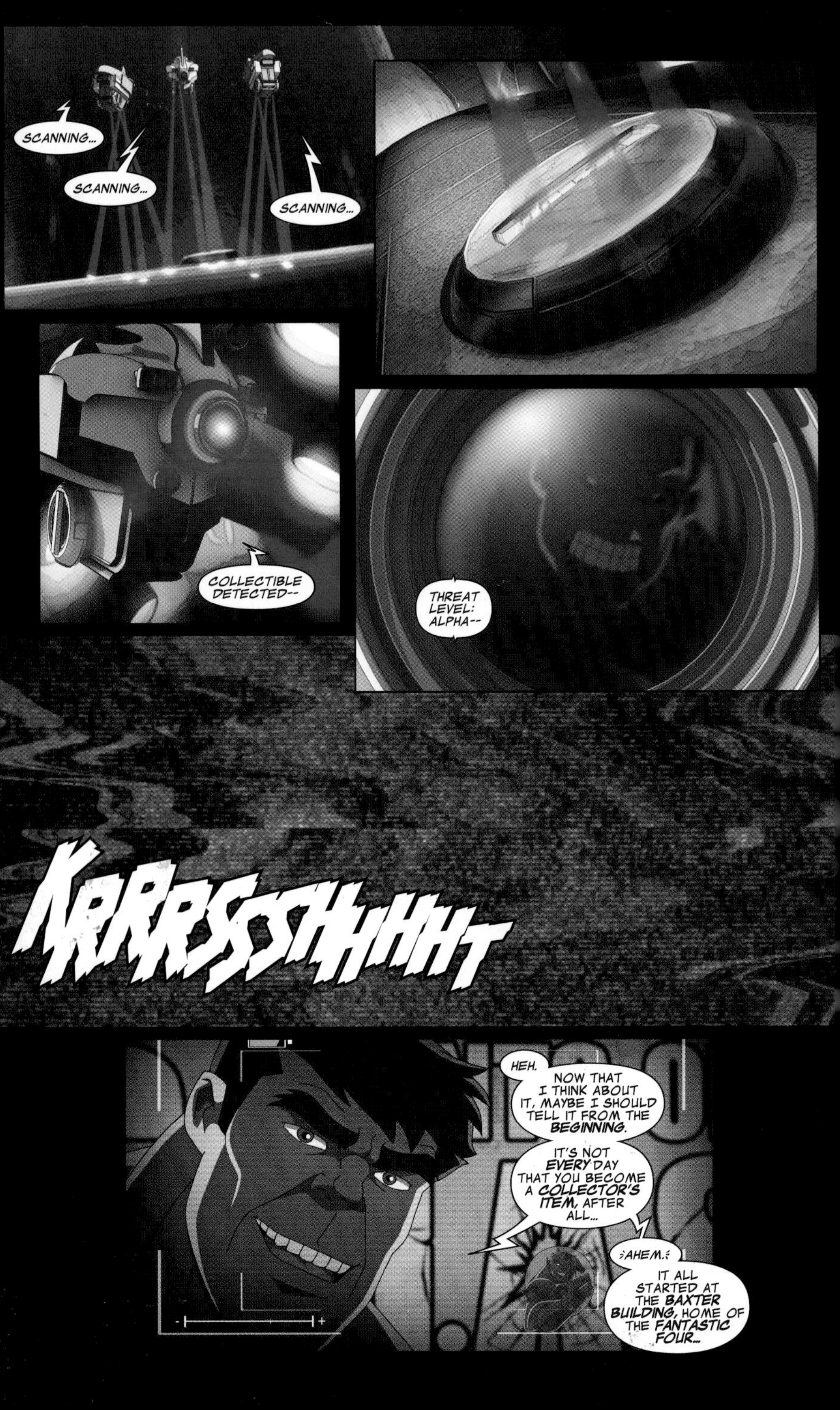
SCANNING...
SCANNING...
SCANNING...
COLLECTIBLE DETECTED--
THREAT LEVEL: ALPHA--
KRRRSSSHHHHT
HEH.
NOW THAT I THINK ABOUT IT, MAYBE I SHOULD TELL IT FROM THE BEGINNING.
IT'S NOT EVERY DAY THAT YOU BECOME A COLLECTOR'S ITEM, AFTER ALL...
AHEM.
IT ALL STARTED AT THE BAXTER BUILDING, HOME OF THE FANTASTIC FOUR...

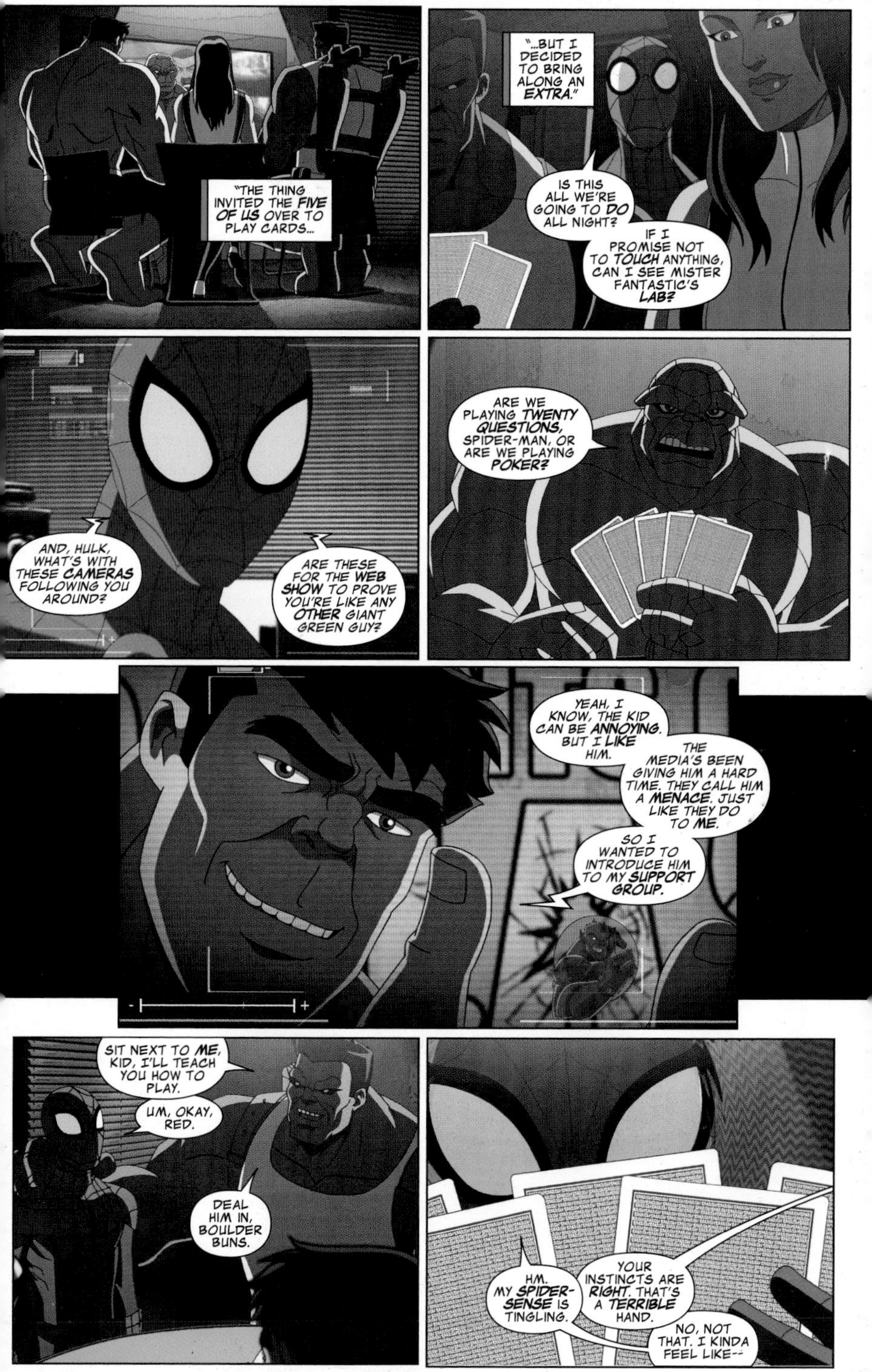
"THE THING INVITED THE FIVE OF US OVER TO PLAY CARDS...
"...BUT I DECIDED TO BRING ALONG AN EXTRA."
IS THIS ALL WE'RE GOING TO DO ALL NIGHT?
IF I PROMISE NOT TO TOUCH ANYTHING, CAN I SEE MISTER FANTASTIC'S LAB?
AND, HULK, WHAT'S WITH THESE CAMERAS FOLLOWING YOU AROUND?
ARE THESE FOR THE WEB SHOW TO PROVE YOU'RE LIKE ANY OTHER GIANT GREEN GUY?
ARE WE PLAYING TWENTY QUESTIONS, SPIDER-MAN, OR ARE WE PLAYING POKER?
YEAH, I KNOW, THE KID CAN BE ANNOYING. BUT I LIKE HIM.
THE MEDIA'S BEEN GIVING HIM A HARD TIME. THEY CALL HIM A MENACE. JUST LIKE THEY DO TO ME.
SO I WANTED TO INTRODUCE HIM TO MY SUPPORT GROUP.
SIT NEXT TO ME, KID, I'LL TEACH YOU HOW TO PLAY.
UM, OKAY, RED.
DEAL HIM IN, BOULDER BUNS.
HM. MY SPIDER-SENSE IS TINGLING.
YOUR INSTINCTS ARE RIGHT. THAT'S A TERRIBLE HAND.
NO, NOT THAT. I KINDA FEEL LIKE--

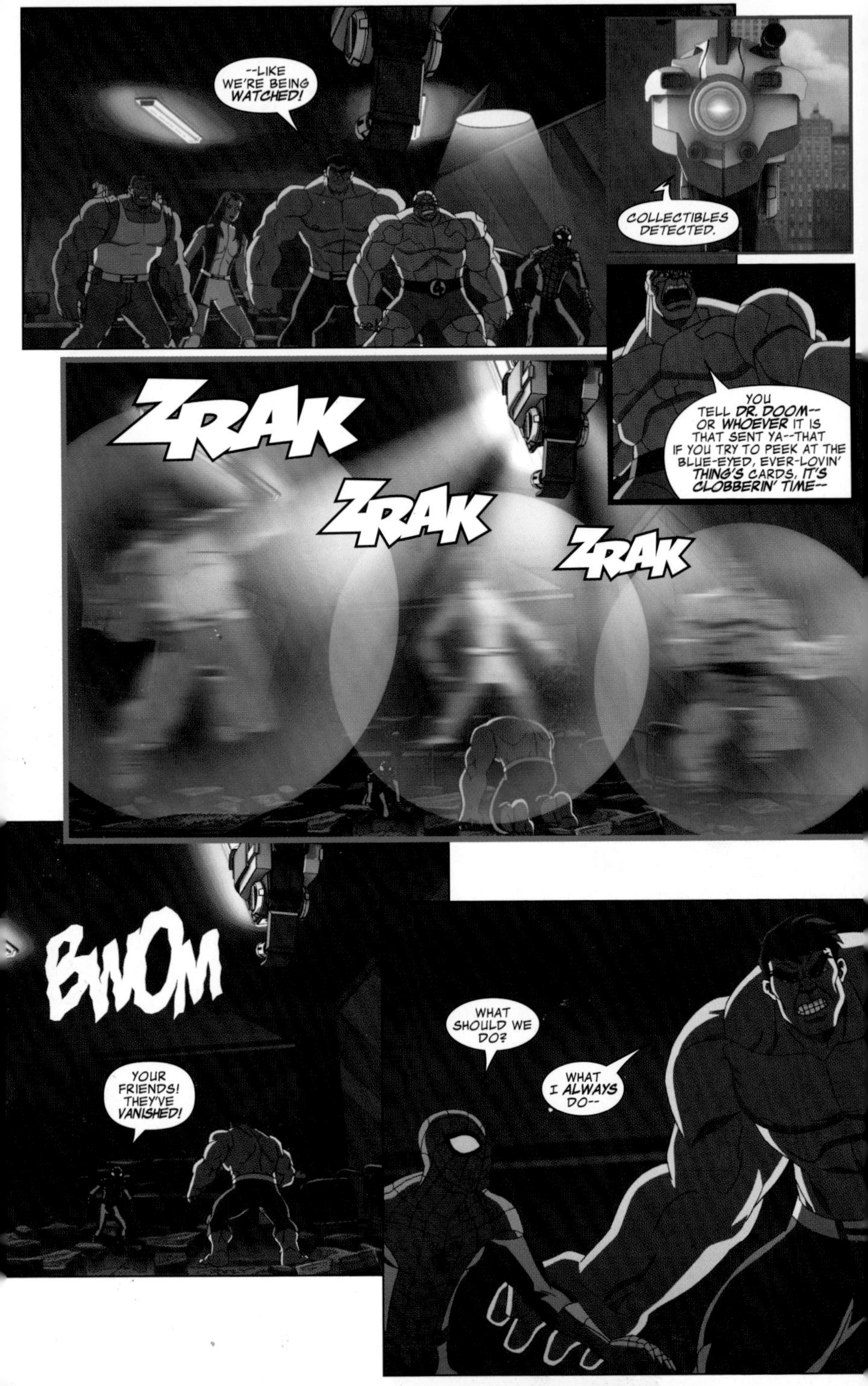
--LIKE WE'RE BEING WATCHED!
COLLECTIBLES DETECTED.
YOU TELL DR. DOOM-- OR WHOEVER IT IS THAT SENT YA--THAT IF YOU TRY TO PEEK AT THE BLUE-EYED, EVER-LOVIN' THING'S CARDS, IT'S CLOBBERIN' TIME--
ZRAK
ZRAK
ZRAK
BWOM
YOUR FRIENDS! THEY'VE VANISHED!
WHAT SHOULD WE DO?
WHAT I ALWAYS DO--

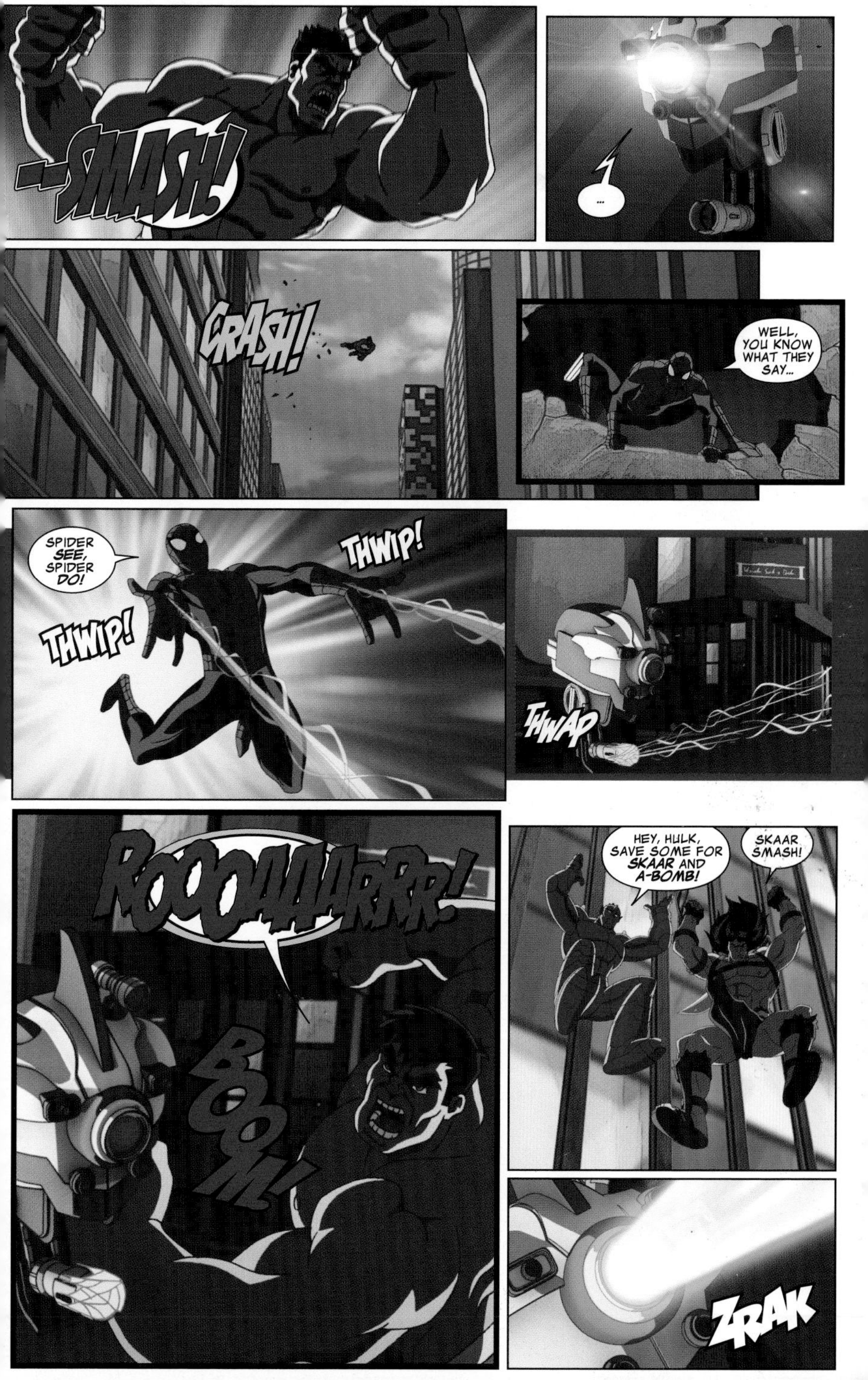
--SMASH!
...
CRASH!
WELL, YOU KNOW WHAT THEY SAY...
SPIDER SEE, SPIDER DO!
THWIP!
THWIP!
THWAP
ROOOAAARRR!
BOOOM!
HEY, HULK, SAVE SOME FOR SKAAR AND A-BOMB!
SKAAR SMASH!
ZRAK

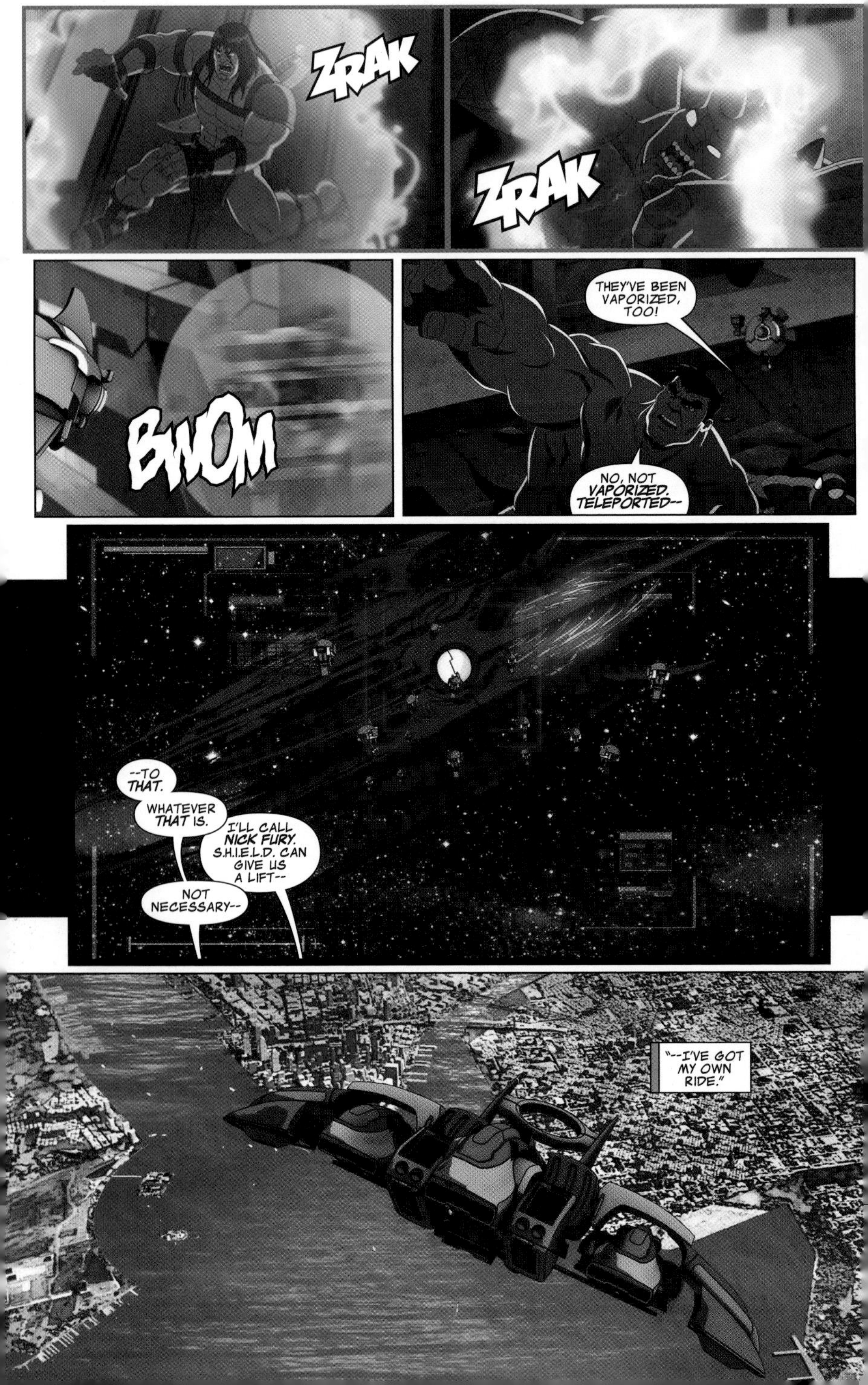
ZRAK
ZRAK
BWOM
THEY'VE BEEN VAPORIZED, TOO!
NO, NOT VAPORIZED. TELEPORTED--
--TO THAT.
WHATEVER THAT IS.
I'LL CALL NICK FURY. S.H.I.E.L.D. CAN GIVE US A LIFT--
NOT NECESSARY--
"--I'VE GOT MY OWN RIDE."

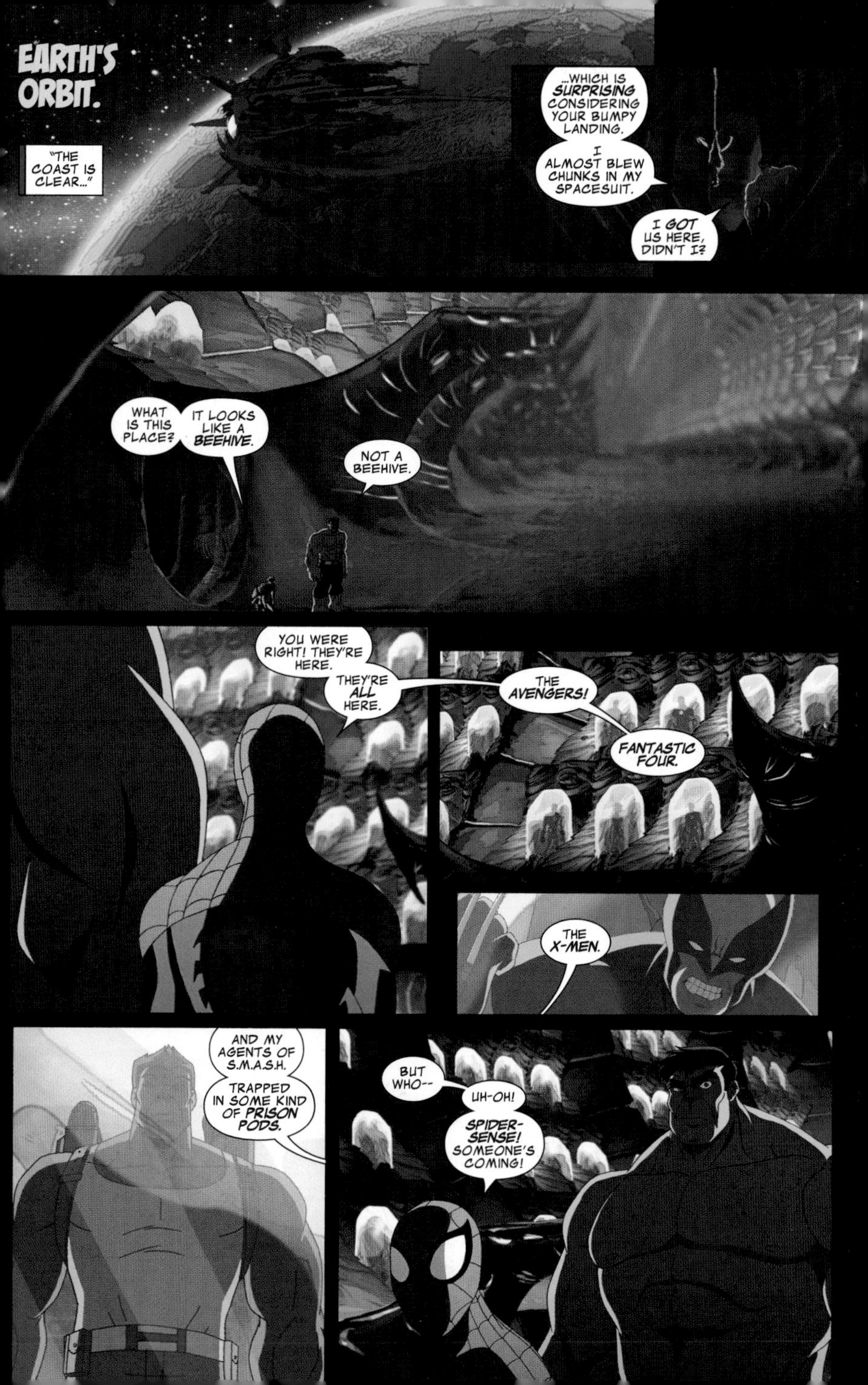
EARTH'S ORBIT.
"THE COAST IS CLEAR..."
...WHICH IS SURPRISING CONSIDERING YOUR BUMPY LANDING.
I ALMOST BLEW CHUNKS IN MY SPACESUIT.
I GOT US HERE, DIDN'T I?
WHAT IS THIS PLACE?
IT LOOKS LIKE A BEEHIVE.
NOT A BEEHIVE.
YOU WERE RIGHT! THEY'RE HERE.
THEY'RE ALL HERE.
THE AVENGERS!
FANTASTIC FOUR.
THE X-MEN.
AND MY AGENTS OF S.M.A.S.H.
TRAPPED IN SOME KIND OF PRISON PODS.
BUT WHO--
UH-OH!
SPIDER-SENSE! SOMEONE'S COMING!

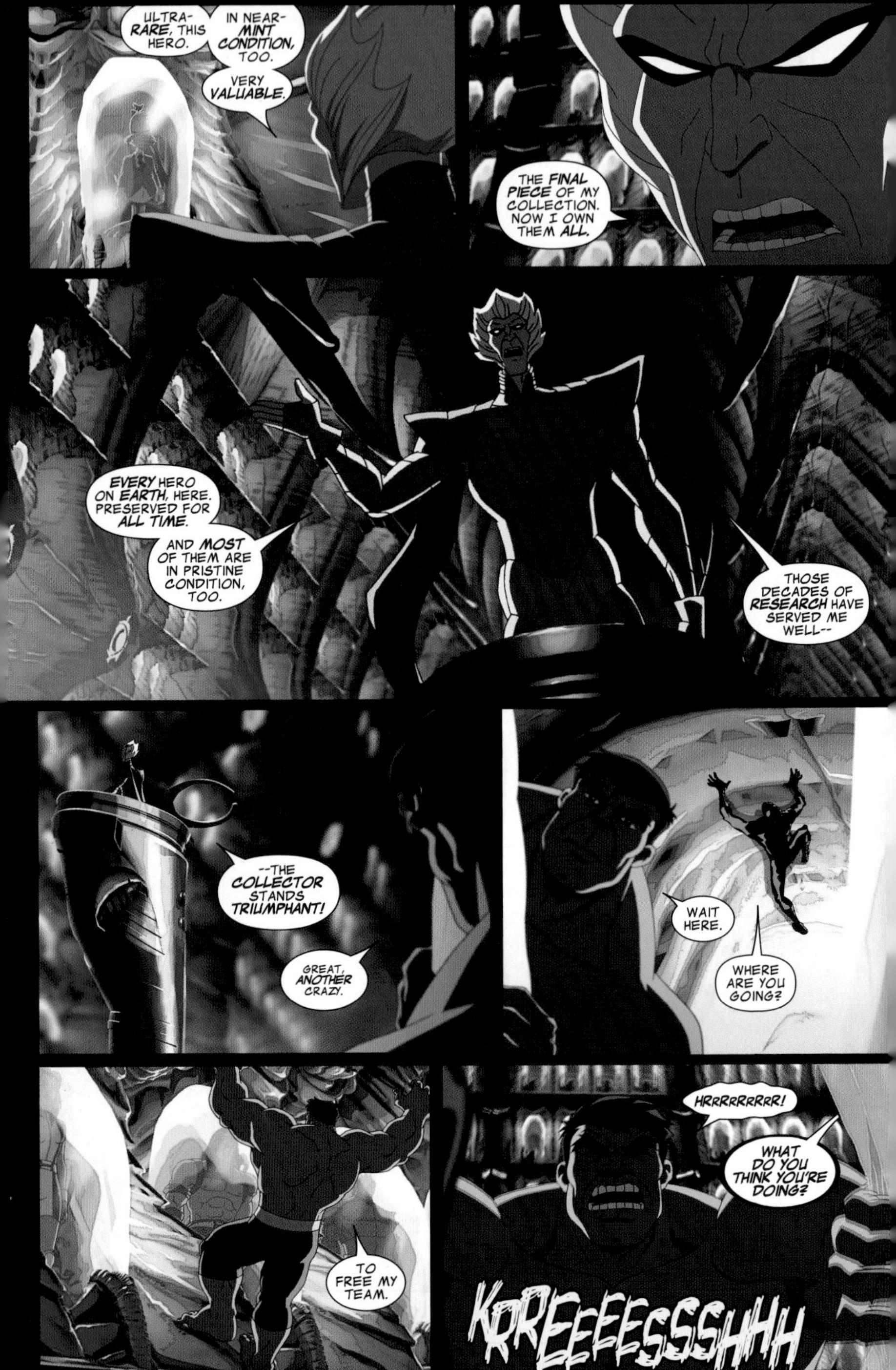
ULTRA-RARE, THIS HERO.
IN NEAR-MINT CONDITION, TOO.
VERY VALUABLE.
THE FINAL PIECE OF MY COLLECTION. NOW I OWN THEM ALL.
EVERY HERO ON EARTH, HERE. PRESERVED FOR ALL TIME.
AND MOST OF THEM ARE IN PRISTINE CONDITION, TOO.
THOSE DECADES OF RESEARCH HAVE SERVED ME WELL--
--THE COLLECTOR STANDS TRIUMPHANT!
GREAT, ANOTHER CRAZY.
WAIT HERE.
WHERE ARE YOU GOING?
TO FREE MY TEAM.
HRRRRRRRR!
WHAT DO YOU THINK YOU'RE DOING?
KRREEEEESSSHHH

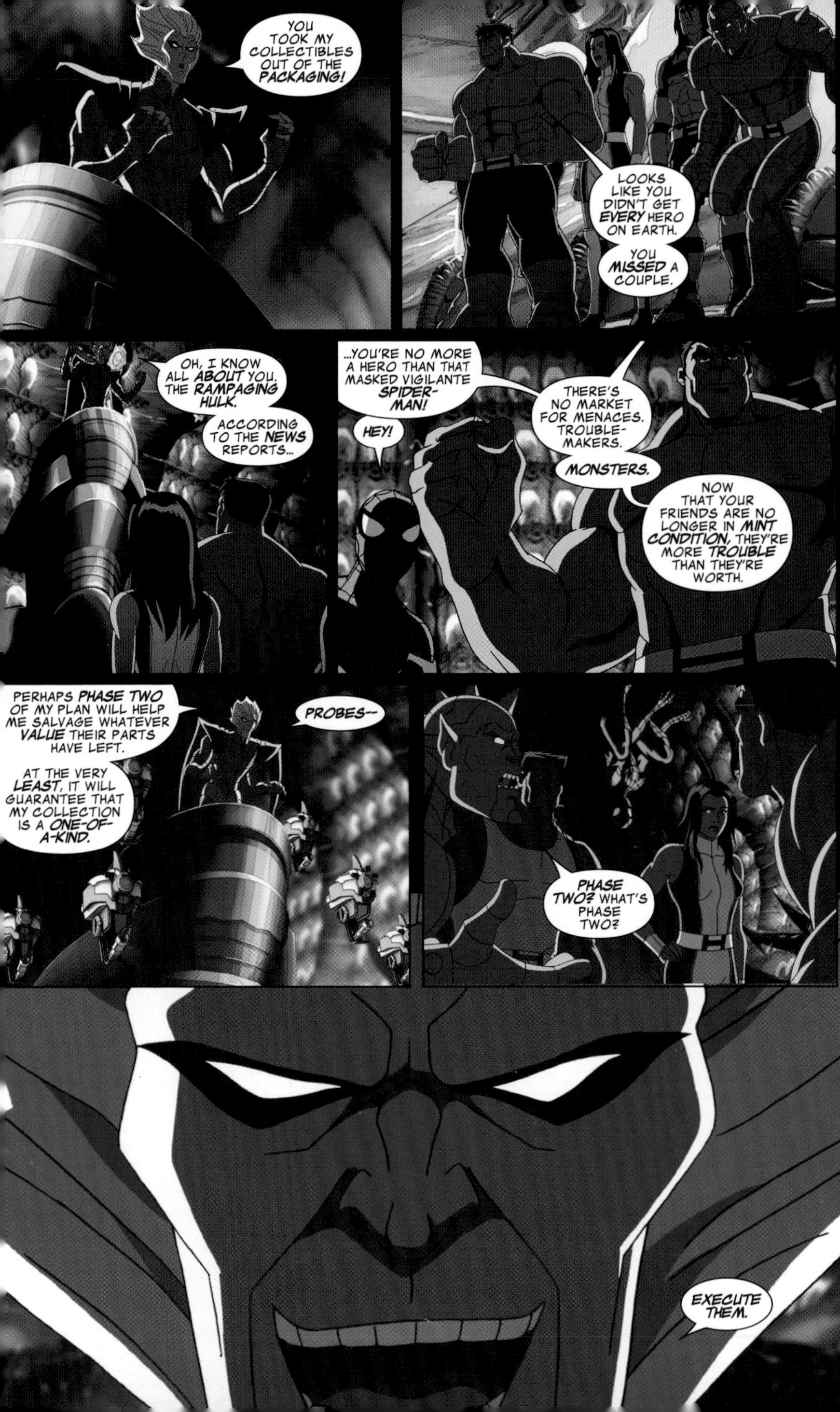

YOU TOOK MY COLLECTIBLES OUT OF THE PACKAGING!
LOOKS LIKE YOU DIDN'T GET EVERY HERO ON EARTH.
YOU MISSED A COUPLE.
OH, I KNOW ALL ABOUT YOU. THE RAMPAGING HULK.
ACCORDING TO THE NEWS REPORTS...
...YOU'RE NO MORE A HERO THAN THAT MASKED VIGILANTE SPIDER-MAN!
HEY!
THERE'S NO MARKET FOR MENACES. TROUBLE-MAKERS.
MONSTERS.
NOW THAT YOUR FRIENDS ARE NO LONGER IN MINT CONDITION, THEY'RE MORE TROUBLE THAN THEY'RE WORTH.
PERHAPS PHASE TWO OF MY PLAN WILL HELP ME SALVAGE WHATEVER VALUE THEIR PARTS HAVE LEFT.
AT THE VERY LEAST, IT WILL GUARANTEE THAT MY COLLECTION IS A ONE-OF-A-KIND.
PROBES--
PHASE TWO? WHAT'S PHASE TWO?
EXECUTE THEM.

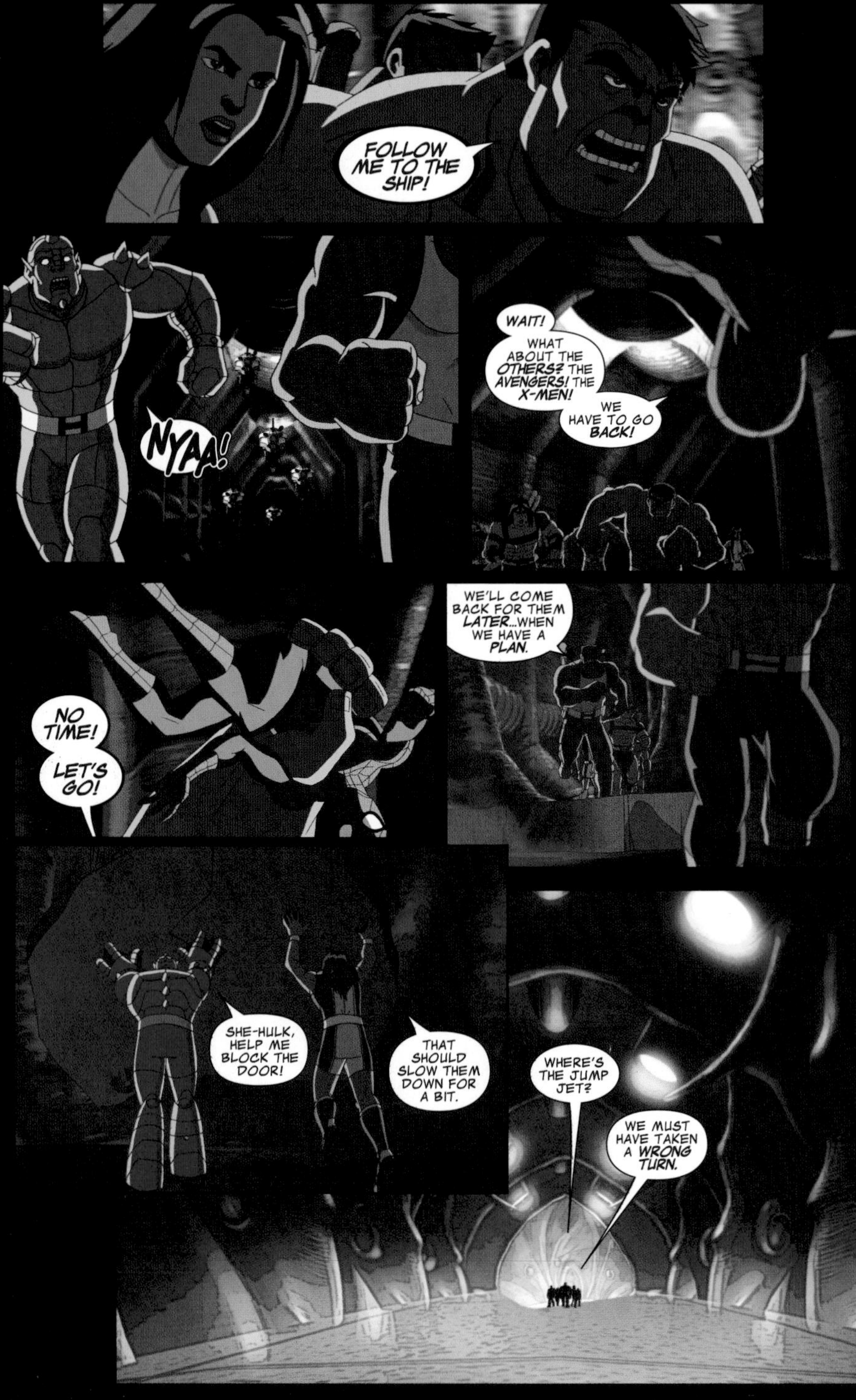
FOLLOW ME TO THE SHIP!
NYAA!
WAIT!
WHAT ABOUT THE OTHERS? THE AVENGERS! THE X-MEN!
WE HAVE TO GO BACK!
NO TIME!
LET'S GO!
WE'LL COME BACK FOR THEM LATER...WHEN WE HAVE A PLAN.
SHE-HULK, HELP ME BLOCK THE DOOR!
THAT SHOULD SLOW THEM DOWN FOR A BIT.
WHERE'S THE JUMP JET?
WE MUST HAVE TAKEN A WRONG TURN.

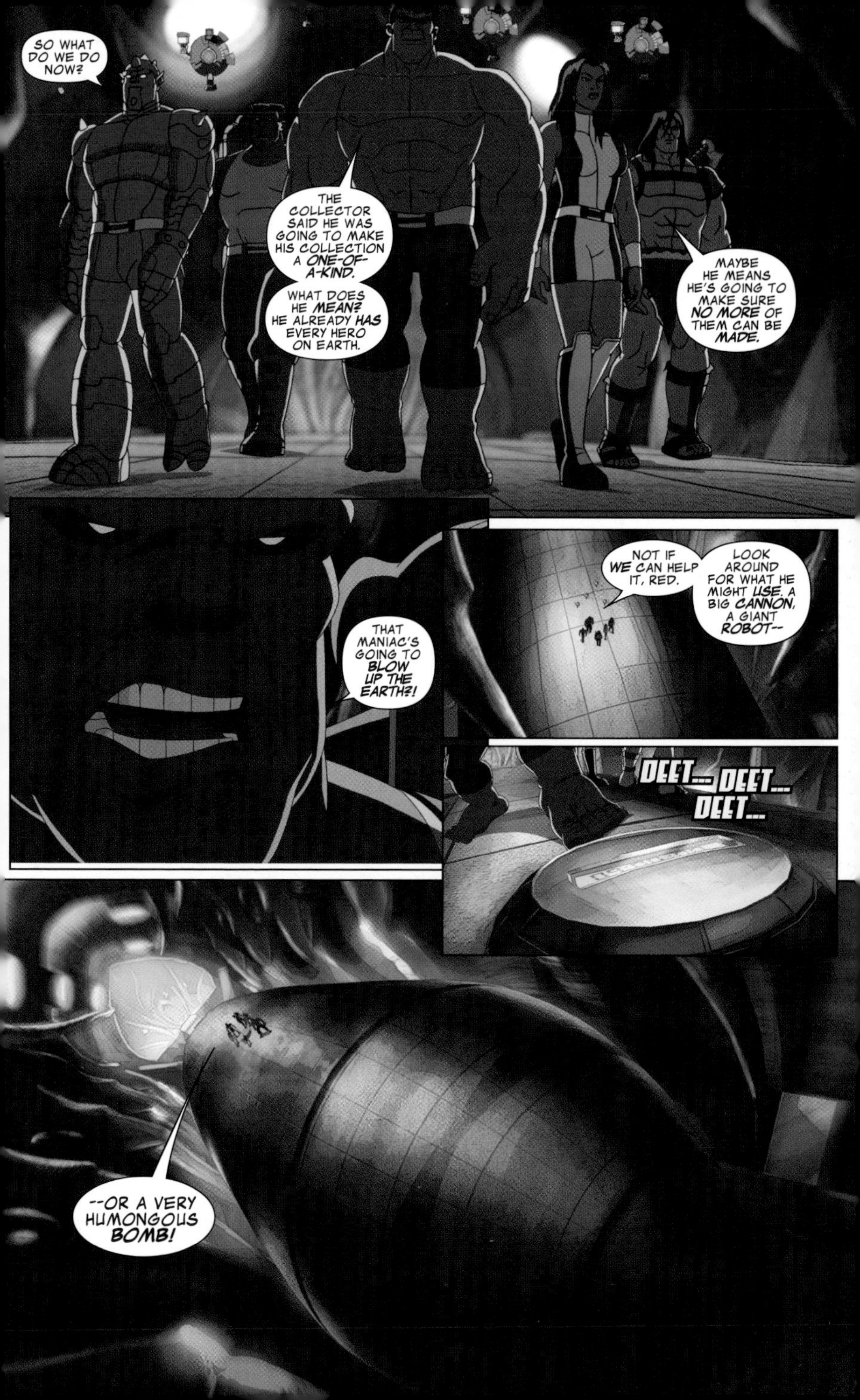
SO WHAT DO WE DO NOW?
THE COLLECTOR SAID HE WAS GOING TO MAKE HIS COLLECTION A ONE-OF-A-KIND.
WHAT DOES HE MEAN? HE ALREADY HAS EVERY HERO ON EARTH.
MAYBE HE MEANS HE'S GOING TO MAKE SURE NO MORE OF THEM CAN BE MADE.
THAT MANIAC'S GOING TO BLOW UP THE EARTH?!
NOT IF WE CAN HELP IT, RED.
LOOK AROUND FOR WHAT HE MIGHT USE. A BIG CANNON, A GIANT ROBOT--
DEET... DEET... DEET...
--OR A VERY HUMONGOUS BOMB!

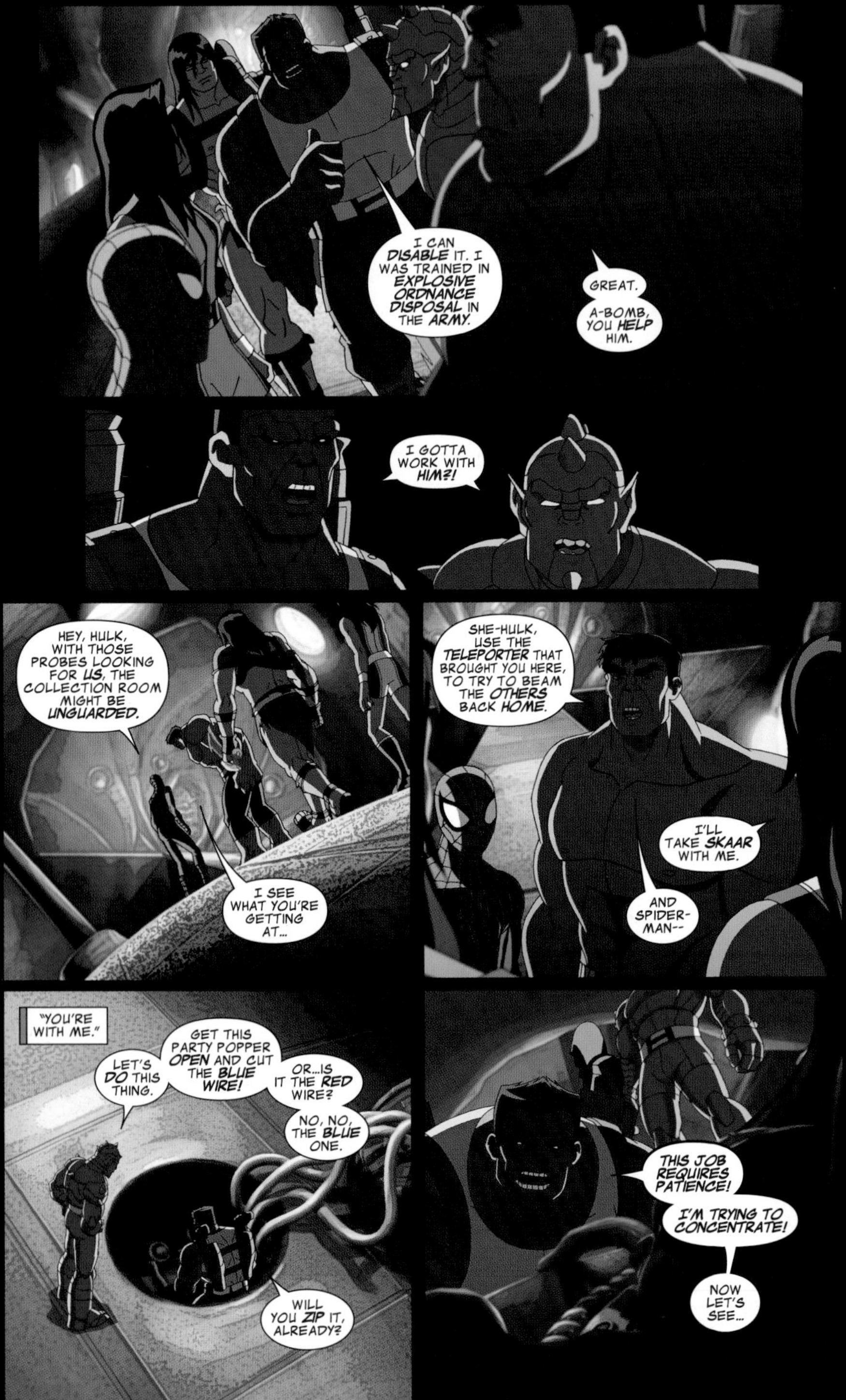
I CAN DISABLE IT. I WAS TRAINED IN EXPLOSIVE ORDNANCE DISPOSAL IN THE ARMY.
GREAT.
A-BOMB, YOU HELP HIM.
I GOTTA WORK WITH HIM?!
HEY, HULK, WITH THOSE PROBES LOOKING FOR US, THE COLLECTION ROOM MIGHT BE UNGUARDED.
I SEE WHAT YOU'RE GETTING AT...
SHE-HULK, USE THE TELEPORTER THAT BROUGHT YOU HERE, TO TRY TO BEAM THE OTHERS BACK HOME.
I'LL TAKE SKAAR WITH ME.
AND SPIDER-MAN--
"YOU'RE WITH ME."
LET'S DO THIS THING.
GET THIS PARTY POPPER OPEN AND CUT THE BLUE WIRE!
OR...IS IT THE RED WIRE?
NO, NO, THE BLUE ONE.
WILL YOU ZIP IT, ALREADY?
THIS JOB REQUIRES PATIENCE!
I'M TRYING TO CONCENTRATE!
NOW LET'S SEE...

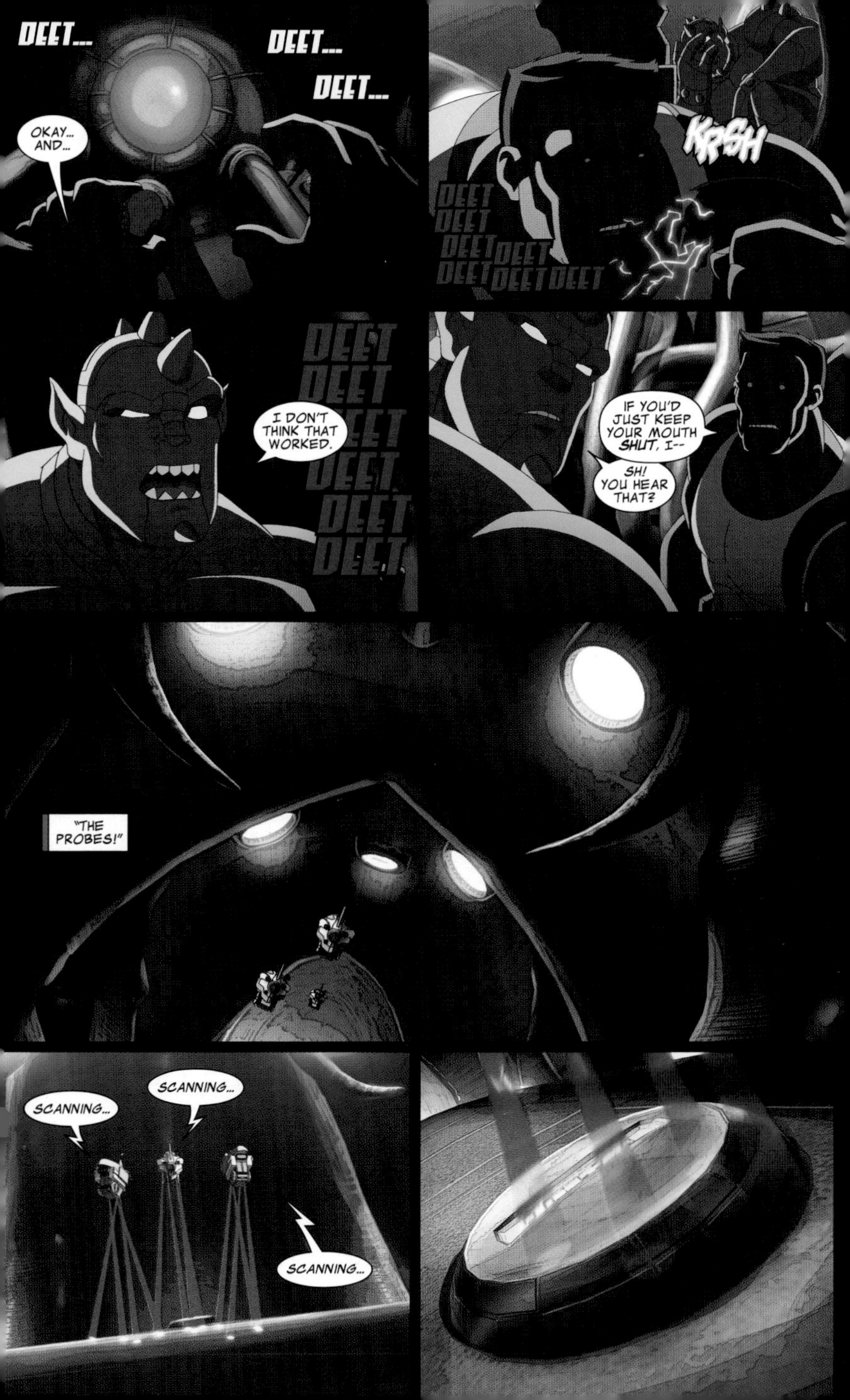
DEET...
DEET...
DEET...
OKAY... AND...
KRSH
DEET DEET DEET DEET DEET DEET DEET
DEET DEET DEET DEET DEET DEET
I DON'T THINK THAT WORKED.
IF YOU'D JUST KEEP YOUR MOUTH SHUT, I--
SH! YOU HEAR THAT?
"THE PROBES!"
SCANNING...
SCANNING...
SCANNING...

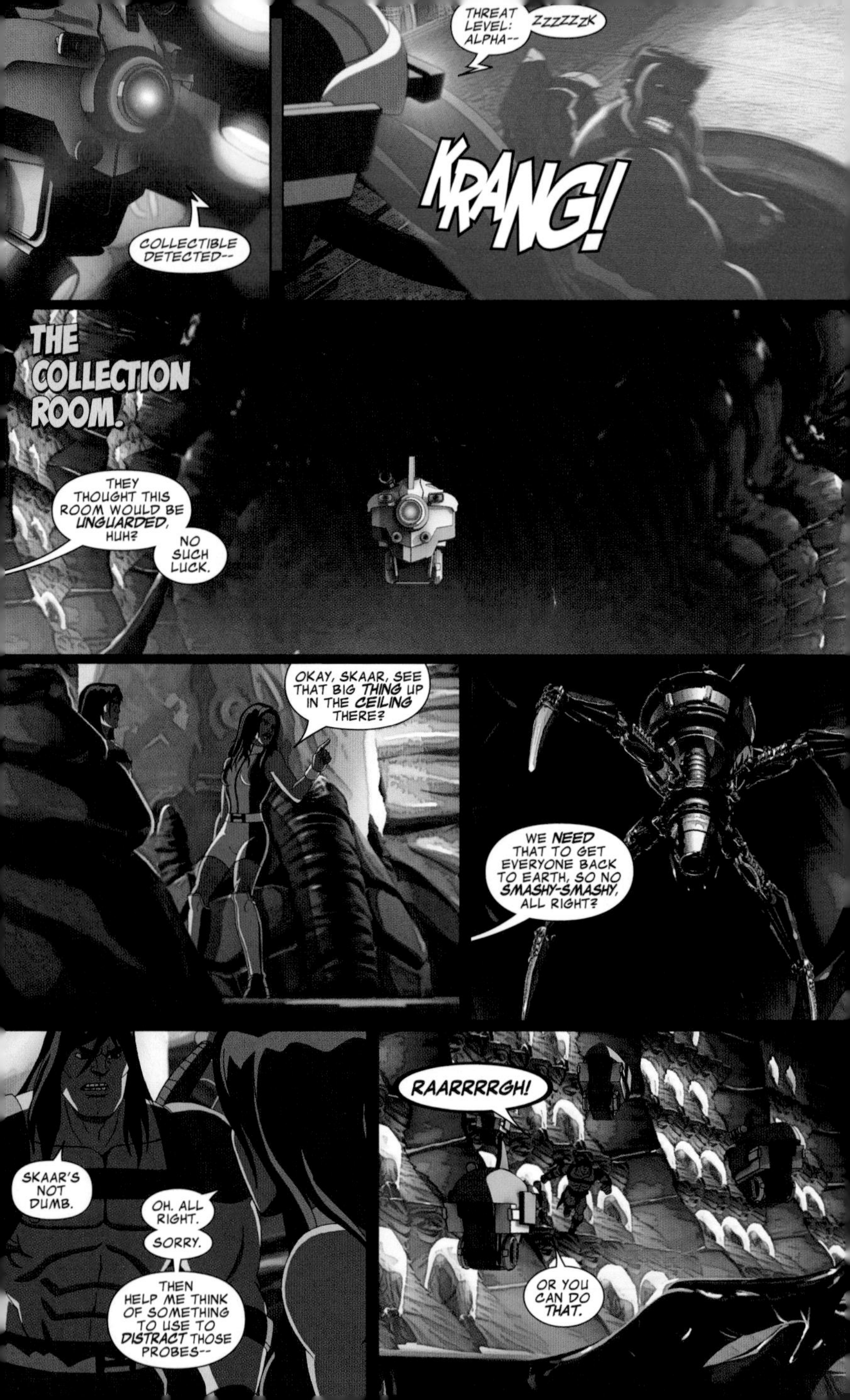
COLLECTIBLE DETECTED--
THREAT LEVEL: ALPHA--
ZZZZZZK
KRANG!
THE COLLECTION ROOM.
THEY THOUGHT THIS ROOM WOULD BE UNGUARDED, HUH?
NO SUCH LUCK.
OKAY, SKAAR, SEE THAT BIG THING UP IN THE CEILING THERE?
WE NEED THAT TO GET EVERYONE BACK TO EARTH, SO NO SMASHY-SMASHY, ALL RIGHT?
SKAAR'S NOT DUMB.
OH. ALL RIGHT.
SORRY.
THEN HELP ME THINK OF SOMETHING TO USE TO DISTRACT THOSE PROBES--
RAARRRRGH!
OR YOU CAN DO THAT.

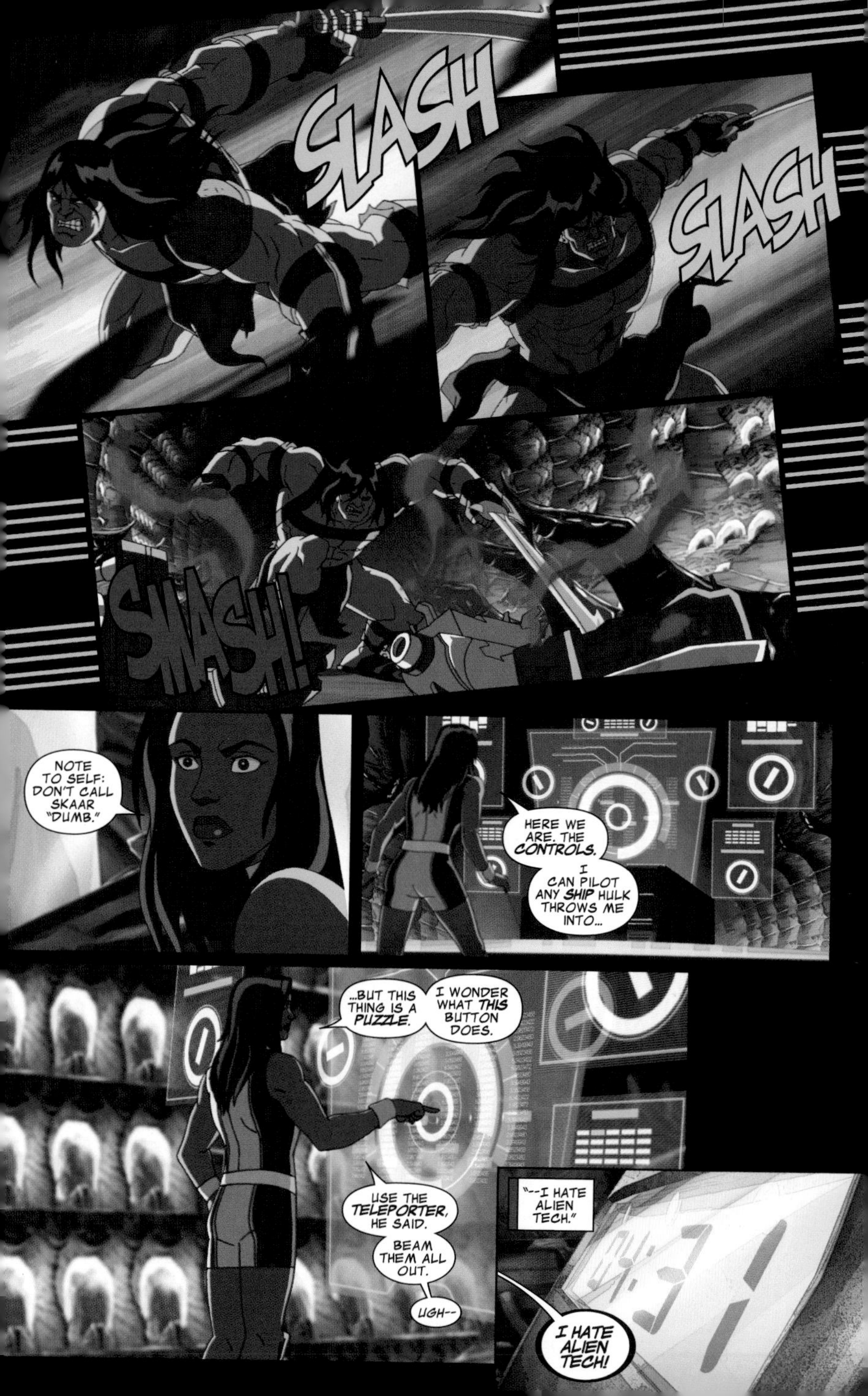
SLASH
SLASH
SMASH!
NOTE TO SELF: DON'T CALL SKAAR "DUMB."
HERE WE ARE. THE CONTROLS.
I CAN PILOT ANY SHIP HULK THROWS ME INTO...
...BUT THIS THING IS A PUZZLE.
I WONDER WHAT THIS BUTTON DOES.
USE THE TELEPORTER, HE SAID.
BEAM THEM ALL OUT.
UGH--
"--I HATE ALIEN TECH."
I HATE ALIEN TECH!

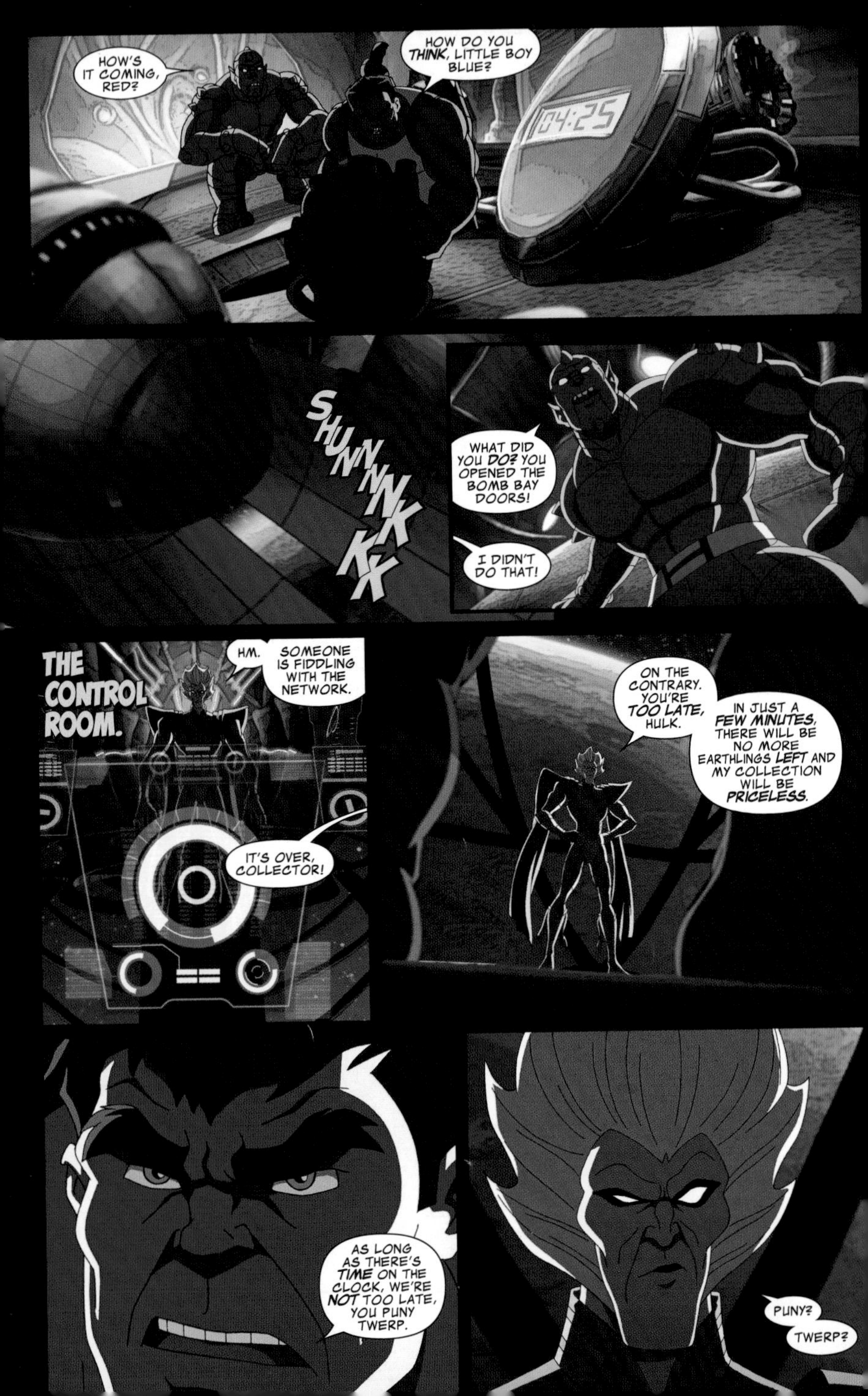
HOW'S IT COMING, RED?
HOW DO YOU THINK, LITTLE BOY BLUE?
104:25
SHUNNNNKKK
WHAT DID YOU DO? YOU OPENED THE BOMB BAY DOORS!
I DIDN'T DO THAT!
THE CONTROL ROOM.
HM. SOMEONE IS FIDDLING WITH THE NETWORK.
IT'S OVER, COLLECTOR!
ON THE CONTRARY. YOU'RE TOO LATE, HULK.
IN JUST A FEW MINUTES, THERE WILL BE NO MORE EARTHLINGS LEFT AND MY COLLECTION WILL BE PRICELESS.
AS LONG AS THERE'S TIME ON THE CLOCK, WE'RE NOT TOO LATE, YOU PUNY TWERP.
PUNY?
TWERP?

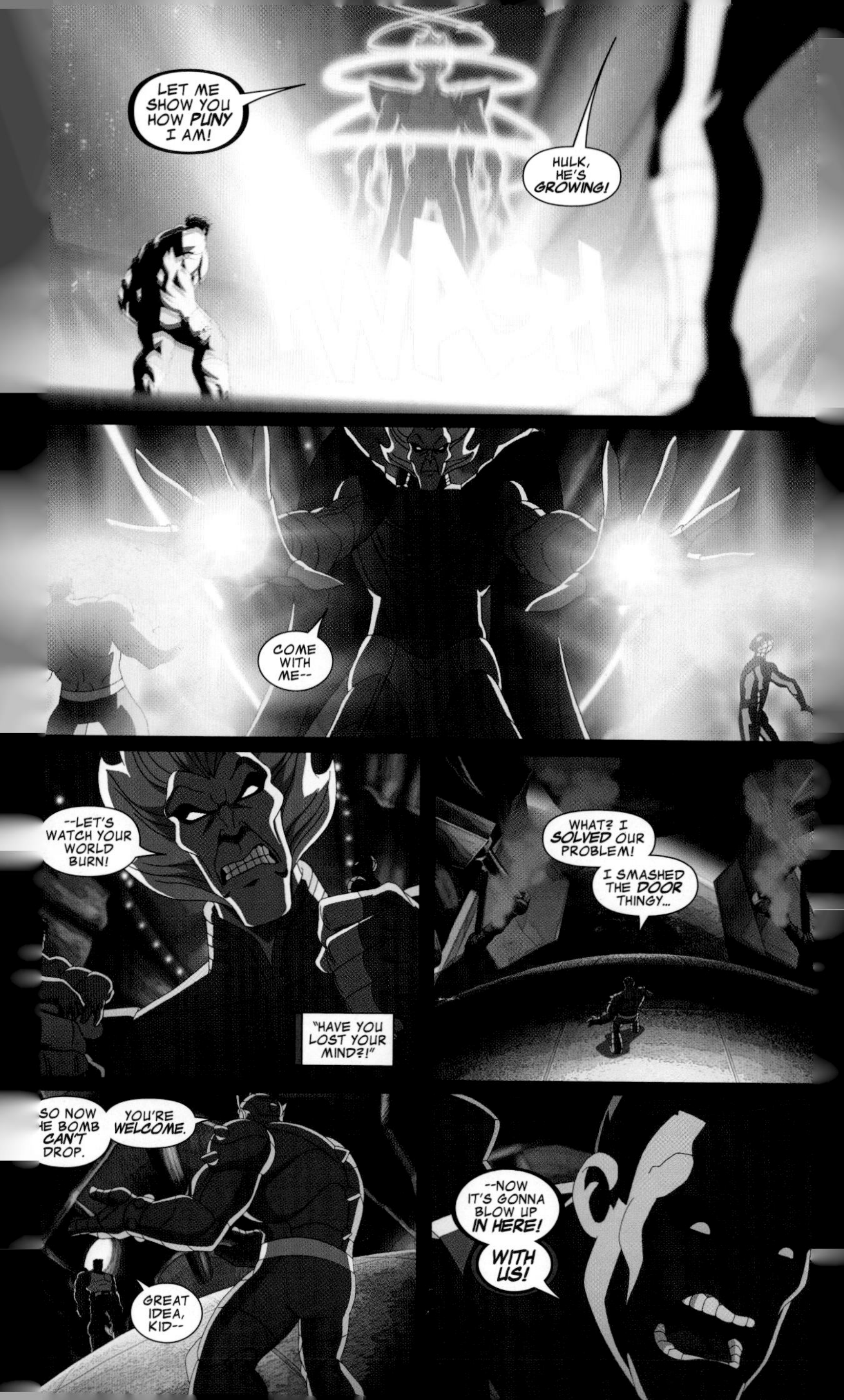
LET ME SHOW YOU HOW PUNY I AM!
HULK, HE'S GROWING!
COME WITH ME--
--LET'S WATCH YOUR WORLD BURN!
"HAVE YOU LOST YOUR MIND?!"
WHAT? I SOLVED OUR PROBLEM!
I SMASHED THE DOOR THINGY...
SO NOW HE BOMB CAN'T DROP.
YOU'RE WELCOME.
GREAT IDEA, KID--
--NOW IT'S GONNA BLOW UP IN HERE!
WITH US!

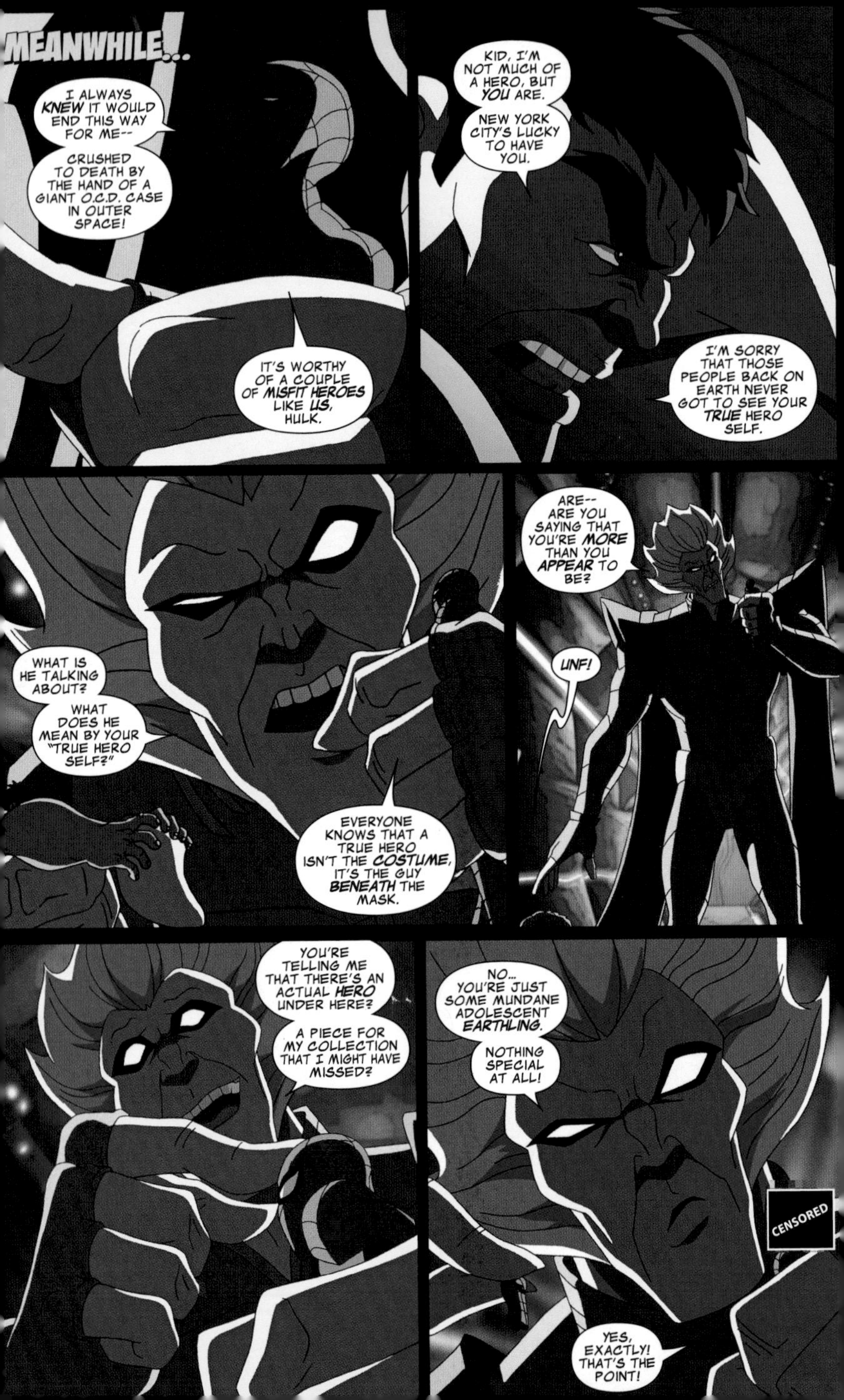
MEANWHILE...
I ALWAYS KNEW IT WOULD END THIS WAY FOR ME--
CRUSHED TO DEATH BY THE HAND OF A GIANT O.C.D. CASE IN OUTER SPACE!
IT'S WORTHY OF A COUPLE OF MISFIT HEROES LIKE US, HULK.
KID, I'M NOT MUCH OF A HERO, BUT YOU ARE.
NEW YORK CITY'S LUCKY TO HAVE YOU.
I'M SORRY THAT THOSE PEOPLE BACK ON EARTH NEVER GOT TO SEE YOUR TRUE HERO SELF.
WHAT IS HE TALKING ABOUT?
WHAT DOES HE MEAN BY YOUR "TRUE HERO SELF?"
EVERYONE KNOWS THAT A TRUE HERO ISN'T THE COSTUME, IT'S THE GUY BENEATH THE MASK.
ARE-- ARE YOU SAYING THAT YOU'RE MORE THAN YOU APPEAR TO BE?
UNF!
YOU'RE TELLING ME THAT THERE'S AN ACTUAL HERO UNDER HERE?
A PIECE FOR MY COLLECTION THAT I MIGHT HAVE MISSED?
NO... YOU'RE JUST SOME MUNDANE ADOLESCENT EARTHLING.
NOTHING SPECIAL AT ALL!
CENSORED
YES, EXACTLY! THAT'S THE POINT!

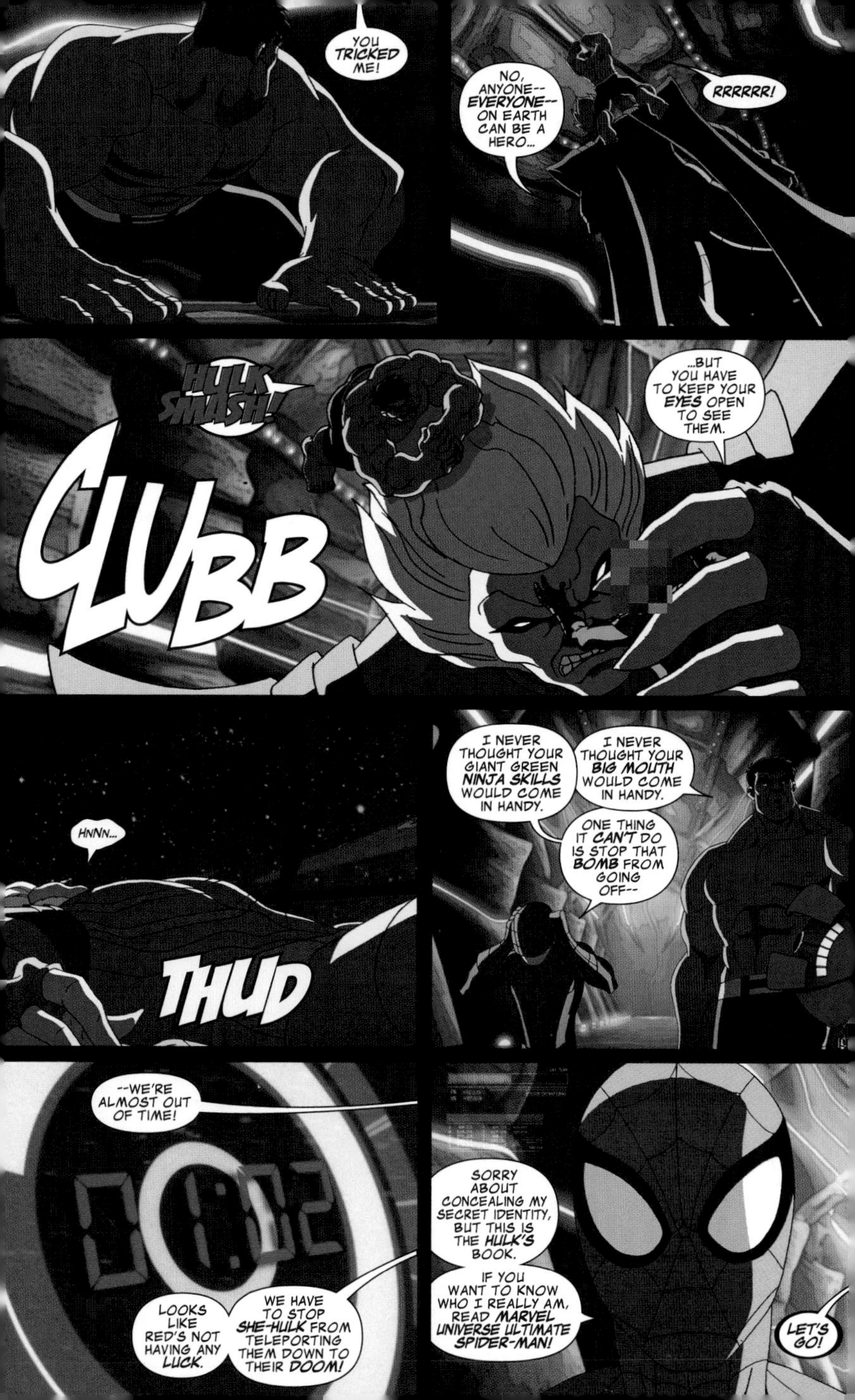

YOU TRICKED ME!
NO, ANYONE-- EVERYONE-- ON EARTH CAN BE A HERO...
RRRRRR!
HULK SMASH!
CLUBB
...BUT YOU HAVE TO KEEP YOUR EYES OPEN TO SEE THEM.
HNNN...
THUD
I NEVER THOUGHT YOUR GIANT GREEN NINJA SKILLS WOULD COME IN HANDY.
I NEVER THOUGHT YOUR BIG MOUTH WOULD COME IN HANDY.
ONE THING IT CAN'T DO IS STOP THAT BOMB FROM GOING OFF--
--WE'RE ALMOST OUT OF TIME!
LOOKS LIKE RED'S NOT HAVING ANY LUCK.
WE HAVE TO STOP SHE-HULK FROM TELEPORTING THEM DOWN TO THEIR DOOM!
SORRY ABOUT CONCEALING MY SECRET IDENTITY, BUT THIS IS THE HULK'S BOOK.
IF YOU WANT TO KNOW WHO I REALLY AM, READ MARVEL UNIVERSE ULTIMATE SPIDER-MAN!
LET'S GO!

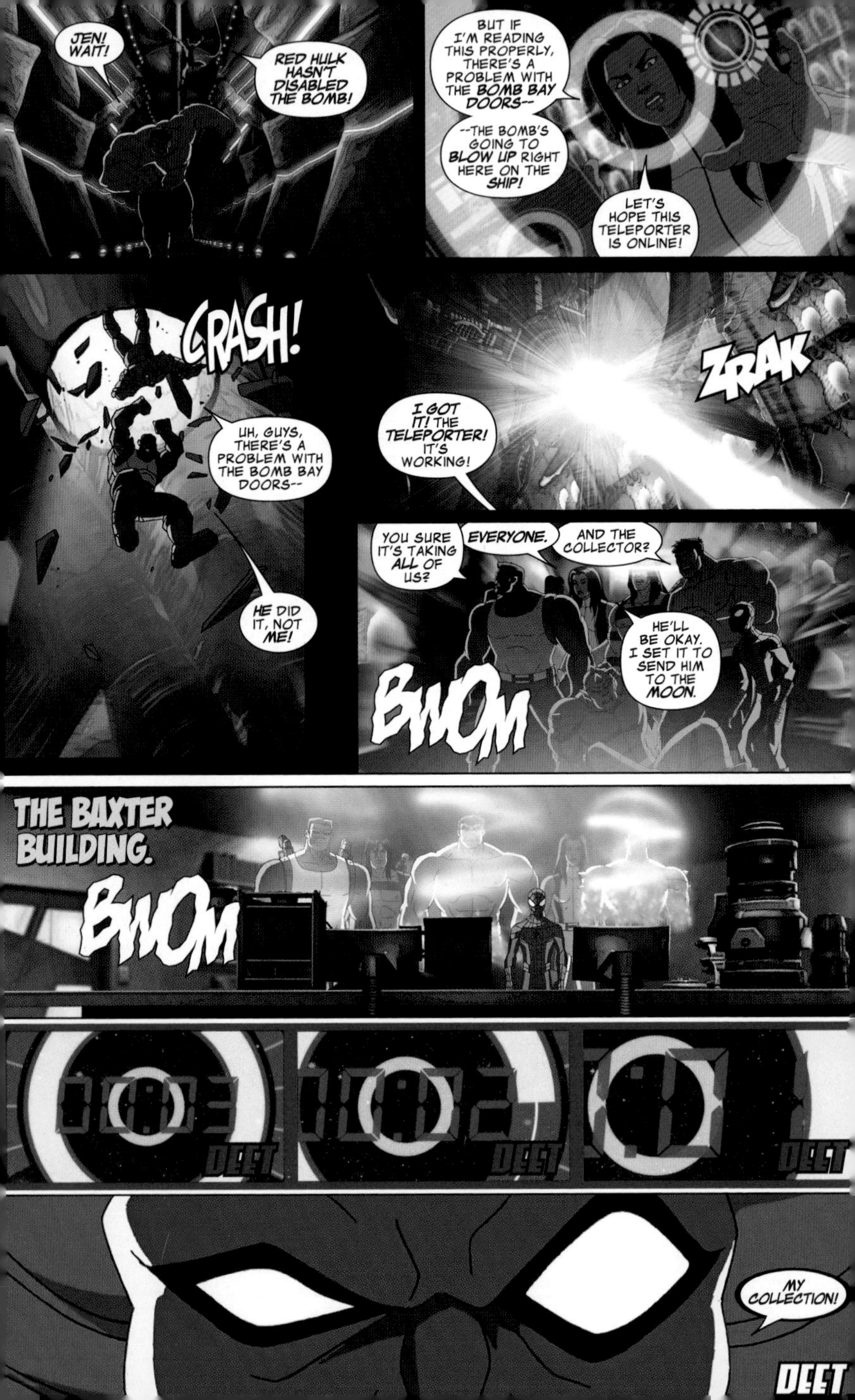
JEN! WAIT!
RED HULK HASN'T DISABLED THE BOMB!
BUT IF I'M READING THIS PROPERLY, THERE'S A PROBLEM WITH THE BOMB BAY DOORS--
--THE BOMB'S GOING TO BLOW UP RIGHT HERE ON THE SHIP!
LET'S HOPE THIS TELEPORTER IS ONLINE!
CRASH!
UH, GUYS, THERE'S A PROBLEM WITH THE BOMB BAY DOORS--
HE DID IT, NOT ME!
ZRAK
I GOT IT! THE TELEPORTER! IT'S WORKING!
YOU SURE IT'S TAKING ALL OF US?
EVERYONE.
AND THE COLLECTOR?
HE'LL BE OKAY. I SET IT TO SEND HIM TO THE MOON.
BWOM
THE BAXTER BUILDING.
BWOM
DEET
DEET
DEET
MY COLLECTION!
DEET

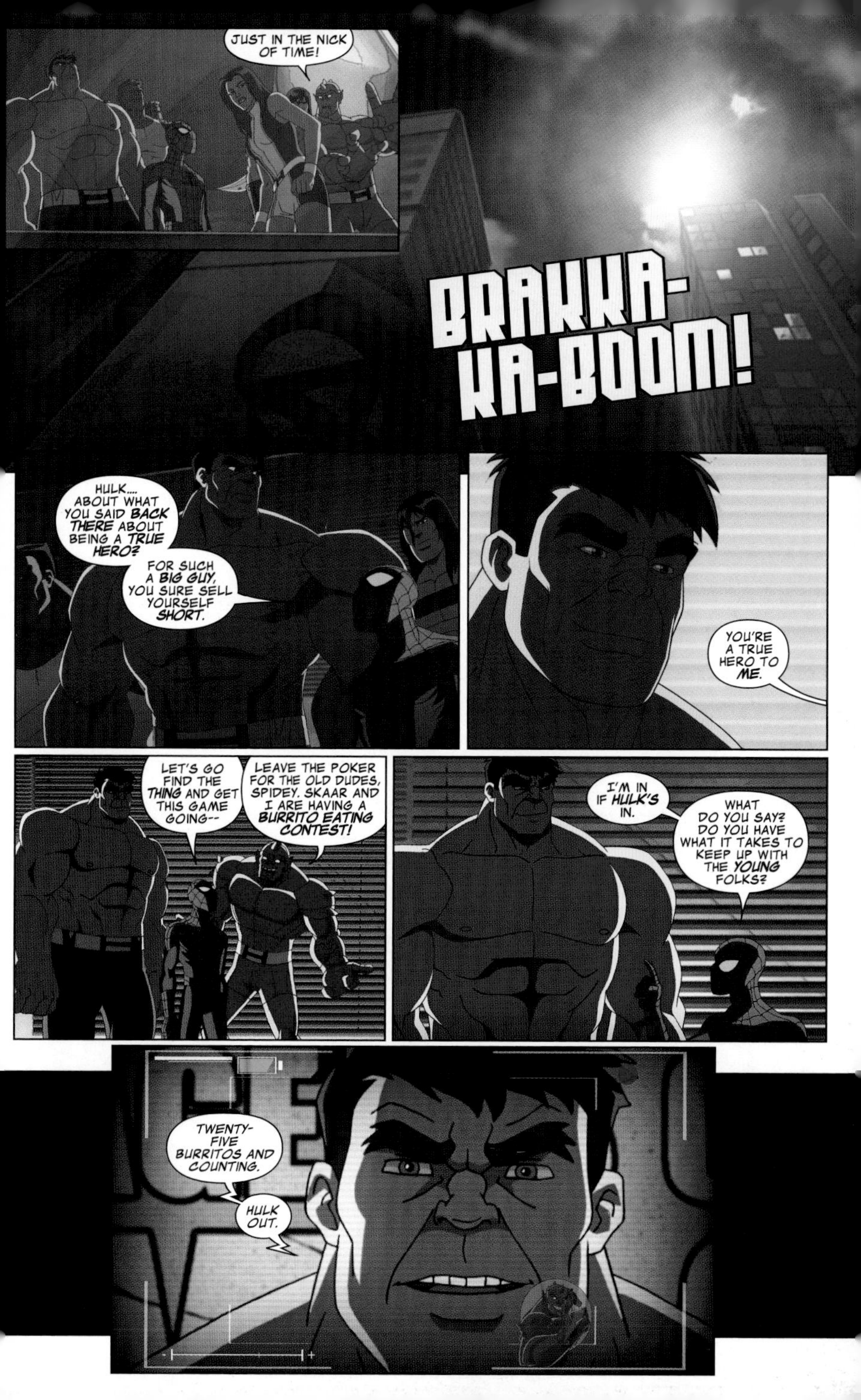
JUST IN THE NICK OF TIME!
BRAKKA-KA-BOOM!
HULK.... ABOUT WHAT YOU SAID BACK THERE ABOUT BEING A TRUE HERO?
FOR SUCH A BIG GUY, YOU SURE SELL YOURSELF SHORT.
YOU'RE A TRUE HERO TO ME.
LET'S GO FIND THE THING AND GET THIS GAME GOING--
LEAVE THE POKER FOR THE OLD DUDES, SPIDEY. SKAAR AND I ARE HAVING A BURRITO EATING CONTEST!
I'M IN IF HULK'S IN.
WHAT DO YOU SAY? DO YOU HAVE WHAT IT TAKES TO KEEP UP WITH THE YOUNG FOLKS?
TWENTY-FIVE BURRITOS AND COUNTING.
HULK OUT.

IT'S A WONDERFUL SMASH

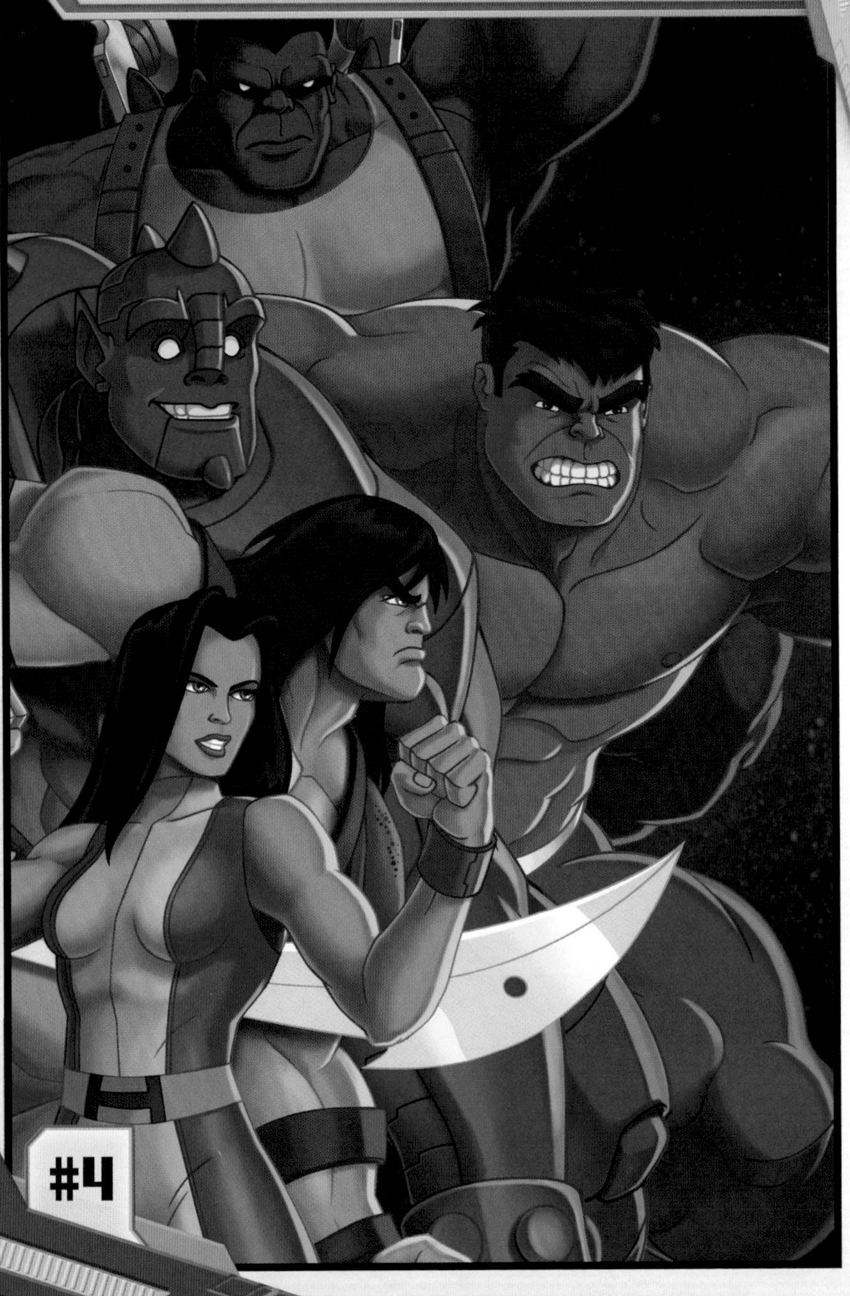
#4

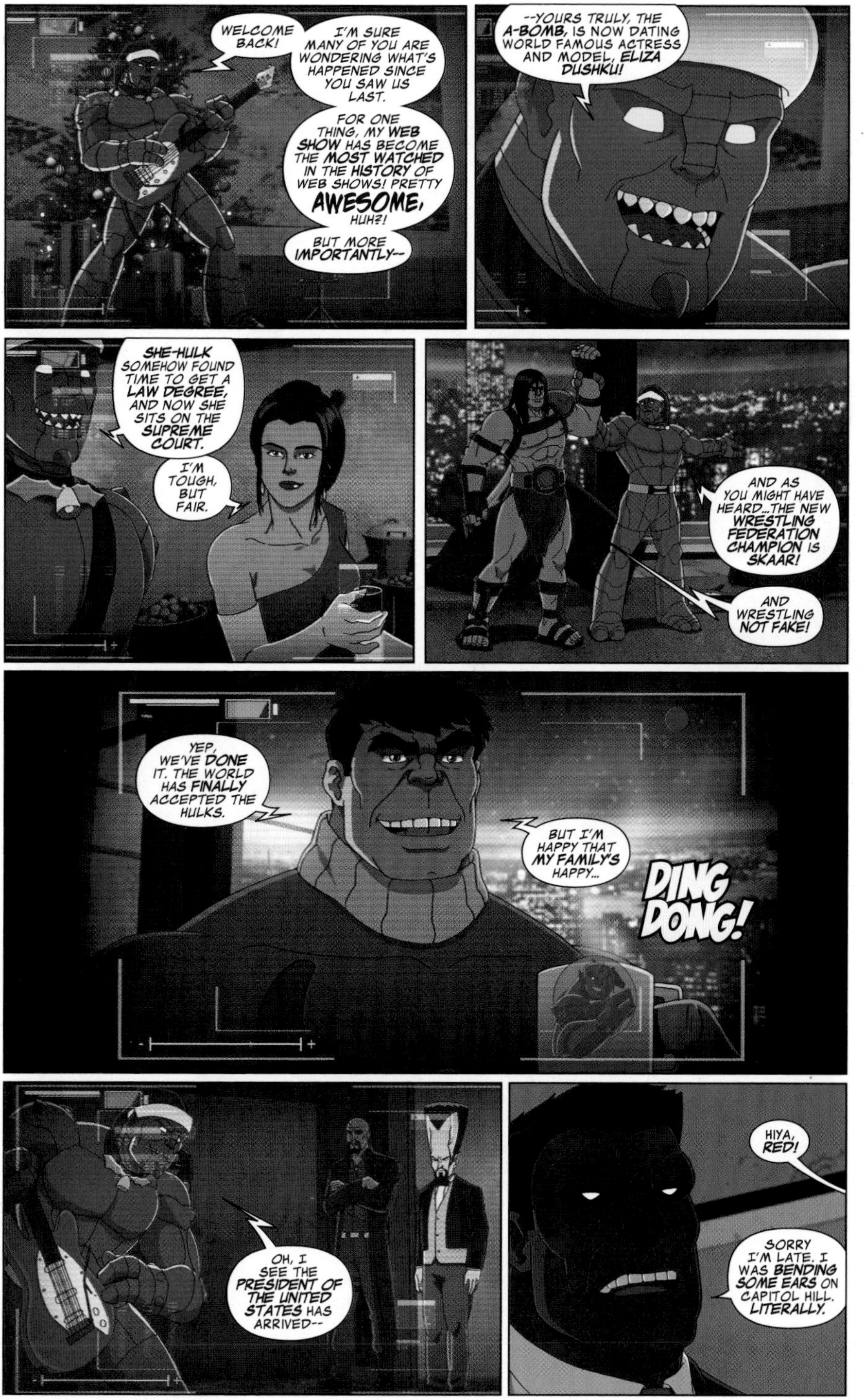
WELCOME BACK!
I'M SURE MANY OF YOU ARE WONDERING WHAT'S HAPPENED SINCE YOU SAW US LAST.
FOR ONE THING, MY WEB SHOW HAS BECOME THE MOST WATCHED IN THE HISTORY OF WEB SHOWS! PRETTY AWESOME, HUH?!
BUT MORE IMPORTANTLY--
--YOURS TRULY, THE A-BOMB, IS NOW DATING WORLD FAMOUS ACTRESS AND MODEL, ELIZA DUSHKU!
SHE-HULK SOMEHOW FOUND TIME TO GET A LAW DEGREE, AND NOW SHE SITS ON THE SUPREME COURT.
I'M TOUGH, BUT FAIR.
AND AS YOU MIGHT HAVE HEARD...THE NEW WRESTLING FEDERATION CHAMPION IS SKAAR!
AND WRESTLING NOT FAKE!
YEP, WE'VE DONE IT. THE WORLD HAS FINALLY ACCEPTED THE HULKS.
BUT I'M HAPPY THAT MY FAMILY'S HAPPY...
DING DONG!
OH, I SEE THE PRESIDENT OF THE UNITED STATES HAS ARRIVED--
HIYA, RED!
SORRY I'M LATE. I WAS BENDING SOME EARS ON CAPITOL HILL. LITERALLY.

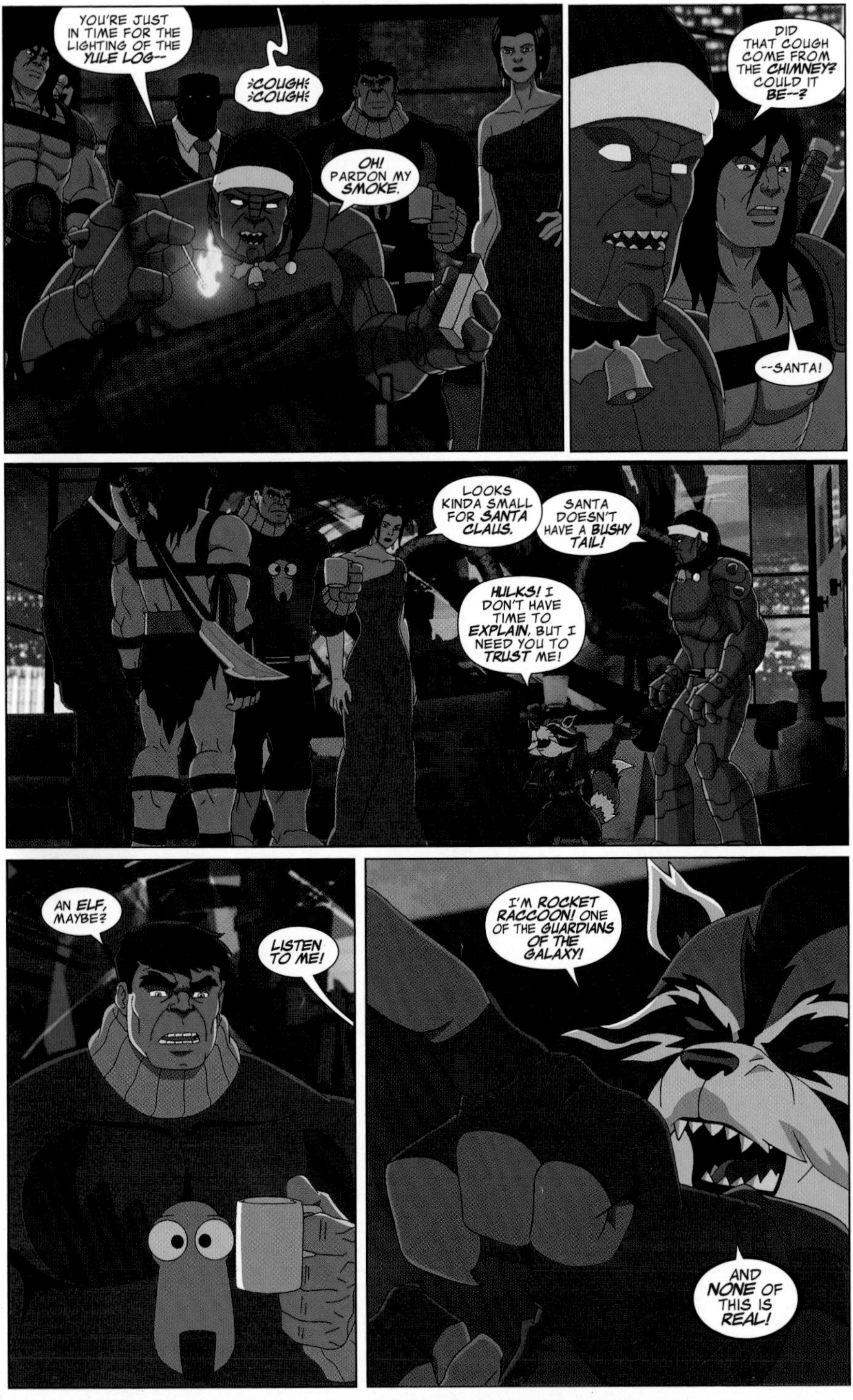

YOU'RE JUST IN TIME FOR THE LIGHTING OF THE YULE LOG--
COUGH *COUGH*
OH! PARDON MY SMOKE.
DID THAT COUGH COME FROM THE CHIMNEY? COULD IT BE--?
--SANTA!
LOOKS KINDA SMALL FOR SANTA CLAUS.
SANTA DOESN'T HAVE A BUSHY TAIL!
HULKS! I DON'T HAVE TIME TO EXPLAIN, BUT I NEED YOU TO TRUST ME!
AN ELF, MAYBE?
LISTEN TO ME!
I'M ROCKET RACCOON! ONE OF THE GUARDIANS OF THE GALAXY!
AND NONE OF THIS IS REAL!

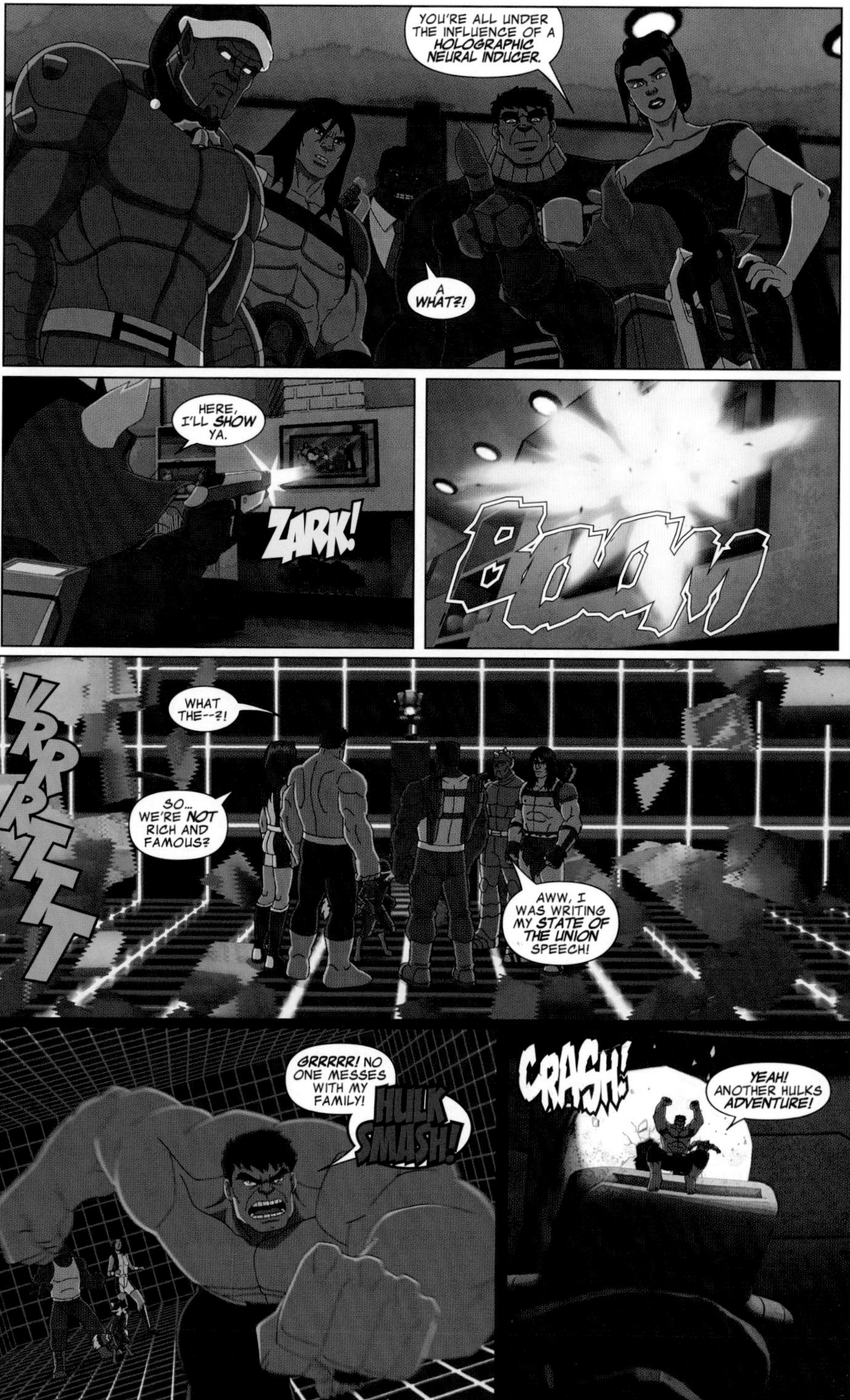
YOU'RE ALL UNDER THE INFLUENCE OF A HOLOGRAPHIC NEURAL INDUCER.
A WHAT?!
HERE, I'LL SHOW YA.
ZARK!
BOOM
VRRRTTT
WHAT THE--?!
SO... WE'RE NOT RICH AND FAMOUS?
AWW, I WAS WRITING MY STATE OF THE UNION SPEECH!
GRRRRR! NO ONE MESSES WITH MY FAMILY!
HULK SMASH!
CRASH!
YEAH! ANOTHER HULKS ADVENTURE!

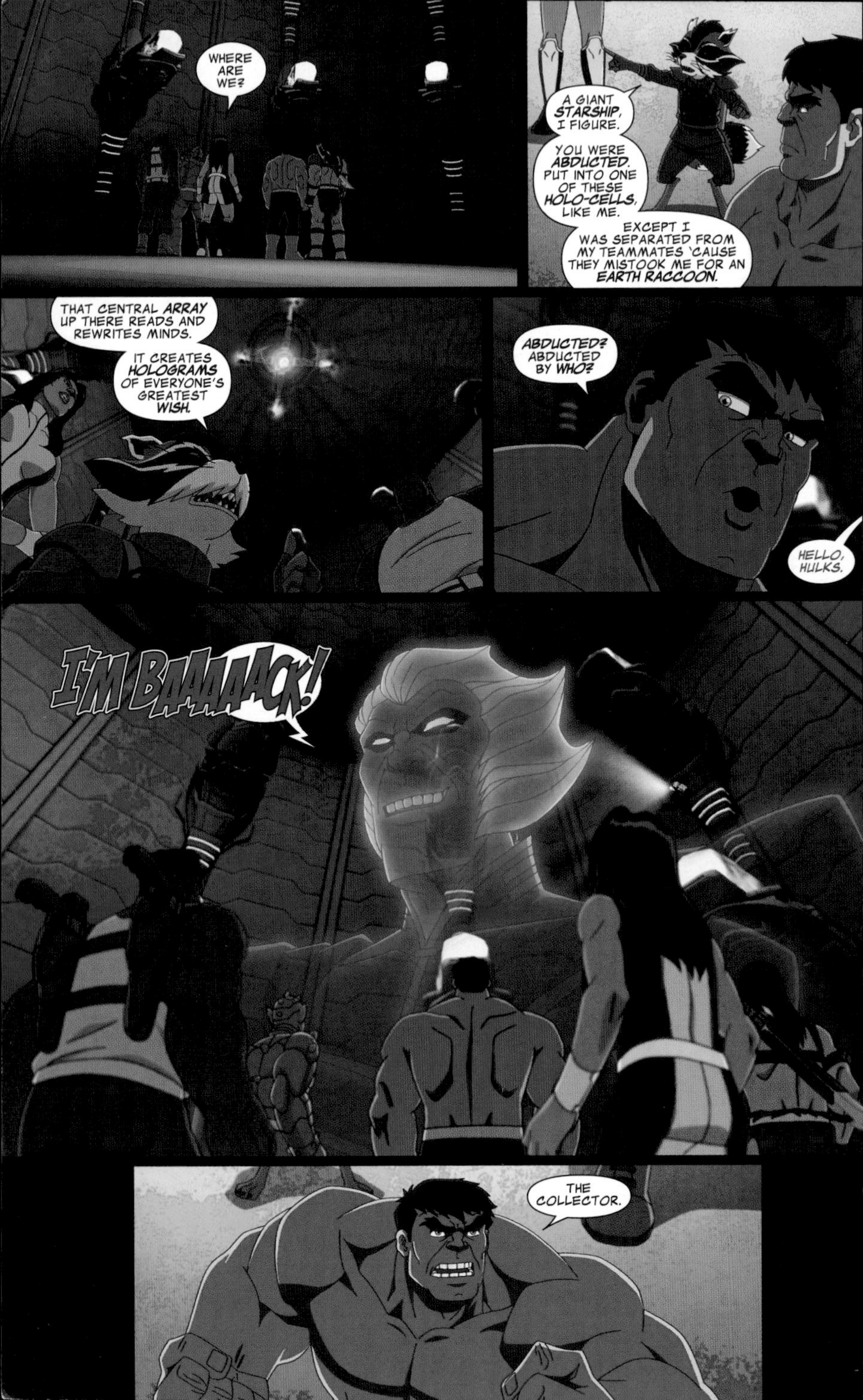
WHERE ARE WE?
A GIANT STARSHIP, I FIGURE.
YOU WERE ABDUCTED. PUT INTO ONE OF THESE HOLO-CELLS, LIKE ME.
EXCEPT I WAS SEPARATED FROM MY TEAMMATES 'CAUSE THEY MISTOOK ME FOR AN EARTH RACCOON.
THAT CENTRAL ARRAY UP THERE READS AND REWRITES MINDS.
IT CREATES HOLOGRAMS OF EVERYONE'S GREATEST WISH.
ABDUCTED? ABDUCTED BY WHO?
HELLO, HULKS.
I'M BAAAAACK!
THE COLLECTOR.

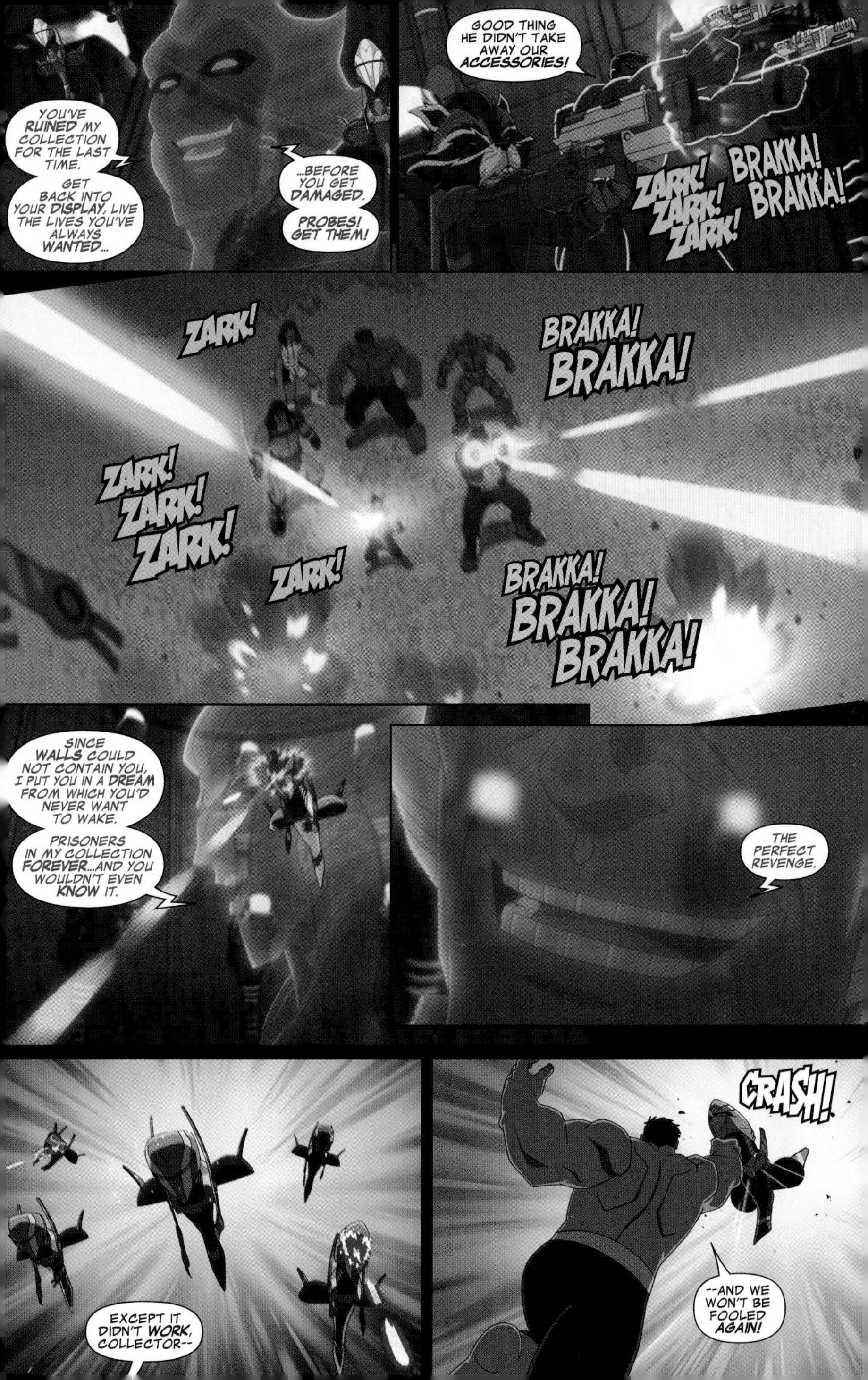
YOU'VE RUINED MY COLLECTION FOR THE LAST TIME.
GET BACK INTO YOUR DISPLAY, LIVE THE LIVES YOU'VE ALWAYS WANTED...
...BEFORE YOU GET DAMAGED.
PROBES! GET THEM!
GOOD THING HE DIDN'T TAKE AWAY OUR ACCESSORIES!
ZARK! ZARK! ZARK!
BRAKKA! BRAKKA!
ZARK!
BRAKKA! BRAKKA!
ZARK! ZARK! ZARK!
ZARK!
BRAKKA! BRAKKA! BRAKKA!
SINCE WALLS COULD NOT CONTAIN YOU, I PUT YOU IN A DREAM FROM WHICH YOU'D NEVER WANT TO WAKE.
PRISONERS IN MY COLLECTION FOREVER...AND YOU WOULDN'T EVEN KNOW IT.
THE PERFECT REVENGE.
EXCEPT IT DIDN'T WORK, COLLECTOR--
CRASH!
--AND WE WON'T BE FOOLED AGAIN!

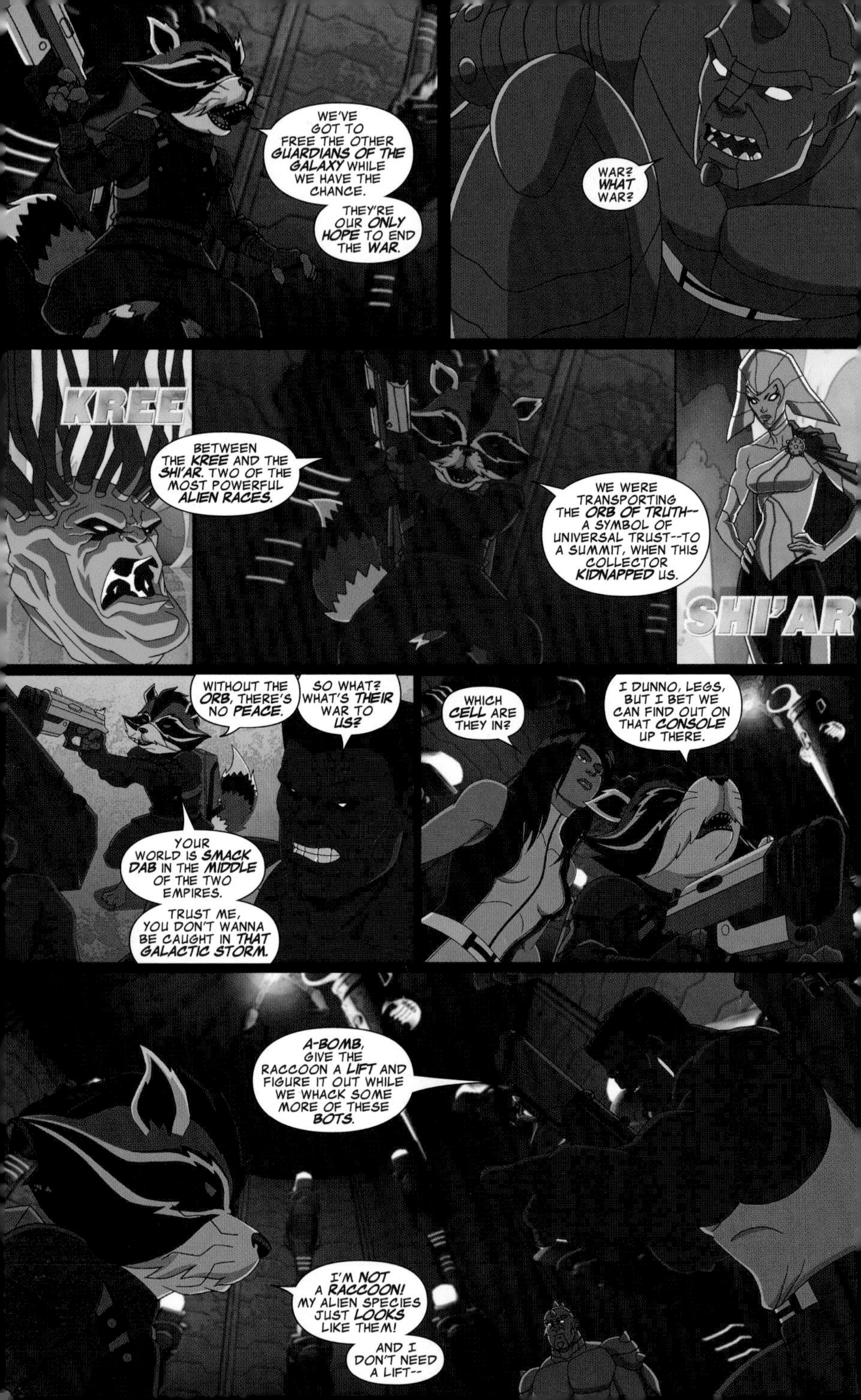
WE'VE GOT TO FREE THE OTHER GUARDIANS OF THE GALAXY WHILE WE HAVE THE CHANCE.
THEY'RE OUR ONLY HOPE TO END THE WAR.
WAR? WHAT WAR?
KREE
BETWEEN THE KREE AND THE SHI'AR. TWO OF THE MOST POWERFUL ALIEN RACES.
WE WERE TRANSPORTING THE ORB OF TRUTH-- A SYMBOL OF UNIVERSAL TRUST--TO A SUMMIT, WHEN THIS COLLECTOR KIDNAPPED US.
SHI'AR
WITHOUT THE ORB, THERE'S NO PEACE.
SO WHAT? WHAT'S THEIR WAR TO US?
YOUR WORLD IS SMACK DAB IN THE MIDDLE OF THE TWO EMPIRES.
TRUST ME, YOU DON'T WANNA BE CAUGHT IN THAT GALACTIC STORM.
WHICH CELL ARE THEY IN?
I DUNNO, LEGS, BUT I BET WE CAN FIND OUT ON THAT CONSOLE UP THERE.
A-BOMB, GIVE THE RACCOON A LIFT AND FIGURE IT OUT WHILE WE WHACK SOME MORE OF THESE BOTS.
I'M NOT A RACCOON! MY ALIEN SPECIES JUST LOOKS LIKE THEM!
AND I DON'T NEED A LIFT--

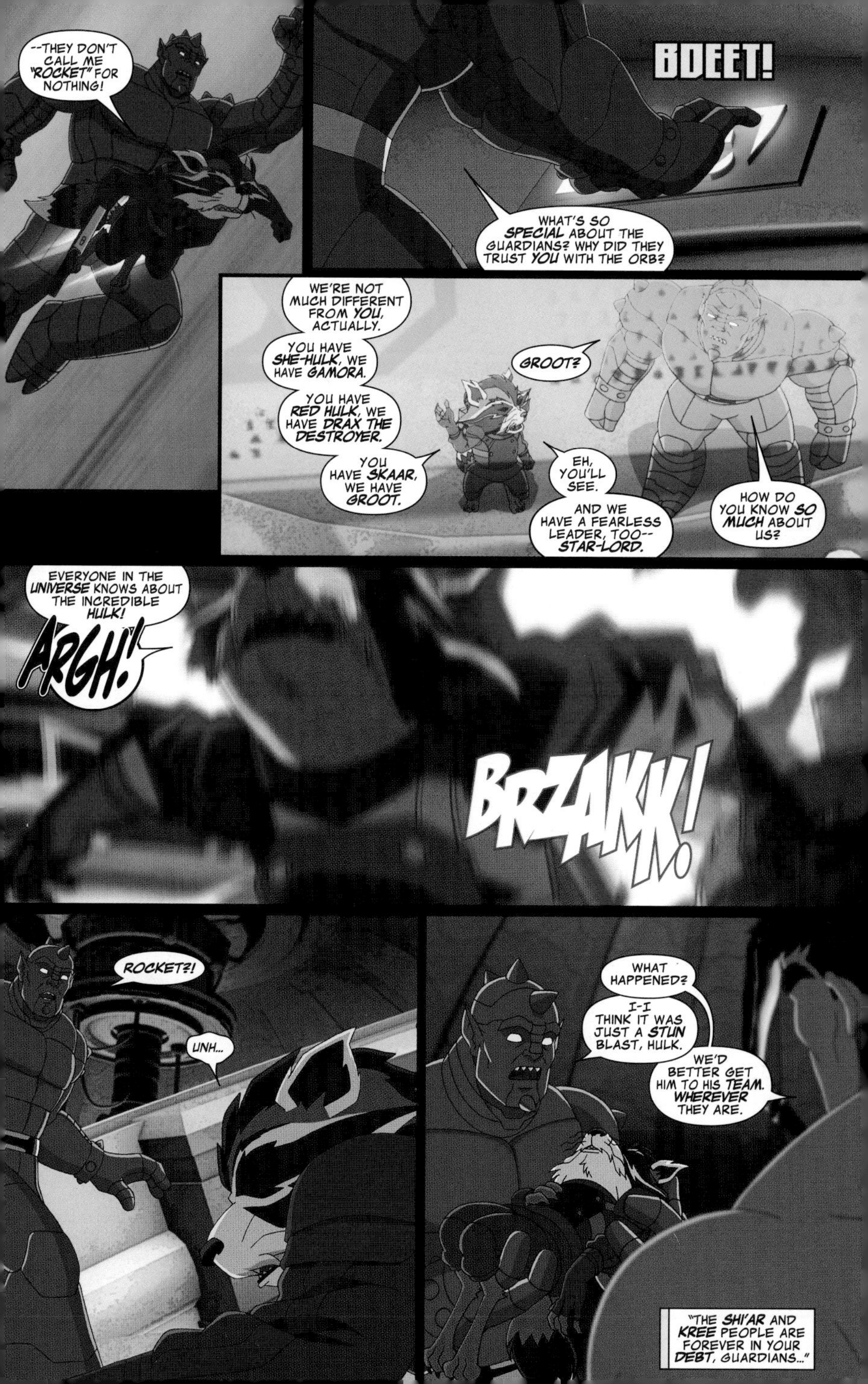
--THEY DON'T CALL ME "ROCKET" FOR NOTHING!
BDEET!
WHAT'S SO SPECIAL ABOUT THE GUARDIANS? WHY DID THEY TRUST YOU WITH THE ORB?
WE'RE NOT MUCH DIFFERENT FROM YOU, ACTUALLY.
YOU HAVE SHE-HULK, WE HAVE GAMORA.
YOU HAVE RED HULK, WE HAVE DRAX THE DESTROYER.
YOU HAVE SKAAR, WE HAVE GROOT.
GROOT?
EH, YOU'LL SEE.
AND WE HAVE A FEARLESS LEADER, TOO-- STAR-LORD.
HOW DO YOU KNOW SO MUCH ABOUT US?
EVERYONE IN THE UNIVERSE KNOWS ABOUT THE INCREDIBLE HULK!
ARGH!
BRZAKK!
ROCKET?!
UNH...
WHAT HAPPENED?
I-I THINK IT WAS JUST A STUN BLAST, HULK.
WE'D BETTER GET HIM TO HIS TEAM. WHEREVER THEY ARE.
"THE SHI'AR AND KREE PEOPLE ARE FOREVER IN YOUR DEBT, GUARDIANS..."

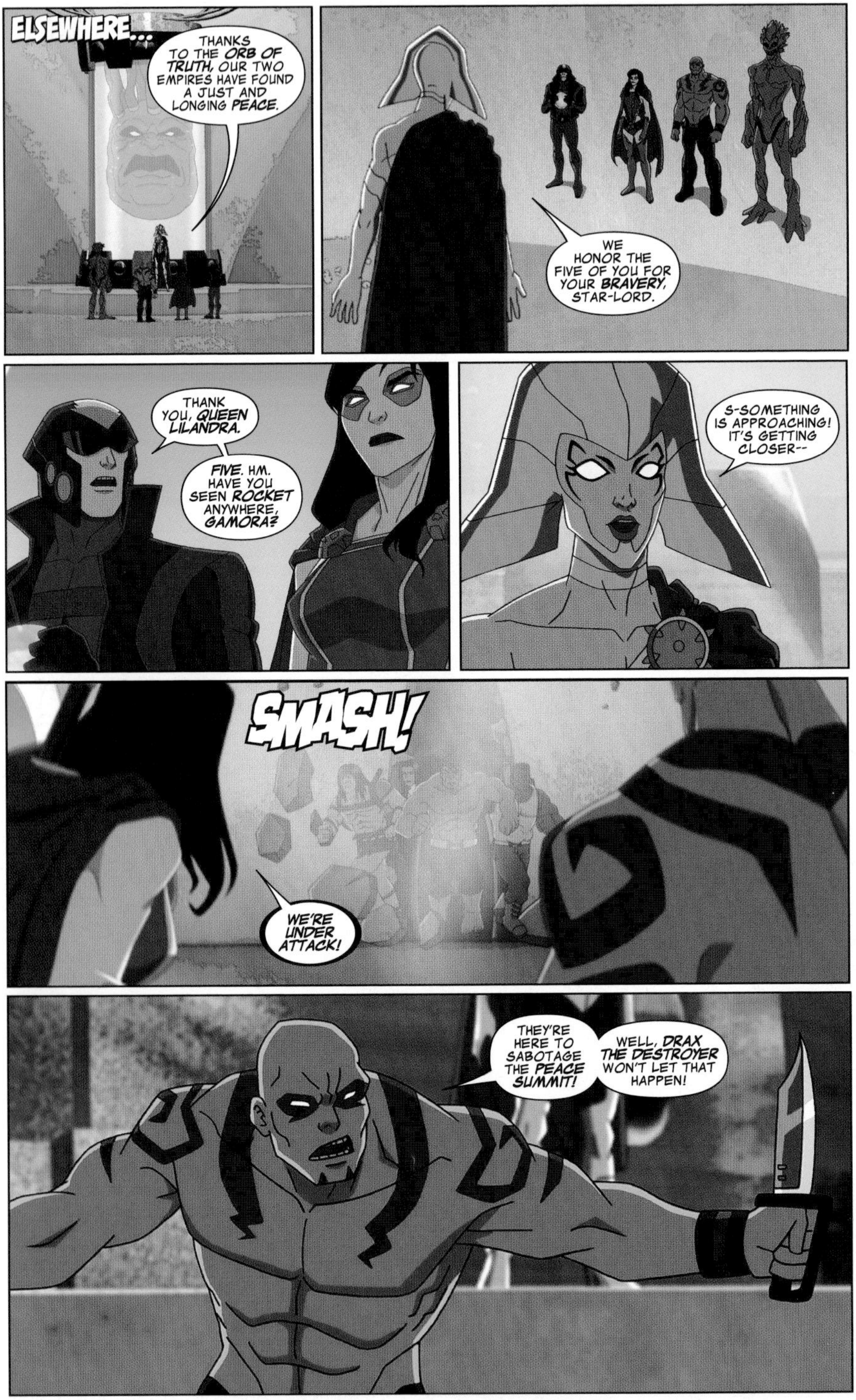
ELSEWHERE...
THANKS TO THE ORB OF TRUTH, OUR TWO EMPIRES HAVE FOUND A JUST AND LONGING PEACE.
WE HONOR THE FIVE OF YOU FOR YOUR BRAVERY, STAR-LORD.
THANK YOU, QUEEN LILANDRA.
FIVE. HM. HAVE YOU SEEN ROCKET ANYWHERE, GAMORA?
S-SOMETHING IS APPROACHING! IT'S GETTING CLOSER--
SMASH!
WE'RE UNDER ATTACK!
THEY'RE HERE TO SABOTAGE THE PEACE SUMMIT!
WELL, DRAX THE DESTROYER WON'T LET THAT HAPPEN!

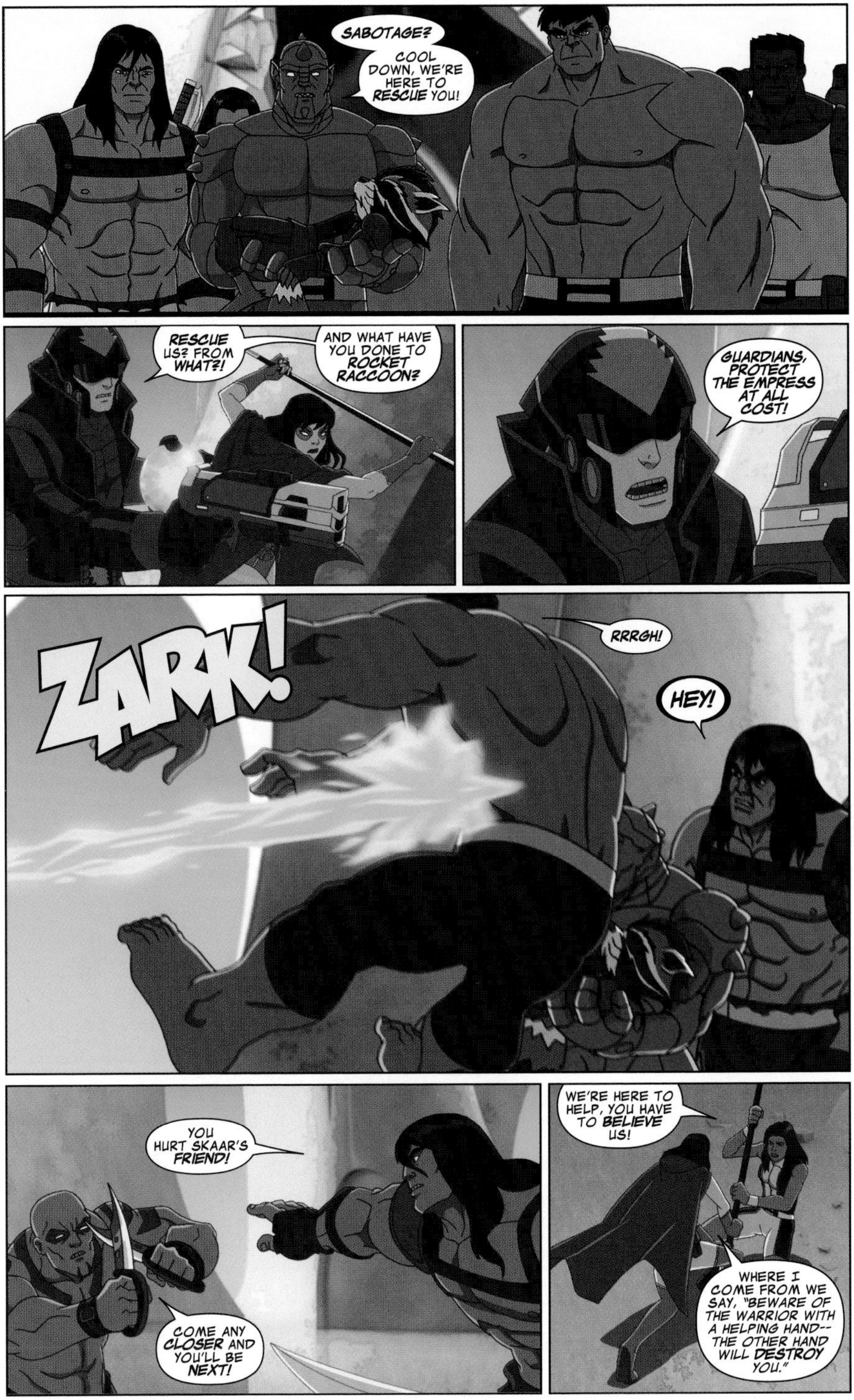
SABOTAGE?
COOL DOWN, WE'RE HERE TO RESCUE YOU!
RESCUE US? FROM WHAT?!
AND WHAT HAVE YOU DONE TO ROCKET RACCOON?
GUARDIANS, PROTECT THE EMPRESS AT ALL COST!
ZARK!
RRRGH!
HEY!
YOU HURT SKAAR'S FRIEND!
COME ANY CLOSER AND YOU'LL BE NEXT!
WE'RE HERE TO HELP, YOU HAVE TO BELIEVE US!
WHERE I COME FROM WE SAY, "BEWARE OF THE WARRIOR WITH A HELPING HAND-- THE OTHER HAND WILL DESTROY YOU."

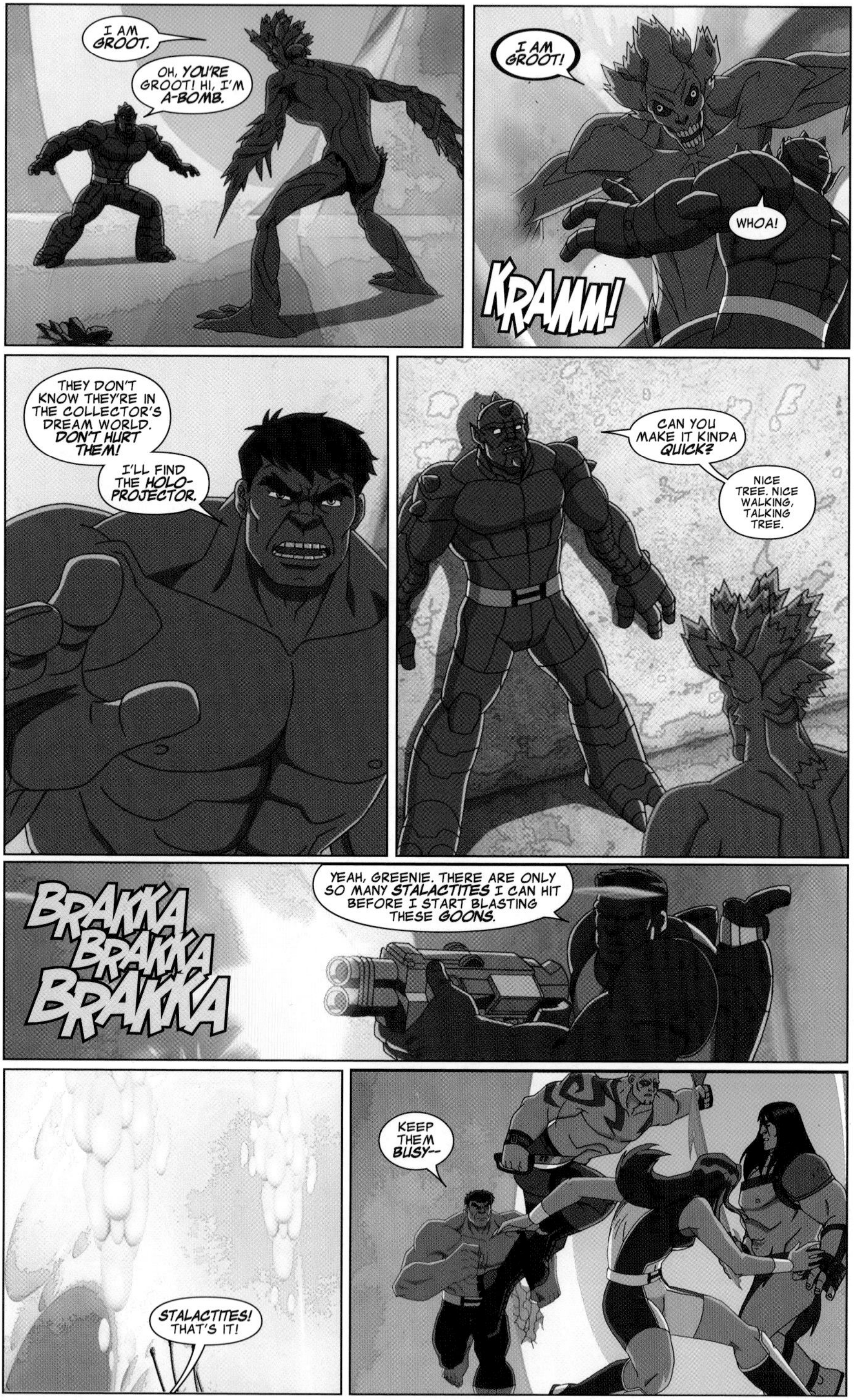
I AM GROOT.
OH, YOU'RE GROOT! HI, I'M A-BOMB.
I AM GROOT!
WHOA!
KRAMM!
THEY DON'T KNOW THEY'RE IN THE COLLECTOR'S DREAM WORLD. DON'T HURT THEM!
I'LL FIND THE HOLO-PROJECTOR.
CAN YOU MAKE IT KINDA QUICK?
NICE TREE. NICE WALKING, TALKING TREE.
BRAKKA BRAKKA BRAKKA
YEAH, GREENIE. THERE ARE ONLY SO MANY STALACTITES I CAN HIT BEFORE I START BLASTING THESE GOONS.
STALACTITES! THAT'S IT!
KEEP THEM BUSY--

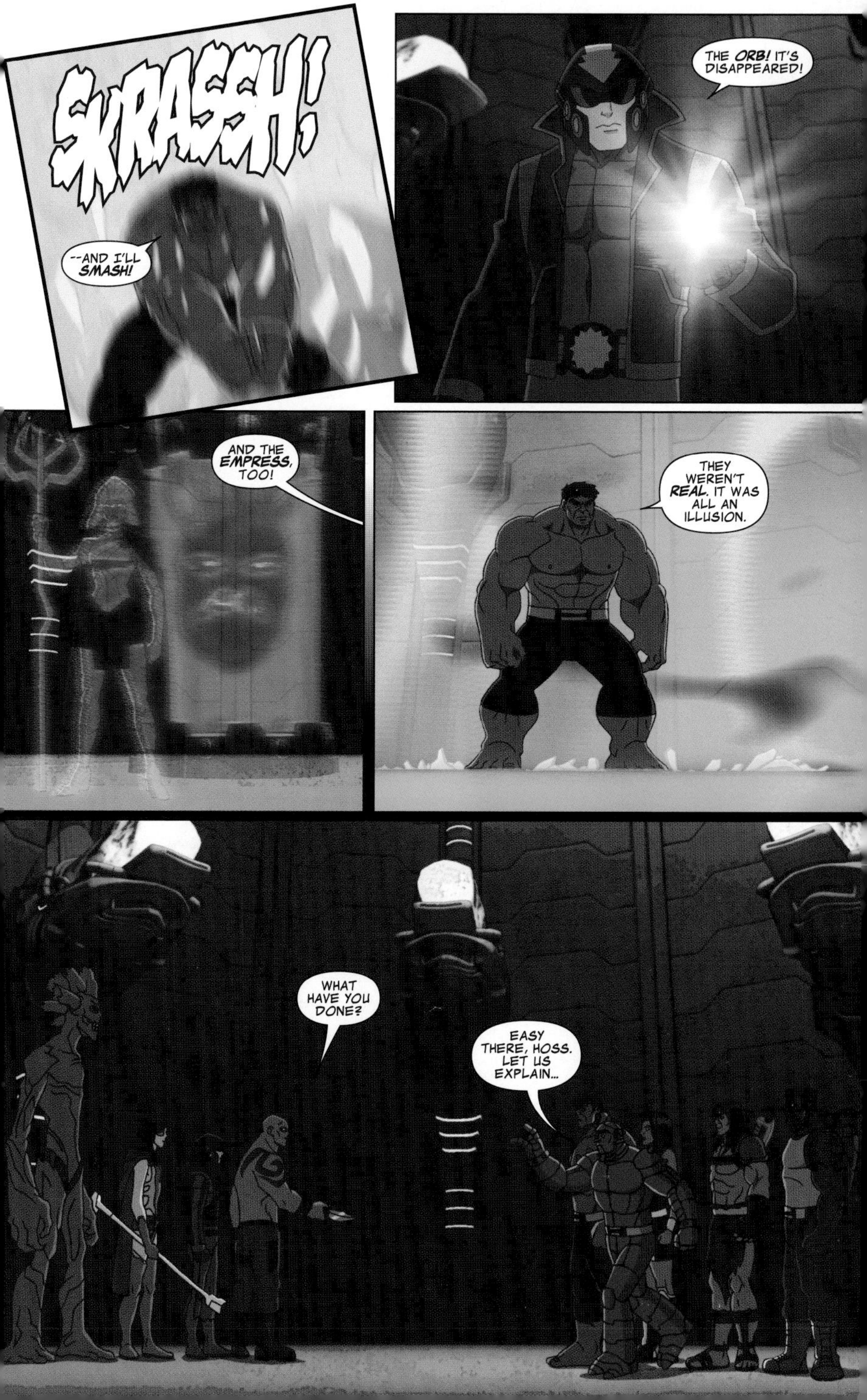
SKRASSH!
--AND I'LL SMASH!
THE ORB! IT'S DISAPPEARED!
AND THE EMPRESS, TOO!
THEY WEREN'T REAL. IT WAS ALL AN ILLUSION.
WHAT HAVE YOU DONE?
EASY THERE, HOSS. LET US EXPLAIN...

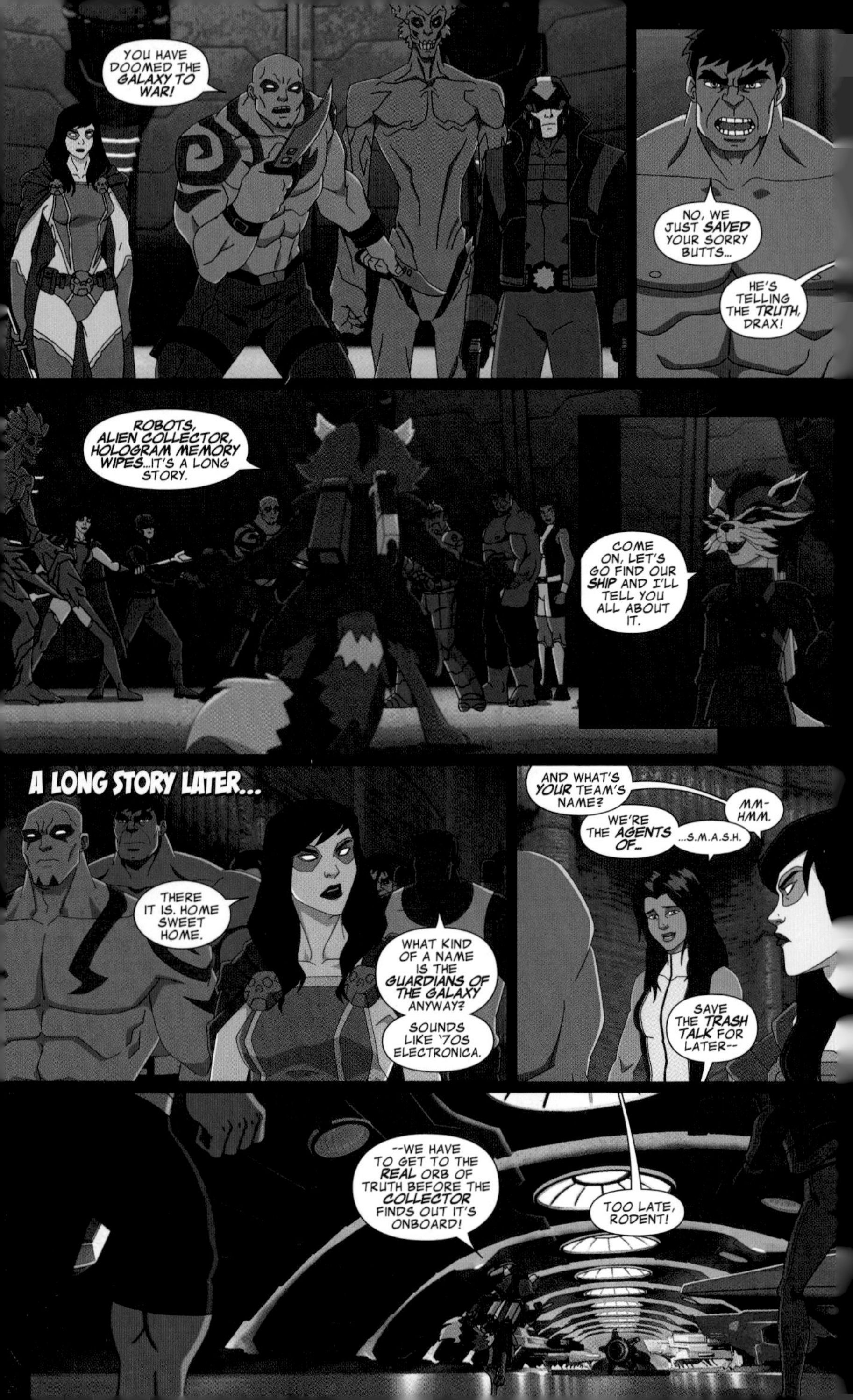
YOU HAVE DOOMED THE GALAXY TO WAR!
NO, WE JUST SAVED YOUR SORRY BUTTS...
HE'S TELLING THE TRUTH, DRAX!
ROBOTS, ALIEN COLLECTOR, HOLOGRAM MEMORY WIPES...IT'S A LONG STORY.
COME ON, LET'S GO FIND OUR SHIP AND I'LL TELL YOU ALL ABOUT IT.
A LONG STORY LATER...
THERE IT IS. HOME SWEET HOME.
WHAT KIND OF A NAME IS THE GUARDIANS OF THE GALAXY ANYWAY?
SOUNDS LIKE '70S ELECTRONICA.
AND WHAT'S YOUR TEAM'S NAME?
MM-HMM.
WE'RE THE AGENTS OF...
...S.M.A.S.H.
SAVE THE TRASH TALK FOR LATER--
--WE HAVE TO GET TO THE REAL ORB OF TRUTH BEFORE THE COLLECTOR FINDS OUT IT'S ONBOARD!
TOO LATE, RODENT!

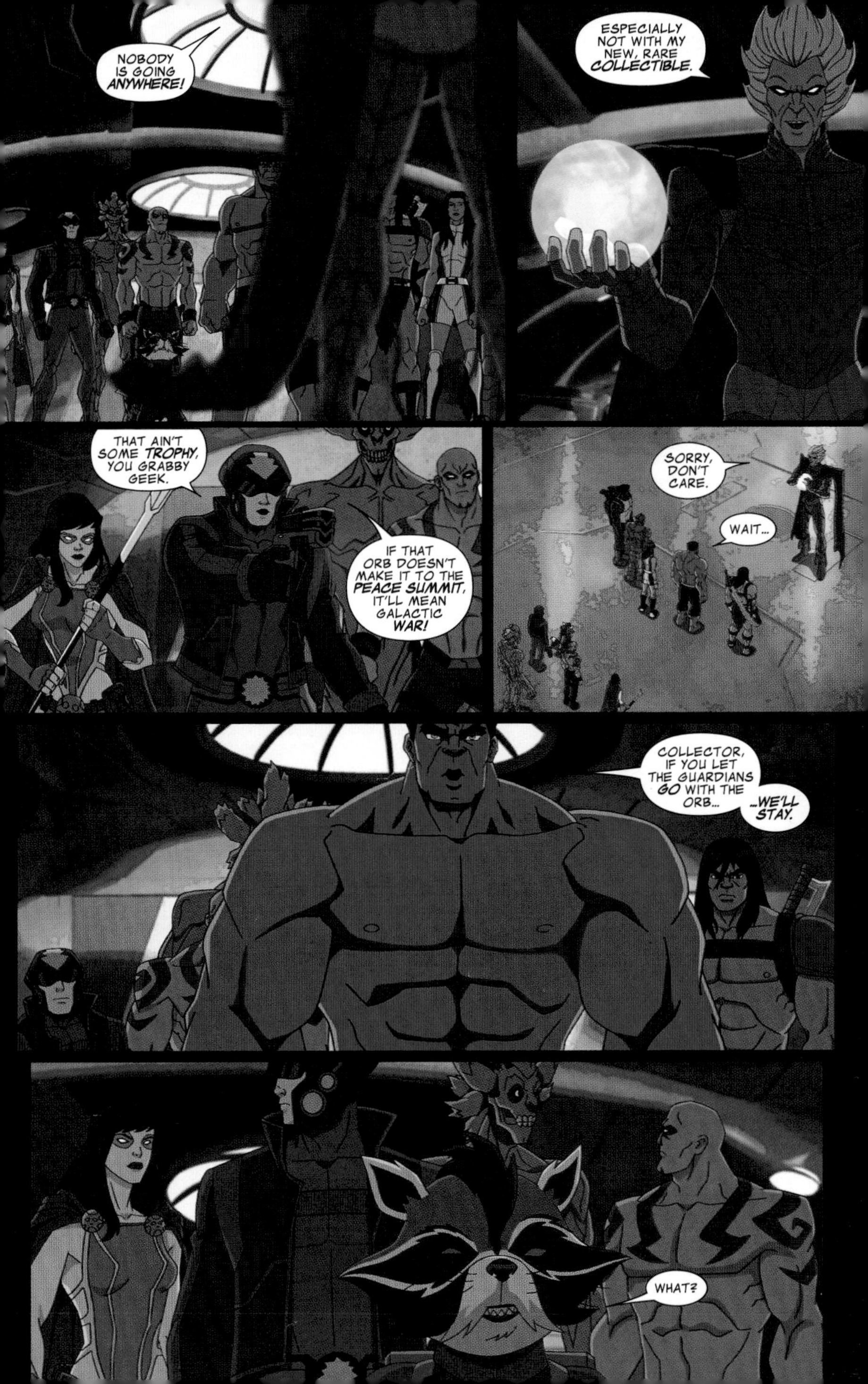
NOBODY IS GOING ANYWHERE!
ESPECIALLY NOT WITH MY NEW, RARE COLLECTIBLE.
THAT AIN'T SOME TROPHY, YOU GRABBY GEEK.
IF THAT ORB DOESN'T MAKE IT TO THE PEACE SUMMIT, IT'LL MEAN GALACTIC WAR!
SORRY, DON'T CARE.
WAIT...
COLLECTOR, IF YOU LET THE GUARDIANS GO WITH THE ORB...
...WE'LL STAY.
WHAT?

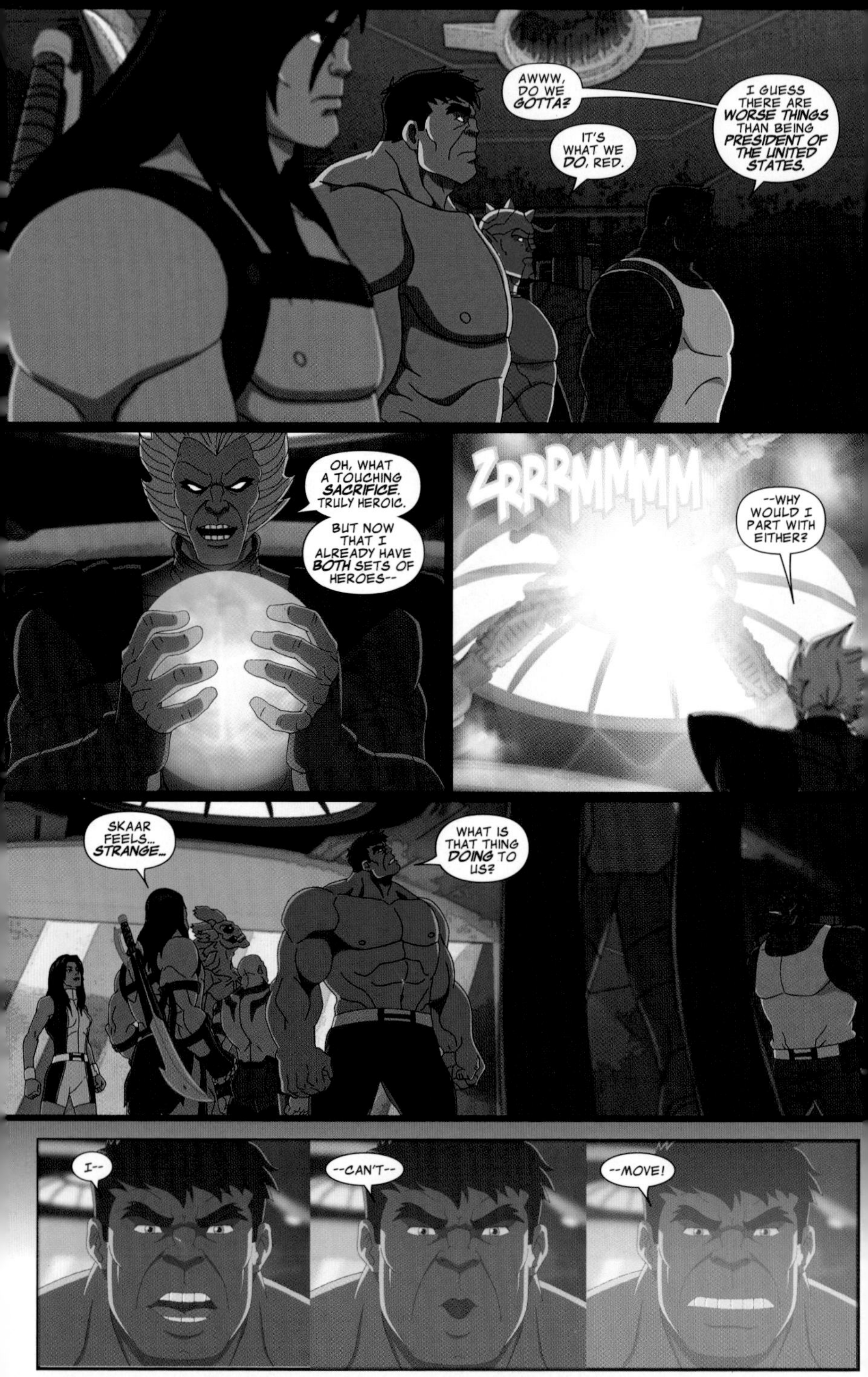
AWWW, DO WE GOTTA?
IT'S WHAT WE DO, RED.
I GUESS THERE ARE WORSE THINGS THAN BEING PRESIDENT OF THE UNITED STATES.
OH, WHAT A TOUCHING SACRIFICE. TRULY HEROIC.
BUT NOW THAT I ALREADY HAVE BOTH SETS OF HEROES--
ZRRRMMMM
--WHY WOULD I PART WITH EITHER?
SKAAR FEELS... STRANGE...
WHAT IS THAT THING DOING TO US?
I--
--CAN'T--
--MOVE!

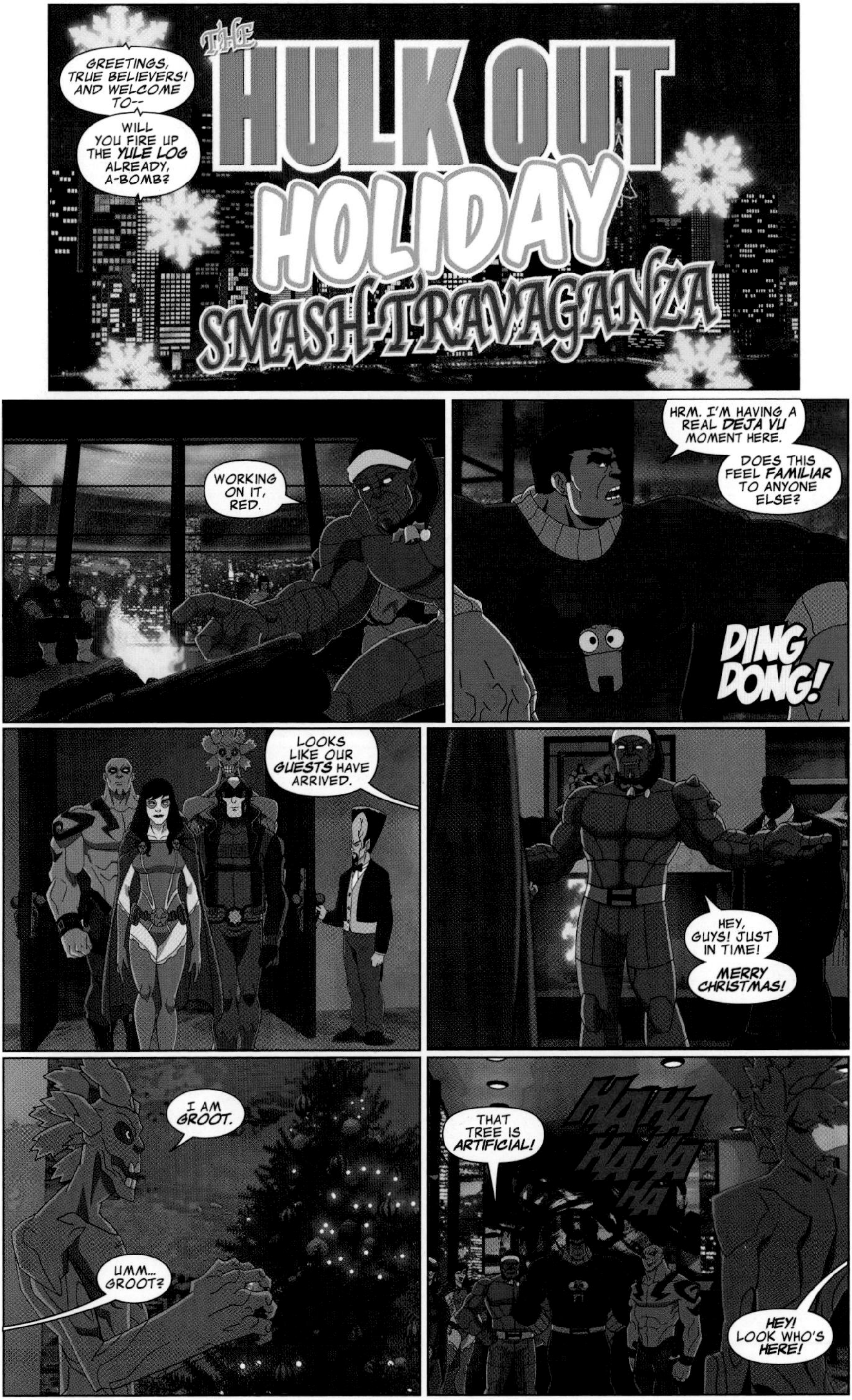
GREETINGS, TRUE BELIEVERS! AND WELCOME TO--
THE HULK OUT HOLIDAY SMASH-TRAVAGANZA
WILL YOU FIRE UP THE YULE LOG ALREADY, A-BOMB?
WORKING ON IT, RED.
HRM. I'M HAVING A REAL DEJA VU MOMENT HERE.
DOES THIS FEEL FAMILIAR TO ANYONE ELSE?
DING DONG!
LOOKS LIKE OUR GUESTS HAVE ARRIVED.
HEY, GUYS! JUST IN TIME!
MERRY CHRISTMAS!
I AM GROOT.
UMM... GROOT?
THAT TREE IS ARTIFICIAL!
HA HA HA HA HA
HEY! LOOK WHO'S HERE!

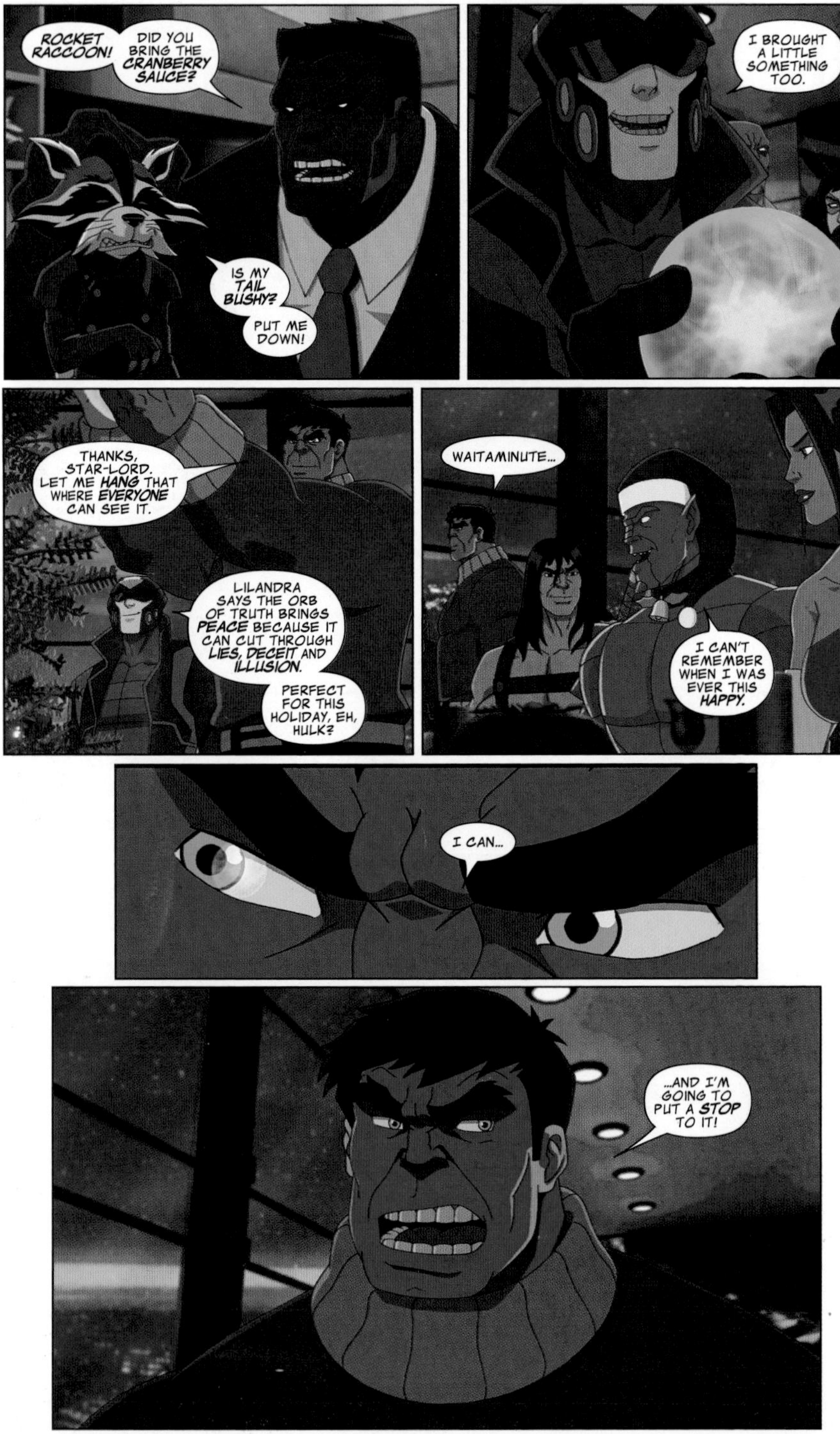
ROCKET RACCOON!
DID YOU BRING THE CRANBERRY SAUCE?
IS MY TAIL BUSHY?
PUT ME DOWN!
I BROUGHT A LITTLE SOMETHING TOO.
THANKS, STAR-LORD. LET ME HANG THAT WHERE EVERYONE CAN SEE IT.
LILANDRA SAYS THE ORB OF TRUTH BRINGS PEACE BECAUSE IT CAN CUT THROUGH LIES, DECEIT AND ILLUSION.
PERFECT FOR THIS HOLIDAY, EH, HULK?
WAITAMINUTE...
I CAN'T REMEMBER WHEN I WAS EVER THIS HAPPY.
I CAN...
...AND I'M GOING TO PUT A STOP TO IT!

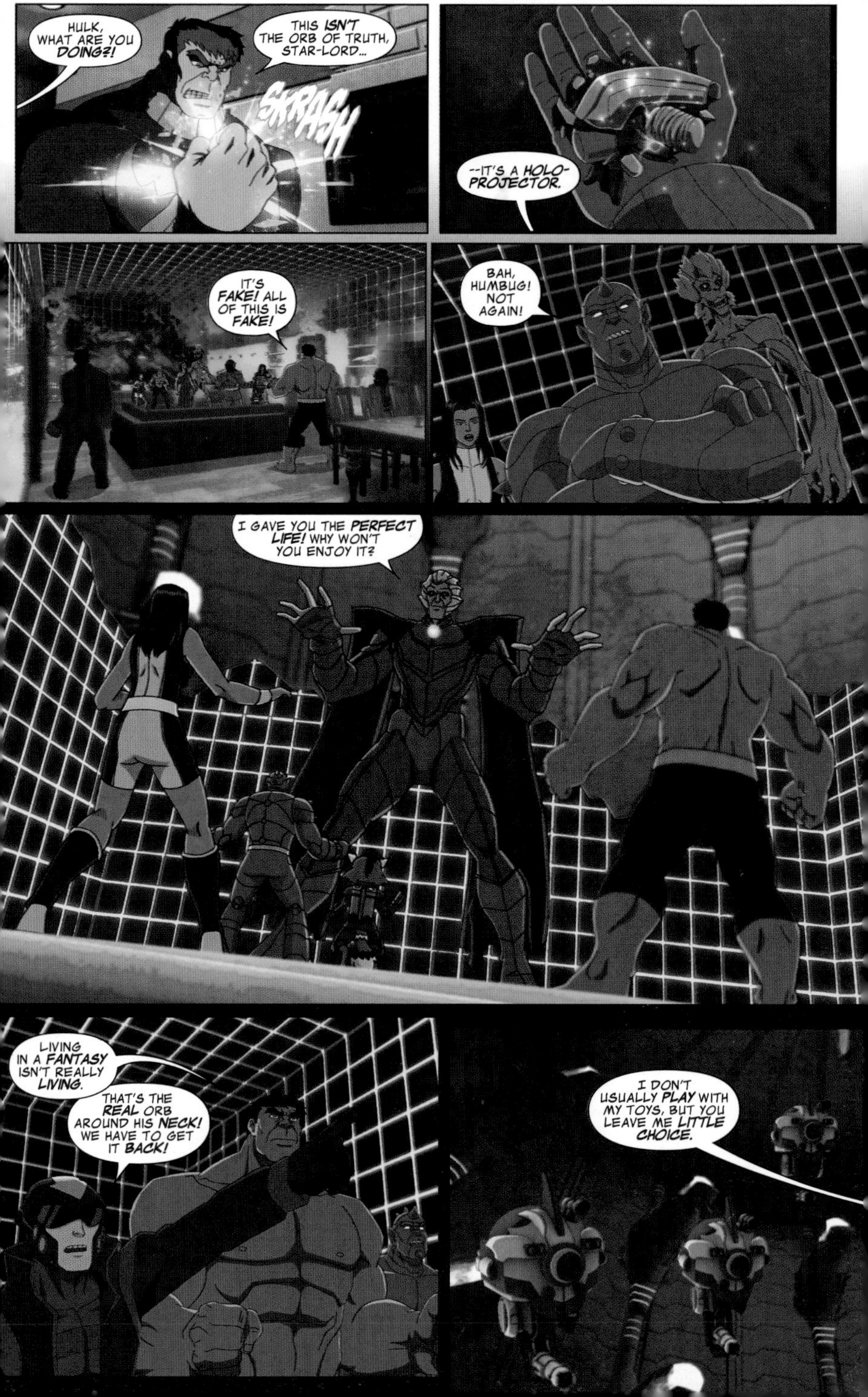
HULK, WHAT ARE YOU DOING?!
THIS ISN'T THE ORB OF TRUTH, STAR-LORD...
SKRASH
--IT'S A HOLO-PROJECTOR.
IT'S FAKE! ALL OF THIS IS FAKE!
BAH, HUMBUG! NOT AGAIN!
I GAVE YOU THE PERFECT LIFE! WHY WON'T YOU ENJOY IT?
LIVING IN A FANTASY ISN'T REALLY LIVING.
THAT'S THE REAL ORB AROUND HIS NECK! WE HAVE TO GET IT BACK!
I DON'T USUALLY PLAY WITH MY TOYS, BUT YOU LEAVE ME LITTLE CHOICE.

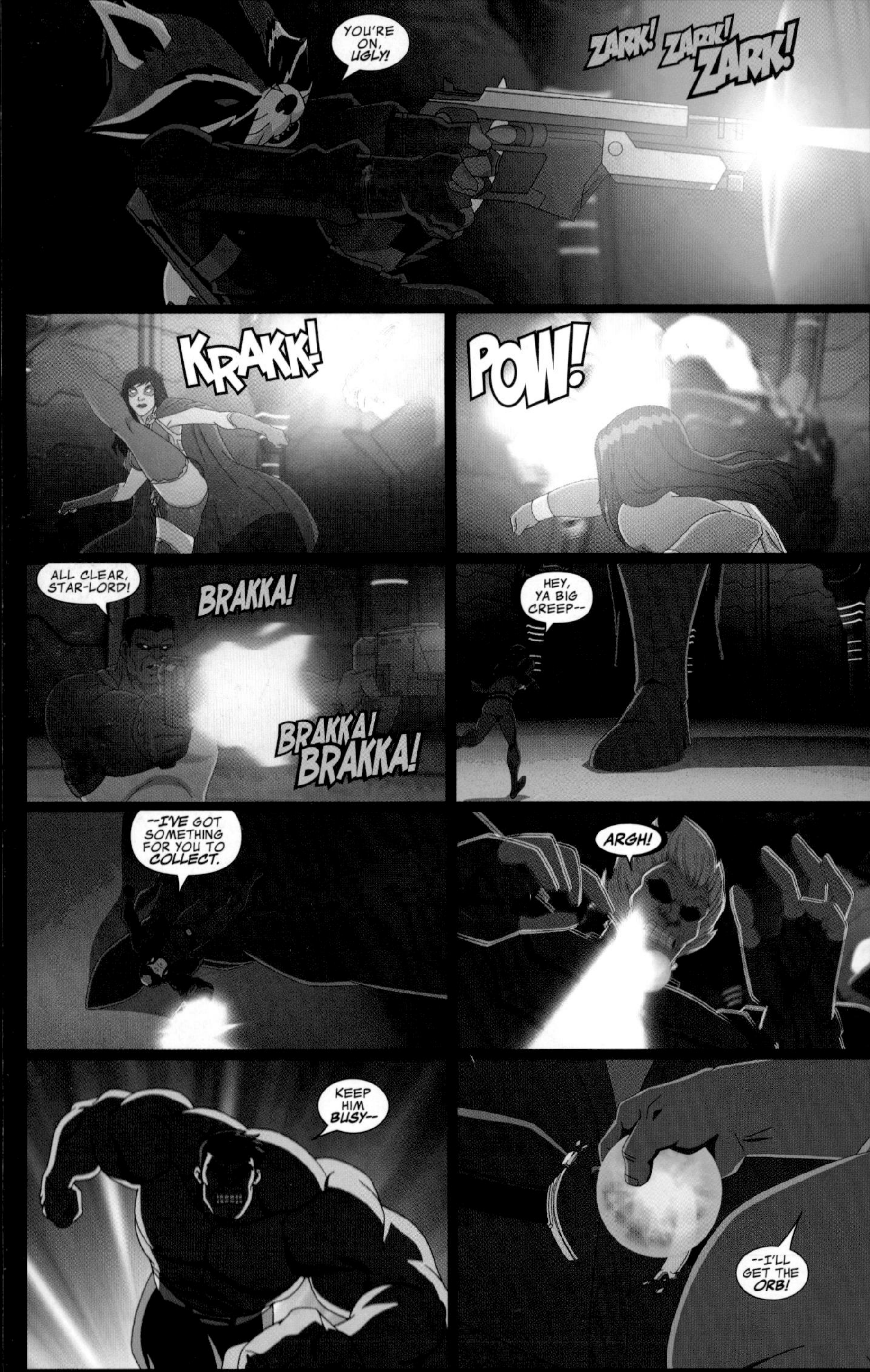
YOU'RE ON, UGLY!
ZARK! ZARK! ZARK!
KRAKK!
POW!
ALL CLEAR, STAR-LORD!
BRAKKA!
BRAKKA! BRAKKA!
HEY, YA BIG CREEP--
--I'VE GOT SOMETHING FOR YOU TO COLLECT.
ARGH!
KEEP HIM BUSY--
--I'LL GET THE ORB!

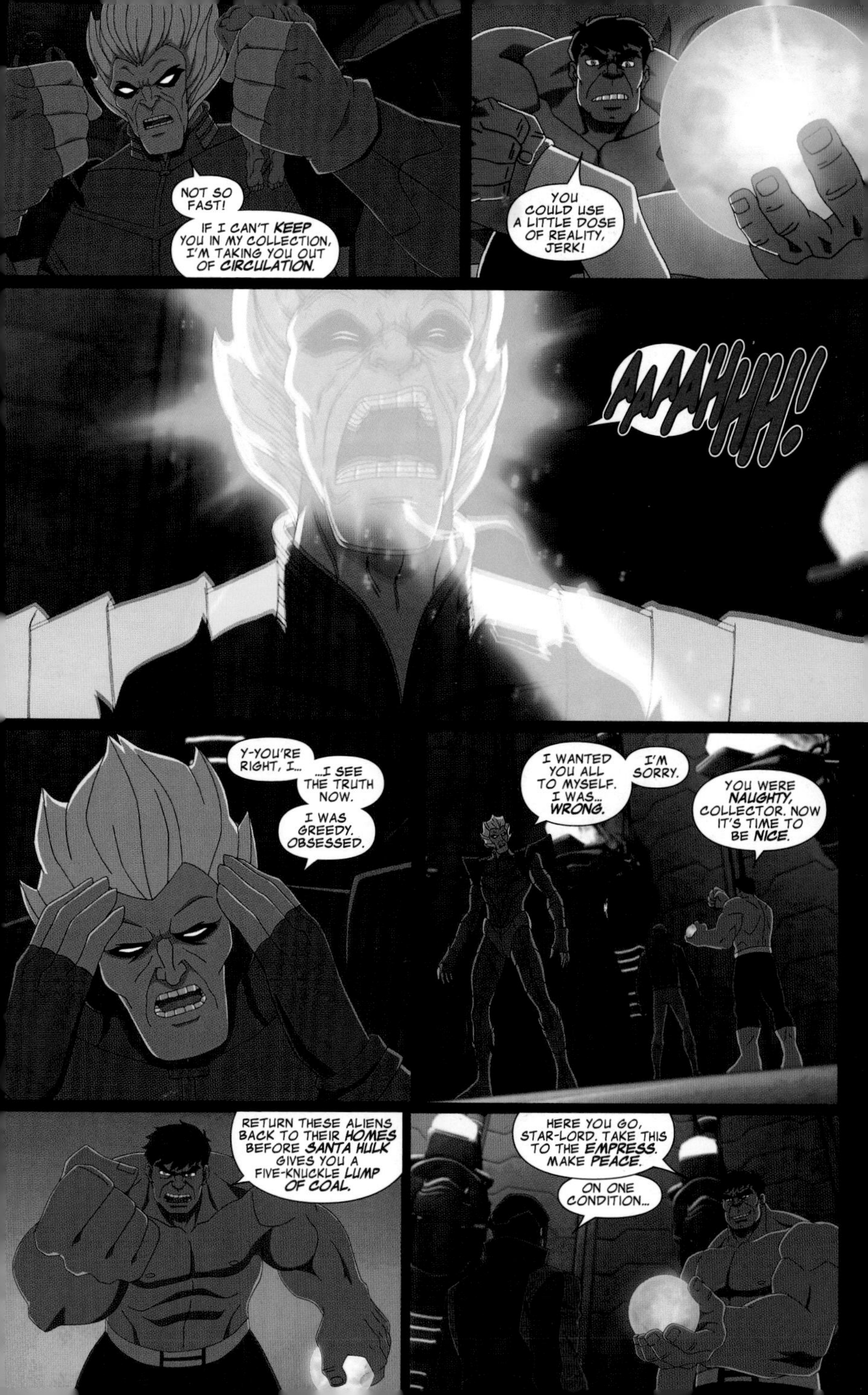
NOT SO FAST!
IF I CAN'T **KEEP** YOU IN MY COLLECTION, I'M TAKING YOU OUT OF **CIRCULATION**.
YOU COULD USE A LITTLE DOSE OF REALITY, JERK!
AAAAHHHH!
Y-YOU'RE RIGHT, I...
...I SEE THE TRUTH NOW.
I WAS GREEDY. OBSESSED.
I WANTED YOU ALL TO MYSELF. I WAS... **WRONG.**
I'M SORRY.
YOU WERE **NAUGHTY,** COLLECTOR. NOW IT'S TIME TO BE **NICE**.
RETURN THESE ALIENS BACK TO THEIR **HOMES** BEFORE **SANTA HULK** GIVES YOU A FIVE-KNUCKLE **LUMP OF COAL.**
HERE YOU GO, STAR-LORD. TAKE THIS TO THE **EMPRESS**. MAKE **PEACE**.
ON ONE CONDITION...

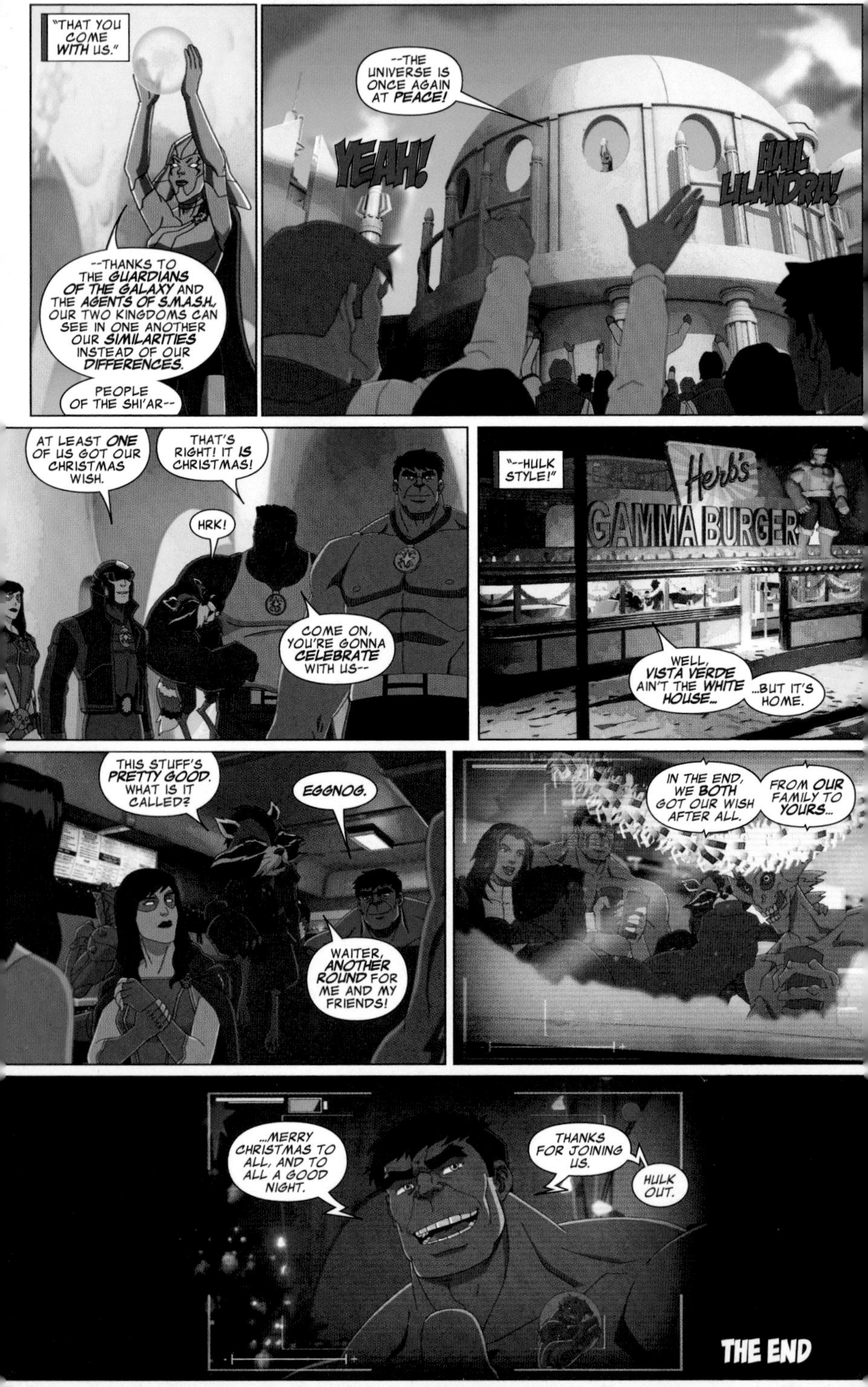
"THAT YOU COME WITH US."
--THANKS TO THE GUARDIANS OF THE GALAXY AND THE AGENTS OF S.M.A.S.H., OUR TWO KINGDOMS CAN SEE IN ONE ANOTHER OUR SIMILARITIES INSTEAD OF OUR DIFFERENCES.
PEOPLE OF THE SHI'AR--
--THE UNIVERSE IS ONCE AGAIN AT PEACE!
YEAH!
HAIL LILANDRA!
AT LEAST ONE OF US GOT OUR CHRISTMAS WISH.
THAT'S RIGHT! IT IS CHRISTMAS!
HRK!
COME ON, YOU'RE GONNA CELEBRATE WITH US--
"--HULK STYLE!"
Herb's
GAMMA BURGER
WELL, VISTA VERDE AIN'T THE WHITE HOUSE...
...BUT IT'S HOME.
THIS STUFF'S PRETTY GOOD. WHAT IS IT CALLED?
EGGNOG.
WAITER, ANOTHER ROUND FOR ME AND MY FRIENDS!
IN THE END, WE BOTH GOT OUR WISH AFTER ALL.
FROM OUR FAMILY TO YOURS...
...MERRY CHRISTMAS TO ALL, AND TO ALL A GOOD NIGHT.
THANKS FOR JOINING US.
HULK OUT.
THE END

HULK

AKA: BRUCE BANNER

The HULK is the biggest, strongest, smashing-est Hero there is, and he's the green glue that holds this family of gamma-fied brawlers together. Gone are the days of anger-driven transformations from scientist Bruce Banner to rampaging monster — he's all-Hulk, all the time. And thanks to the documentary web-series his best pal A-Bomb is making, the world will finally see him for the Hero he is. But the ever-humble Hulk isn't interested in the spotlight. He's out there doing the job he needs to do...saving the world from destruction by smacking down every angry alien, roaring sea creature and talking planet from here to the Big Bang. Hulk is a man of few words, but that's because he only needs two: HULK SMASH!!!

SHE-HULK

AKA: JENNIFER WALTERS

Hulk likes to think of his team as a family, but Jen is the real gamma-blood-related deal. Before joining the Agents of S.M.A.S.H., the sensational SHE-HULK had a hard time fitting in with the rest of the world because she stuck out like a 6 foot, indestructible green thumb. As a stunt-woman, she was wrecking stuff professionally, but now she's moved on to better work as the pilot of the team's heavily armed Jump Jet. She-Hulk is tougher than she looks — which is saying a lot because she could rip an 18-wheeler in half — and has no problem keeping up with (and sometimes getting ahead of) the boys! A stubborn thrill-seeker, She-Hulk never backs down from a fight, arm-wrestling match or burping contest. This girl hasn't met a ship she wouldn't crash or a baddie she can't smash.

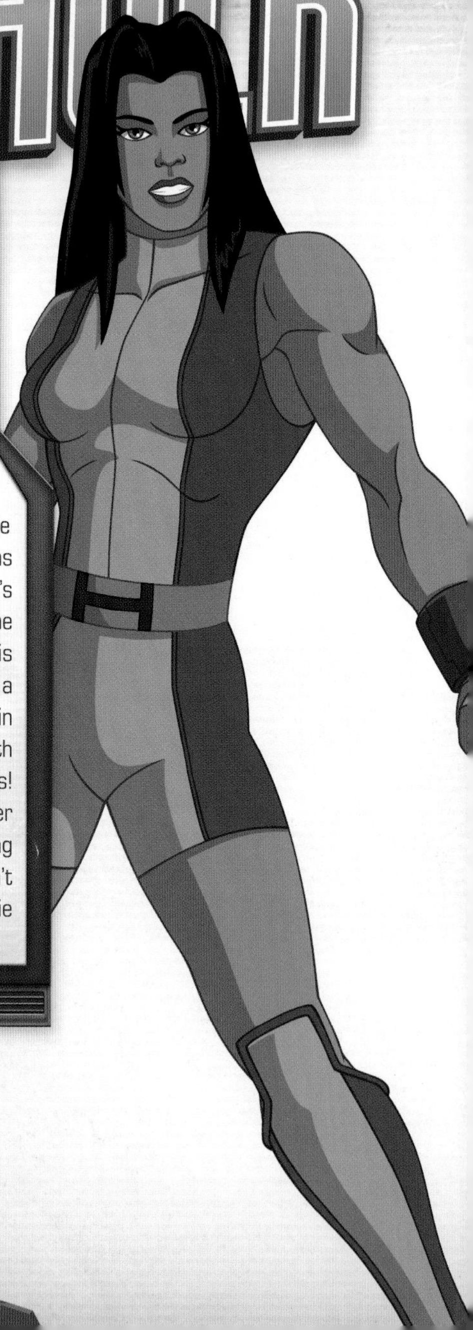

RED HULK

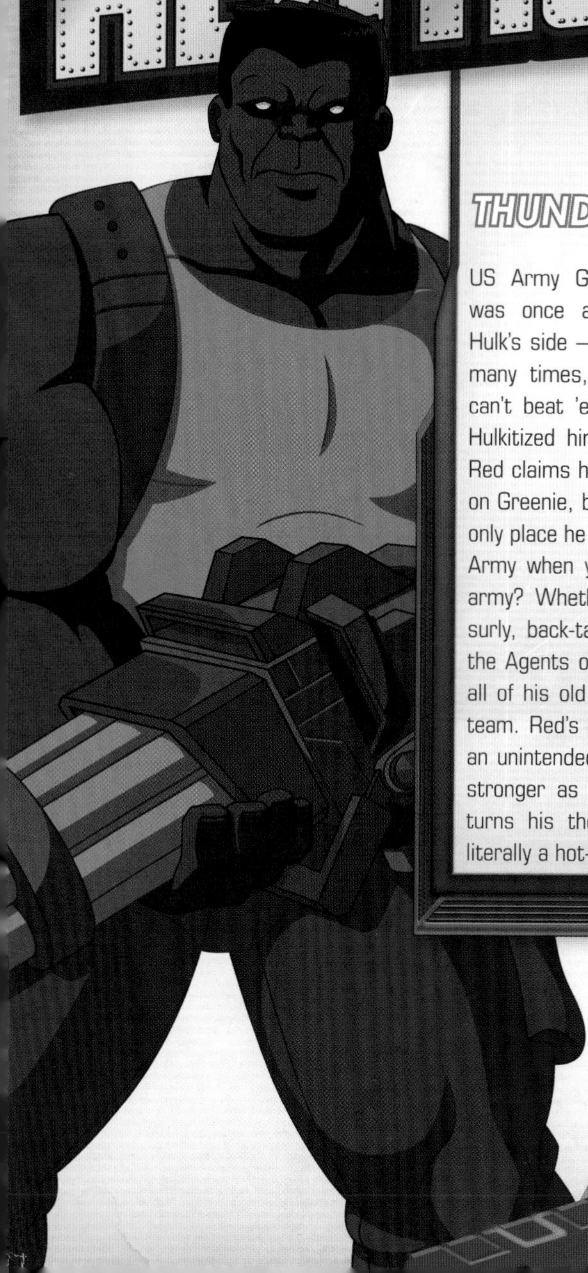

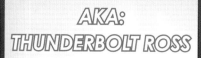

AKA: THUNDERBOLT ROSS

US Army General Thunderbolt Ross was once a loud-mouthed thorn in Hulk's side — but after losing one too many times, he took the old "if you can't beat 'em, join 'em" approach and Hulkitized himself to become RED HULK. Red claims he's hanging out to keep an eye on Greenie, but the truth is that this is the only place he fits in now. But who needs the Army when you're a one man (one HULK) army? Whether he'll admit it or not, the surly, back-talking Red loves being part of the Agents of S.M.A.S.H. and even shared all of his old Hulkbuster weapons with the team. Red's gammification also came with an unintended side effect: While Hulk gets stronger as he gets angrier, Red's anger turns his thermostat up to boiling. He's literally a hot-head!

SKAAR

The savage sword-slinger's origins remain a mystery, but SKAAR's love of smashing is no secret. His war cry "Skaar slash!" lets you know he'll slice and dice everything from a dangerous robot to a buffet table. Skaar is Hulk unchained. All that mindless rage Hulk lost must have found its way into this primitive teen's brain, which makes him a great asset in the fight against evil. However, Skaar's sword is double-edged because he's the same whirlwind of destruction on the battlefield as he is at home. He's more "house breaker" than "housebroken." Even though he's not the brightest, he's sharp where it counts and just the wild card the team needs.

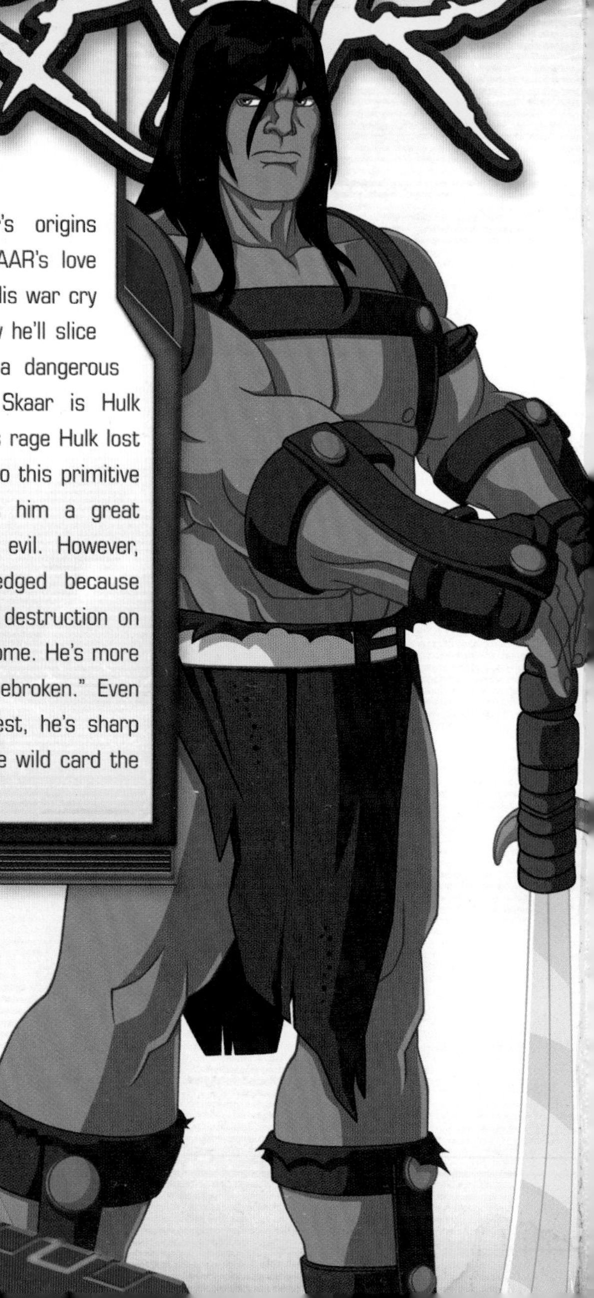